INFLUENTIALS IN TWO
BORDER CITIES

Influentials in two BORDER CITIES

A Study in Community Decision-Making

WILLIAM V. D'ANTONIO and
WILLIAM H. FORM

UNIVERSITY OF NOTRE DAME PRESS

© by UNIVERSITY OF NOTRE DAME PRESS—1965

LIBRARY OF CONGRESS CATALOG CARD NO. 65-17775

MANUFACTURED IN THE U.S.A. BY NAPCO, MILWAUKEE

Contents

Acknowledgments   x

CHAPTER 1
Societal Backgrounds of Community Power   1

CHAPTER 2
A Profile of Two Border Cities   17

CHAPTER 3
Identification of Business and Political Influentials   57

CHAPTER 4
Integration and Cleavage Among Business and
Political Influentials   88

CHAPTER 5
Stability and Change in Influence: 1955–1958   106

CHAPTER 6
Decision-Making in El Paso   130

v

CHAPTER 7
    Decision-Making in C. Juarez   160

CHAPTER 8
    Decision-Making in an International Context   193

CHAPTER 9
    Influentials, Community Power and Democracy   217

Appendix
    Methodology   249

Figures

FIGURE 1

El Paso-C. Juarez metropolitan area   21

FIGURE 2

Chamizal boundary agreement   45

FIGURE 3

*Aerial view of international boundary showing
public and railroad bridges*   195

FIGURE 4

*Typical traffic congestion on the International
Bridge in El Paso*   196

FIGURE 5

*International boundary area showing Cordova
Island and 1963 Chamizal Agreement*   198

Tables

I General Characteristics of Adult Spanish Surname and Anglo Population El Paso Urban Area, 1960   24

II Characteristics of El Paso and C. Juarez Populations, 1960   42

III El Paso Business Influentials Ranked According to Number of Votes Received in 1955   61

IV El Paso Political Influentials Ranked According to Number of Votes Received in 1955   62

V C. Juarez Business Influentials Ranked According to Number of Votes Received in 1955   63

VI C. Juarez Political Influentials Ranked According to Number of Votes Received in 1955   64

VII Nominations for Influentials in El Paso and C. Juarez as Given by Judges in the Opposite City   67

VIII Economic Affiliations of Business Influentials   68

IX Characteristics of Influentials in Two Border Cities, 1955   70

X   Percentage Distribution of Business and Political Influentials Who Were Members of Selected Local Organizations in Two Border Cities, 1955   71

XI   Occupations of Political Influentials in Two Border Cities, 1955   75

XII   Summary of Images of American and Mexican Business Held by American and Mexican Influentials   94

XIII   Summary of Images of American and Mexican Politics Held by American and Mexican Influentials   95

XIV   Institutional Identification of Business and Political Influentials in Two Border Cities   103

XV   General Influentials in El Paso, 1958, Arranged According to Number of Votes Received as Key Influentials; and Showing Their Influence Position in 1955   108–109

XVI   General Influentials in 1958 Who Were Influentials in 1955; Key Influentials in 1958 Who Were Key Influentials in 1955   110

XVII   Top 20 Choices for the "Ideal Hospital Committee" in El Paso in 1958, Number of Votes Received, and Whether or Not the Individual Had Been Selected as Influential in 1955 or 1958   113

XVIII   General Influentials in C. Juarez, 1958, Arranged According to Number of Votes Received as Key Influentials; and Showing Their Influence Position in 1955   116

XIX   General Influentials in 1958 Who Were Influentials in 1955; Key Influentials in 1958 Who Were Key Influentials in 1955   117

XX   Top 20 Choices for the "Ideal Hospital Committee" in C. Juarez in 1958, Number of Votes Received, and Whether or Not the Individual Had Been Selected as Influential in 1955 or 1958   123

XXI   Number of Issues in Which Influentials Played Key Roles in Two Border Cities   240

XXII   Percentages of Reputed Influentials Who Played Key Roles in the Resolution of Six Issues in Each of the Two Border Cities   241

Acknowledgments

The researchers are indebted to a great many people in El Paso and C. Juarez* who are the main actors in this study. Their trust and co-operation made this study possible. Much as we would like to acknowledge their help individually, we cannot do so, because only anonymity provides the protection they need for revealing their inner thoughts and observations to us. Of course, many will recognize themselves and other prominent people even under fictitious names.

We recognize a heavy responsibility in telling this "tale of two cities" objectively. Our analysis cannot, of necessity, please all the people in these two communities. We have tried to be as accurate as possible, and we hope that those who were courageous enough to help will find herein a sympathetic portrayal of their thoughts and behavior. We hope they appreciate that our major concern throughout was to understand the patterns

* C. Juarez appears unaccented throughout the book.

of leadership and decision-making in the communities and not to expose individuals to personal criticism. It is our belief that the patterns we found have broad implications, for both the communities and the countries involved. Of course, we accept full responsibility for the presentation and interpretation of events which took place. Also, as co-authors, we are equally responsible for the entire work.

The authors wish to acknowledge in particular their personal and professional indebtedness to Professor Charles P. Loomis for his intellectual leadership of the wider research of which this study is a part. We are also grateful for his continued interest and sponsorship of this study. Through Dr. Loomis, funds were made available by the Carnegie Corporation for the Study of Social Change on the United States-Mexican Border, and by the United States Public Health Service for Project W-108, Anglo-Latino Relations in Hospitals and Communities. Funds provided Professor D'Antonio by the Social Science Research Council and the University of Notre Dame for the visit to Mexico in 1962 are also acknowledged.

Dr. Julian Samora, Head of the Department of Sociology of Notre Dame, read in its entirety an earlier draft of this manuscript and made extensive editorial comments and suggestions. We are also indebted to Professors Ralph Goldman of San Francisco State College, Peter H. Rossi, Director of the National Opinion Research Center, and Howard J. Ehrlich, of the National Institute of Mental Health, for their helpful criticisms. Professors Frank Fahey and William Liu of Notre Dame also read and commented on various sections of this manuscript.

Professors Eugene C. Erickson, Clyde McCone, and James Officer assisted in various aspects of the project from 1958 to 1962, as did Dr. Ann Olmsted of Michigan State University. Mr. Jesse Daffron provided valuable field assistance during the summer of 1962.

We want also to thank members of the staff of the University of Notre Dame for help in preparing the manuscript for publication. We are especially grateful to Mr. William Irwin, Mrs. F. R. Lawrence and her staff, and Sister Roseanne Murphy for their assistance in processing the manuscript. Katherine Lehman of Michigan State University was especially helpful in preparing the final draft. Mr. Joseph Schlangen was responsible for preparing the Index.

We are, of course, profoundly indebted to our wives and children, who have demonstrated so ably that they too can adjust to the mobility often required in social research. Perhaps part of the reward for them, as for us, has been the opportunity to become acquainted with and love the Rio Grande border region and its people.

W. V. D'ANTONIO
Associate Professor of Sociology
University of Notre Dame

W. H. FORM
Professor of Sociology
School of Labor and Industrial Relations
Michigan State University

To

CHARLES P. LOOMIS

CHAPTER 1

Societal Backgrounds of Community Power

INTRODUCTION

THIS IS A STUDY of leadership and decision-making in the border cities of El Paso, Texas, and C. Juarez, Chihuahua, Mexico. More precisely, our focus is on the use of power in decision-making both within and between these two border cities, as seen through the eyes and actions of the communities' leaders. These leaders were the influentials, the men of high position, the elites of business, politics and the professions, and some of their subordinates, whose activities and attitudes in one way or another helped to shape the destinies of these "twin" cities during the decade of the 1950's.

Studies of community leadership and decision-making now occupy an important place in social science research. These studies reflect a continuing concern, dating back to the earliest philosophers, about who can, should and does govern the local community. Many social scientists feel that the development and maintenance of democratic institutions at the national level rests upon viable democratic patterns at the local community level.[1]

Two major social currents challenge whether democratic decision-making is possible now at the local level. First, subjugated groups at home and abroad, impatient with the slow evolution of democratic forms, want their social revolution now, whatever the political consequences. Second, the growth of large cities raises the question whether responsive participative democracy is feasible in the bureaucratic settings which arise. Social scientists studying these currents have begun to evolve a theory of community power. This book represents a modest attempt to come to grips with certain aspects of this general theory, and hopefully it may contribute something to it. Our study is a partial approach because it focuses primarily on the leaders of El Paso and C. Juarez, the reputation they had for power, and the roles they played in important community decision-making. From this limited approach we hope to evaluate the problems of community leadership in this border setting, and to relate our findings to the larger problem of democratic decision-making in the two nations represented. We realize that these two communities do not adequately represent their nations, but they do contain the kinds of problems which nations face in their attempts to meet their problems responsibly.

An enormous amount of speculation exists about the requisites for democracy. Current theory[2] tends to stress that a community or society is able to function democratically if it is characterized by a minimum of social class cleavages, a basic agreement on values emphasizing controlled conflict, and a

[1] See for example, Morris Janowitz (ed.), *Community Political Systems* (Glencoe, Ill.: The Free Press, 1961), p. 17.

[2] See, for example, S. M. Lipset, *Political Man* (Garden City: Doubleday, 1960); W. V. D'Antonio and H. J. Ehrlich (eds.), *Power and Democracy in America* (Notre Dame: University of Notre Dame Press, 1961); and P. Cutright, "National Political Development: Measurement and Analysis," in *American Sociological Review*, XXVIII (April 1963), 253–264.

cross-cutting set of independent voluntary associations which are controlled by their members. These three attributes are, of course, interrelated.

It seems as valid today, as when Aristotle first made the observation, to hold that a stable democracy is not possible when great disparities in wealth exist. When the middle classes predominate and are not too far removed from the rich above them or the poor below them, a broad value consensus can develop among all groups which permits orderly dissent or conflict in the body politic. In a society with a small group of extremely wealthy people and a small middle class, the vast majority of the poor are subject to various kinds of economic and political exploitation. When men are freed from hunger and ignorance, they may be able to develop self-restraints which permit the institutionalization of social conflict. When economic conditions are *generally* favorable and secure, there can be a consensus around such values as freedom of speech, of the press, of religion, open and honest elections, and equal justice under law. Such a consensus permits and limits conflict so that the basic stability of the society itself is not threatened.

Indeed, conflict and consensus are the vital stuff of democracy. By definition, society exists because it possesses some degree of consensus on basic beliefs and values which structure its goals and the means to achieve them. Consensus can exist either in dictatorships or democracies. The peculiar characteristic of democracy is that it permits or even encourages conflict within a broad system of consensus.[3] It does not assume that total consensus must exist, but only that there must be sufficient

[3] The persistence of conflict or at least some degree of dissent, disagreement, or discontent with the status quo may be predicated on the assumption that man in human society will always create new problems even as he resolves old ones. A society dominated by an educated middle class would seem to be in a better position to meet and solve these problems than any other kind of society, and thus to move the people gradually to higher levels of material, intellectual and moral fulfillment.

agreement on enough basic values and beliefs to make orderly conflict possible. Thus, opposition to those in control at any given time is restrained by the legitimate expectation on the part of those not in control, that they can reasonably expect to achieve power or at least influence current decision-making. Extreme ideological conflict between those in and out of power prevents the establishment of sufficiently strong norms of consensus. On the other hand, the democratic society may be imperiled by a consensus that becomes all-encompassing. Only recently has American society recognized the threat of over-conformity, and become concerned that controversy not be regarded as a disloyal act. Overconformity is as much a danger in a business-oriented middle-class society as is lack of a basic consensus in a society undergoing a sociopolitical revolution.

One of the most astute observations made by Tocqueville more than a century ago was that Americans were addicted to the development of independent voluntary associations, which sought to pursue specific ends or interests. Among the most outstandingly successful of these have been our two political parties, the Chamber of Commerce, the service clubs, and the labor unions. Social scientists have found evidence that these voluntary associations which parallel and cut across class lines may be vital to the preservation of democracy in a modern, complex, urban-industrial society.[4] As autonomous units governed by their own membership they can serve as moulders of public opinion and leadership. Historically, most of these associations have had a strong middle- and upper-class orientation, but the labor unions and ethnically-oriented political clubs have articulated lower-income groups to the political process and educated

---

[4] See Arnold Rose, *Theory and Method in the Social Sciences* (Minneapolis: University of Minnesota Press, 1954); Seymour M. Lipset, Martin A. Trow and James S. Coleman, *Union Democracy: The Internal Politics of the International Typographical Union* (Glencoe, Ill.: The Free Press, 1956); and Herbert Maccoby, "The Differential Political Activity of Participants in a Voluntary Association," *American Sociological Review*, XXIII (October 1958), 524–532.

them into the ways of democracy. These voluntary associations may be as important as any other factor in assuring, as Professor Dahl puts it, that existing inequalities are no longer cumulative. That is, the possession of great wealth or prestige does not automatically guarantee political power or vice-versa. The ideal of a democratic society is that power and decision-making are diffused and that there is no solidary power, prestige or income elite which makes all the important decisions. A basic question of our research was the degree to which El Paso and C. Juarez conformed to this theory of democracy.

DIVERGENT PATHS IN THE STRUGGLE TOWARD DEMOCRACY

The United States may well be regarded as one of the world's first experiments in political democracy.[5] The nation developed gradually from a simple agricultural base into a giant industrial complex. In the process, political freedoms became diffused to larger and larger numbers of people, at the same time that economic and social mobility became a standard part of the "American Dream." Built on a Protestant foundation, and continually reshaped by new European ethnic stocks, there gradually emerged among institutional sectors a consensus built around the values of free enterprise, individualism, achievement, political equality, religious tolerance and voluntary co-operation. These values support a strong business orientation and an evenly balanced two-party system which cuts across economic, religious and ethnic lines. Despite the stresses and strains between business and government, a substantial consensus has been established between them.

This portrayal of American democracy roughly describes the society in general. Wide variations from this general pattern exist in different communities in various regions of the country.

[5] See   Seymour Martin Lipset, *The First New Nation* (New York: Basic Books, 1963).

Research has suggested that in some parts of the country at least, democracy is still more a dream than a reality. In the 1930's the Lynds found Middletown to be ruled by something approaching a one-family oligarchy.[6] The Useems and Tangent found strong and bitter cleavages between the upper- and lower-income groups in Prairietown.[7] Variations on these themes were described by Warner for Jonesville and West for Plainville.[8] Mills found in middle-sized cities that the small businessman supported an economic and political rhetoric advantageous to the big businesses.[9] In 1953 Hunter published his now classic *Community Power Structure*, a power study of a southern Regional City. He found that Regional City was dominated by loose coalitions of business-professional groups. Political pluralism appeared to be a luxury enjoyed by the upper-income leaders in the community. The increasing demand of Negroes, Puerto Ricans, and Spanish-speaking groups for equality of economic and political rights further documents the existence of nondemocratic control-patterns in hundreds of American communities.

Hunter's book stimulated a great amount of research on community power during the 1950's and early 1960's.[10] Although the pattern of business class control was documented in many cities, other studies showed that power was more diffused[11]

[6] Helen and Robert Lynd, *Middletown in Transition* (New York: Harcourt, Brace, 1937).

[7] John and Ruth H. Useem and Pierre Tangent, "Stratification in a Prairie-town," in *American Sociological Review*, VII (June 1942), 331–342.

[8] W. L. Warner, *Democracy in Jonesville* (New York: Harper, 1949), and James West, *Plainville, U.S.A.* (New York: Columbia University Press, 1945).

[9] C. Wright Mills, "The Middle Classes in Middle-Sized Cities," *American Sociological Review* (October 1946), 520–529.

[10] See the excellent annotated bibliography of Charles Press, *Main Street Politics: Policy Makers at the Local Level* (East Lansing: Michigan State University, 1962).

[11] D. C. Miller, "Industry and Community Power Structure," in *American Sociological Review*, XXIII (February 1958), 9–15.

and that the various groups had power in one issue and not in another. Neither the model of a small, ruling elite or oligarchy, nor the model of a broadly diffused political democracy was completely validated. However, some more recent efforts, growing out of dissatisfactions with Hunter's methodology, have given stronger support to the democratic theory. Dahl found that New Haven had evolved from oligarchy to pluralism in the last 150 years.[12] He presented strong evidence that today most groups have some power, and that economic and status elites are not necessarily the power leaders. Burgess found that Negroes could be influential in community decision-making in a southern city.[13] However, regardless of the support given to more monolithic or more pluralistic patterns of power, most studies have shown that relatively few people participate actively in any single community decision.[14] Power is often concentrated—as much by default as by design—a situation which Dahl calls a "passive consent" for the system as it is. In this way conflict is minimized and the community enjoys a sufficiently high level of integration among its parts to assure solution of some important and most routine problems.

The relatively integrated character of American society[15] comes more clearly into focus when contrasted with the Mexican situation.[16] Although Mexico has been moving in the direc-

[12] R. A. Dahl, *Who Governs?* (New Haven: Yale University Press, 1961). For an analysis of power and decision-making in Chicago see P. Rossi and R. Dentler, *The Politics of Urban Renewal* (Glencoe, Ill.: The Free Press, 1961), and Robert Banfield, *Political Influence* (Glencoe, Ill.: The Free Press, 1961).

[13] M. E. Burgess, *Negro Leadership in a Southern City* (Chapel Hill: University of North Carolina Press, 1962).

[14] This has been most thoroughly explored by Robert Presthus, *Men at the Top* (New York: Oxford University Press, 1964), pp. 239–367.

[15] The word "American" is used here in the narrow sense of referring only to the United States. The authors are aware of its broader usage to cover both North and South Americans.

[16] The recent work by Presthus suggests that there may also be a wide range in degree of consensus in American cities. *Op. cit.*, pp. 321–367.

tion of an urbanized industrial society, the movement has been impaired by problems not encountered in the United States. The values and beliefs of the earlier Spanish and Indian cultures continue to exert influence in Mexico. The ancient heritage led to a system of stratification and paternalistic control by a small wealthy group which limited both economic development and participative democracy. Opposing ideas and programs slowly gained strength and they resulted in a significant reform movement led by Benito Juárez and his followers in the 1850's and 1860's. However, this was followed by a "counter-reform," and thirty-five years of paternalistic dictatorship under Porfirio Díaz. While industrialization and some semblance of law and order were established, the most significant facts of the dictatorship were that the vast majority of Mexicans became propertyless and the political franchise was nonexistent. Then came the Revolution of 1910 led by Francisco Madero, under the pledge of "effective suffrage and no re-election." The clamor for more extensive reforms mounted and culminated in the Constitution of 1917, the now historic document which still governs Mexican life, and which did so much to overturn the traditional system.

After several years of near chaos, a strong political party emerged, and brought a semblance of order and unity to the country. This party (now called the *Partido Revolucionario Institucional*) has dominated all phases of Mexican life since the 1920's. Its avowed aim is to institutionalize a reform process in the economic, social, and political life of all Mexico. Slowly, and especially since 1940, the Revolution has solidified its economic base. Land reform, which reached its peak under Cárdenas in the 1930's, has necessarily slowed down as Mexico has become more concerned with industrialization by both governmental and private initiative.

As a consequence of this history, several strains are found in contemporary Mexican society: traditional paternalism attenuated but not yet destroyed; indigenous socialism, aggressive capitalism, and political centralism. Understandably, the society —and business and politics in particular—is in a state of transition in which traditional values are rapidly being cast aside or radically reinterpreted. In this situation the communists have sought to take every possible advantage. Their potential danger stems not from any mass following or strong internal organization, but from an ability to exploit the social disequilibrium brought about by social change. The personal and social significance of this disequilibrium is dramatized in two penetrating studies of life in changing Mexico by Oscar Lewis. In *Five Families* and then in *The Children of Sanchez,* Lewis has depicted the consequences of urbanism, rapid population growth, and inadequate industrialization on Mexican life. The ensuing culture of poverty simultaneously breeds attitudes of fatalism and political opportunism.[17]

Recent research in Mexico by American political scientists has been more optimistic, arguing that the Revolution is leading to a more and more democratic life.[18] Although Scott recognizes the dangerous transitional period through which Mexico is now passing, he is encouraged by the strengthening of the middle class, the growing vitality of opposition parties, and the growing ability of interest groups to act on their own behalf.

[17] Oscar Lewis, *Five Families* (New York: Basic Books, 1959); and *Children of Sanchez* (New York: Random House, 1961).

[18] See for example, L. V. Padgett, "Mexico's One Party System: A Re-Evaluation," *The American Political Science Review,* II, No. 4 (December 1957), 995–1008; Robert Scott, *Mexican Government in Transition* (Urbana: University of Illinois Press, 1959). Scott states that "given the conditions under which social and political integration must take place in Mexico, the amount [of social integration] that has already occurred is an encouraging sign that, with enough time, the process will continue and an even more workable homogenous social-political system will evolve" (p. 95). For an excellent account of the historical background and current status of municipal government in Mexico, see Leonard Cardenas, Jr., "The Municipality in Northern Mexico," in *Southwestern Studies,* I, No. 1 (Spring 1963) (El Paso: Texas Western College Press).

This view is further supported in Glade and Anderson's analysis of Mexico's rapidly developing economy, which they perceive as now self-propelling.[19]

RESEARCH QUESTIONS

With the above as background on the problems which democracy faces in the United States and Mexico, we turn to questions we raised concerning problems of power in the two communities selected for study. All of the questions were not raised a priori. Rather, new questions emerged as we attempted to answer earlier ones. This work, then, represents a diary of research questions which arose over almost a decade's time.

The questions came up, roughly, in this order: Who are the men of greatest reputed influence in the economic and governmental spheres of El Paso and C. Juarez? How broadly representative are these men of the various social groupings found in their respective communities? What image do they have of the critical business-politics nexus in their communities? Do their social backgrounds and interpersonal relations reflect inter-institutional relationships of the community and nation? Are business and politics seen as distinct spheres of power activity, or are they perceived as more or less integrated? Do the ones who reputedly have the most power actually play the major roles in resolving important community issues? Finally, how is power manifested in the international context of the border?

The Central Concepts

The central phenomenon around which this study was developed is power. Power has many meanings, but for our purposes it refers to the ability to control the decision-making process in the community. While force or the threat of force

[19] William P. Glade, Jr., and Charles W. Anderson, *The Political Economy of Mexico* (Madison: University of Wisconsin Press, 1963).

may occasionally be applied to secure control, this is rarely the case in community decision-making. Most often, control is exercised as part of the legal or traditional rights of a person, office, or group. This type of control is known as authority and it involves the acceptance of the legitimacy of control on the part of those who obey. Although sanctions are not generally applied to secure adherence to authority, they are always there in the form of ability to affect the economic or social status of persons and groups, positively or negatively. Less obvious than force or authority is that more subtle phenomenon of power manifested in the willingness of people to obey others who lack formal authority. They obey because they have respect or esteem for or fear of the person, office, or group. This type of power is called influence. In its extreme form it becomes charisma. It may be partially derived from a position of authority, but it is not limited thereby. It is a more personal kind of power, manifested for example in knowledge, charm, persuasiveness or wealth. People who have such influence have been traditionally called influentials. An influential may or may not be a formal authority leader. For us the influential is a person who is capable of significantly affecting the decision-making process in the community. His will may not always prevail, but his views are usually considered before a final decision is reached.

When issues arise in the community, people are faced with problems in the *distribution* of power. Politics is the process of resolving contested issues, the process whereby control is achieved. This research focuses on this process as it involves influentials in the give and take of community decision-making. Community decisions are indeed the testing grounds for those who are reputed to have power, that is, authority, and/or influence. Much of what passes as these phenomena represents at best a *potential* for control or sometimes only a reputation for control. By studying community decisions, the potential is tested. Thus, this study endeavors to correlate potential with actual power.

Conflict over who will control derives from many sources, only a few of which may be identified here. First, the authority of several interrelated positions, agencies or institutions is seldom so clearly defined as to eliminate a struggle over who has the right to decide. Second, and very important in a democracy, people in positions of authority have to justify themselves continually to those who may be affected by their decisions. Thus, the city council's right to levy taxes is restricted by its ability to convince the electorate or specific interest groups that the tax is needed and is reasonable. Failure to do so creates an issue—a question of *who* will control—for both the council and the people have some authority in this case. Third, the influence of persons or groups may operate either to activate authority or to impede its application. For example, respected citizens or groups may call on the city council to act in a given way. The council has to weigh the consequences of obeying or not obeying. Although such persons of influence do not have legitimate authority over the council, they may, in fact, constitute an informal government. Fourth, and this is the obverse of the third, there is a tendency for persons in authority to extend their control beyond its legitimate limits by acquiring the "influence of office." Here again an issue may arise over the limits of this kind of power.

It should be obvious from the above that authority and influence are closely related phenomena. Authority without influence gravely impairs imaginative action in unanticipated situations. Influence without authority creates instabilities and uncertainties in organizational operations. Clearly both are needed, but they rarely coexist in optimum balance, thus creating issues in the distribution of power. This research is concerned with studying the interrelations of authority and influence to community decision-making.

Assumptions and Methods

There are several ways to study decision-making in a community. The particular method which a scientist uses depends to a great extent on his assumptions about a community. We approached the whole problem of power and decision-making in El Paso and C. Juarez with several assumptions. First, we assumed that El Paso and C. Juarez could be studied by means of the same methods although the cities were in different countries and represented differing sociocultural systems; second, that the phenomena of power and influence could be identified simply and directly by asking people about it; third, that the people who knew most about community power were in high business and government posts near the centers of decision-making; fourth, that power was unequally distributed in community decisions, and that it tended to flow more toward business and political leaders than toward any other persons or groups in the community.

While a more detailed statement of our field experiences appears in the Appendix, we may state here that the data for this study were gathered over a period of almost eight years. During this time more than 300 people were interviewed in the two communities. The authors began their research on the border in the fall of 1954, and spent the entire academic year there. A return visit was made in the summer of 1958; another visit in the spring of 1961, and a fourth during the summer of 1962. Some persons were interviewed during each visit, and these people spent as many as 100 hours telling us about their activities in community projects and related activities. While other materials were also used, the interviews with community leaders provided most of the data for this study.[20]

The first three months of our stay on the border were devoted to exploratory research. El Paso seemed to be a booming city,

[20] See the Appendix.

with a business-oriented leadership and a loosely organized conservative Democratic Party which believed in close co-operation between business and government. A large number of voluntary associations bound the leaders of business and government in their many public pursuits. While these leaders admitted that they had to face certain internal problems, as well as problems with their Mexican neighbors, they felt they had control of the situation and the organizational equipment to resolve problems. To them the large Spanish-speaking population seemed like a faceless mass, a mass which must be attended to but not be reckoned with.

RESEARCH HYPOTHESES

Based upon these early impressions and the existing primitive theory on community power, we developed two guiding hypotheses for El Paso. First, we expected to verify that El Paso was indeed ruled more or less monolithically by a business-professional coalition. Second, we hypothesized that systematic research would demonstrate that the business and political leaders formed a single, well-integrated unit in the community. This would be reflected in their value orientations, associational memberships, positions on community problems, and general community activities. Insofar as conflict and competition in community decisions were concerned, we did not expect them to be between business and government but only among different cliques of influential persons. We did not expect to find representatives of the Spanish-speaking and the lower-income groups to be in seats of influence.

The exploratory research in C. Juarez suggested that Mexican border cities displayed institutional strains between business, government and other institutions. As the PRI came into conflict with the ideology of local business leaders, its reform ideology seemed to prevent the formation of coalitional structures so common in United States cities. This situation polarized, rather than articulated, such other institutional sectors as religion, education, and the press, around either business or government. The emerging patterns seem to portend continual strife with the rise of business and government bureaucracies, built on the coexisting and contradictory values of personalism and universalism. We expected to find this disjunctiveness in organizational structures preventing both consensus on local problems and the building of joint structures to solve them as well.

On the basis of preliminary investigation and knowledge of recent Mexican history, we hypothesized that community decision-making in C. Juarez would be dominated by the governmental institution and PRI (the official Revolutionary Party) in a more or less monolithic manner. We also expected that local business and political leaders would form two more or less discrete social systems with pronounced cleavages between them, which would be reflected in their values and beliefs, associational patterns, and attitudes and actions toward local problems.

In comparing the two communities, we expected to find community decision-making more structured and narrowly based in C. Juarez than in El Paso, with political leaders dominating one city and business-professional leaders dominating the other.[21] We also expected to find a higher degree of integration among the leaders of El Paso.

Another research objective was to study the inter-city relations. Very early, it was impressed upon us that the domestic aspects of international relations on the border might affect the structure of power and decision-making in the two cities. Thousands of people of Spanish-Mexican and/or Indian origin

[21] The American study most similar to ours in comparative research design is that of Presthus, op. cit. Unfortunately, we were not in communication with one another during the entire period of research and writing.

were residing in El Paso. Some of them had lived in the United States for generations, others had arrived very recently. How "Anglos" and Spanish-name persons got along in general concerned some leaders in both communities, and how the two peoples got along in El Paso was a matter of concern to all Spanish-name persons on both sides of the border.

Early in the research several Juarez leaders commented that, in evaluating their city's growth, they more and more tended to compare themselves with El Paso rather than with Chihuahua City, the capital city of their state. This led us to speculate whether the American pattern of business and government relations might have an impact on C. Juarez. This might be expected if there were a great deal of contact between leaders of the two communities. Conceivably, the businessmen or the political leaders of the American city could serve as models to be imitated or avoided, depending on the values of the leaders and their evaluations of the American scene.

It was clear that the two cities were closely tied by economic bonds. Both profited by tourist trade traveling north and south. American business needed Mexican labor as much as Mexican business needed American dollars. Besides economic interdependence, governmental and other leaders of both communities were co-operating on common problems such as the control of crime, narcotics, auto and pedestrian traffic, prostitution and health.

Our study then attempted to explore and probe power and decision-making within and between the two largest cities on the United States-Mexican border. The cultural, organizational, and societal similarities and divergences in the international setting provided a challenge for an unusual comparative study. We shall elaborate the specific problems studied in the subsequent chapters. To provide an adequate background for interpreting the findings, a brief sketch of certain historical and contemporary features of each city is presented in the following chapter.

CHAPTER 2

A Profile of Two
Border Cities

THE FIRST KNOWN WHITE visitors to explore the American southwest border area were Juan de Oñate and his group, who came
upon the Pass to the North in 1598. Later, a small settlement
was founded on the southern side of the Rio Grande (Rio Bravo
to the Mexicans) where C. Juarez stands today. A missionary
church, still standing, was dedicated to Nuestra Señora de
Guadalupe Mexicana in 1668. Since military and religious activity were limited in this arid outpost of Spain, the pass to the
American Southwest remained largely unsettled during the
next two centuries.

The Texas War of Independence with Mexico in 1836, and
the Peace Treaty following the United States-Mexico war of
1846–1848 led to the formation of two separate towns, Paso del
Norte, in Mexico, and Franklin, in the United States.[1] Until

[1] See Howard F. Cline, *The United States and Mexico* (Cambridge, Mass.:
Harvard University Press, 1961), for a detailed history of the relations between
the two countries.

the coming of the railroads in the latter part of the nineteenth century the two towns grew very slowly. Since then, and especially since the Second World War, they have grown very rapidly.

The two cities have been the locale for important historical events. From 1861–1867 President Benito Juárez made Paso del Norte his headquarters, while he resisted the French drive to make Prince Maximillian the emperor of Mexico. In 1909 President Porfirio Díaz met with President Howard Taft, first in one city and then in the other, to symbolize the peace and friendship between the two nations. In 1911 the Treaty of Peace between the government forces of Porfirio Díaz and the insurgent Francisco Madero was signed in C. Juarez, ending Díaz' thirty-five year rule. One historian of the period recounted that while Francisco Madero was preparing his army on the Mexican side of the Rio Grande, sympathizers in El Paso provided food, tobacco, and little luxuries.[2] The two cities continued to be linked as important centers for Mexican revolutionary activity until the 1920's.

Since 1940, the rate of growth for both cities has been impressive. The large influx of migrants has given the entire area a boom-town atmosphere. Urbanization and industrialization have proceeded at a rapid pace despite the chronic water shortage in this semi-arid region. By 1960, the El Paso-C. Juarez metropolitan area had a total population of more than half a million people. Although only a shallow river separates the two cities, they differ considerably in their ecology, social organization and cultural characteristics. The following profile helps illuminate some of these differences.

EL PASO

History

The history of El Paso, like all southern border cities, cannot be written without constant reference to the native Spanish-

[2] Ernest Peixotto, *Our Hispanic Southwest* (New York: Scribners, 1916).

speaking population which inhabited the area prior to the
independence of Texas and prior to the constant stream of
migrants which have come from Mexico since. Unlike other
cities in the United States, border cities have not been able to
assimilate their ethnic groups. The proximity to Mexico, and
the constant influx of Mexican migrants assures a permanent
culture of ethnicity. Thus, border cities cannot look forward to
a period when all Spanish-name people will be socially and
culturally assimilated. Permanent bi-ethnicity is a basic fact of
border society which manifestly affects the functioning of the
communities.

The first permanent settlement on the present site of El Paso
was made by Juan María Ponce de León in 1827. James Magoffin
settled in the area in 1830 and called it Magoffinsville. A post
office was established in 1852 after the signing of the Gadsden
Treaty with Mexico, and the town was named Franklin after
its first postmaster until 1859 when the present name was
adopted. El Paso was formally chartered as a town in 1873,
when it had a population of twenty-three Anglo-Americans
and 150 "Mexicans." The town became an important stop on
the Old Overland Trail from St. Louis to San Francisco. With
the coming of the railroads in the late 1880's the population
began to increase rapidly and the town's facade changed from
one of adobe buildings to one built of brick and lumber. By
1910 El Paso had 40,000 persons and was the site of one of the
largest copper smelting refineries in the world. From that time
to the present, most of the employees of this smelting company
have been Mexicans, and many of them have continued to
reside in C. Juarez.

By 1940, El Paso's population had risen to almost 100,000,
and when we began our research in 1954, it had grown to more
than 200,000. By 1960, the population was around 270,000
persons, some 45 per cent of whom had Spanish surnames. This
rapid growth may be largely attributed to immigration and
annexation. Immigration has been extensive both from Mexico

and northern and eastern United States. The rapid rise in the last decade was also caused by the annexation of nearby small towns in El Paso County, with the result that county and city populations are fast becoming one. El Paso is now the fifteenth largest American city in land area, and it is also the largest city in population and economic importance within a radius of five hundred miles.

Ecology and Economy

The ecology of the city reflects the local ethnic situation. Stretching along the Rio Grande River, the city is split into two spurs by the insistence of Mt. Franklin close to the city center (see Figure 1). Highway 80 is roughly a north-south axis. Below this highway the population is made up primarily of recent Mexican arrivals. They are mostly unskilled and semi-skilled workers and represent the poorest segment of the community. This area, which includes the *Chamizal* (a piece of territory now in the process of being returned to Mexico), generally contains sub-standard overcrowded houses, warehouses, small factories, stores and garages. It also contains a large shopping district which is patronized mainly by the local residents and "Juarenses" (citizens of C. Juarez). Very close by is the central shopping district of the city.

As one moves north of Highway 80 up the spurs to the higher territory, the proportion of Mexican and Spanish-name residents decreases. There is no strict residential ethnic segregation in El Paso, as is commonly found in other Texas cities. In general, Spanish-name persons reside in areas commensurate with their social and economic status. Since few of them are in the upper middle or upper classes, residential areas of this level are populated primarily by Anglos. A few pre-Independence Spanish families reside in elegant but older areas closer to the city center.

The local economy is built principally around cattle, copper,

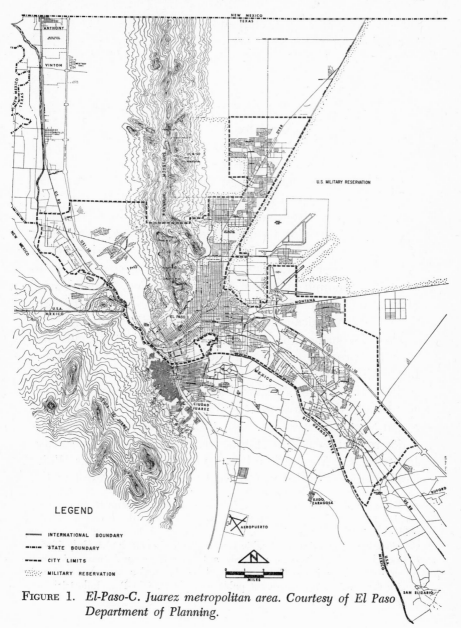

LEGEND

▪▪▪▪▪▪▪ INTERNATIONAL BOUNDARY

▪▬▪▬▪ STATE BOUNDARY

▬▪▬▪▬ CITY LIMITS

▒▒▒ MILITARY RESERVATION

FIGURE 1. *El-Paso-C. Juarez metropolitan area. Courtesy of El Paso Department of Planning.*

natural gas, cotton, and retail and wholesale trade. The following major industries have been developed: copper, lead and
other ore refining; oil refining; cement, tile and brick manufacturing; cotton and denim clothes; meat packing; natural gas
and butane; leather goods; lumber; and food processing.[3] Large
banks and other financial institutions have developed to support
the needs of these and related industries.

El Paso is also a major transportation terminal serving the
Southern Pacific Railroad; the Atcheson, Topeka and the Santa
Fe; the Texas and Pacific; the National Railways of Mexico;
and the Mexican Northwestern Railroad. The city is more than
600 miles distant from any competing rail terminal. It is also
an important trucking terminal. Despite the increasing import
and monetary restrictions which the Mexican government has
decreed in order to stabilize its economy, El Paso continues to
exert its economic influence deep into Mexico. Thousands of
Mexicans from the interior annually make shopping trips to
this nearest American metropolis.

Also of considerable economic importance to the city has
been the presence of three military installations: Fort Bliss,
Biggs Air Force Base, and William Beaumont Army Hospital.
In 1957, these together housed some 40,000 military personnel
and provided employment for more than 3,000 civilians. In
recent years, El Paso has been trying to establish itself as a
major recreation center offering sunshine, a dry climate, easy
access to "Ol' Mexico," and such nearby attractions as White
Sands National Park and Carlsbad Caverns. As a result of the

[3] For a detailed description of the El Paso economy, see *The El Paso Times'*
Special Annual Edition devoted to the city's economic development, usually
published in April of each year. Also, see Howard J. Nelson, "A Service
Classification of American Cities," in *Economic Geography*, XXXI (July 1955).
Nelson classified El Paso as primarily a transportation and communications
center. Using his criteria, C. Juarez would be classified as a commercial and
service center. Also consult recent publications by the El Paso Industrial Development Corporation.

aggressive efforts of the Chamber of Commerce, tourist trade
has been increasing in importance.

As suggested above, the occupational and industrial division
of labor of the city somewhat parallels the ethnic divisions. All
of the leading industries are managed by Anglo-Americans,
as are most of the large banks, wholesale, and commercial
establishments. A few of the leading retailers are "old-line"
Jewish families. An estimated nine tenths of the professionals
in medicine, education, law, and engineering are Anglos. Only
recently have Spanish-name people invaded the professions,
and they tend to serve the ethnic community.[4]

Since the Second World War, relatively large numbers of
bilingual, Spanish-name second- and third-generation workers
have invaded the clerical occupations, both sales and office.
Similarly, second- and third-generation Spanish-name men
have begun to invade the service and repair industries. These
bilingual workers are needed to handle customers who speak
little English or only Spanish. In general, other white-collar
and skilled occupations are held by Anglo-Americans. The
overwhelming proportion of semi-skilled, unskilled, domestic
and service workers are Spanish-name persons of first- and
second-generation Mexican background, many of whom cannot
speak English. Table I compares the Spanish-speaking of El
Paso with Anglos in the city. The differences are striking.
For example, while 60 per cent of the Spanish-speaking had
completed seven years or less of schooling, a slightly higher
percentage of Anglos had achieved a high school education
or beyond. The former were less likely to own the dwelling

[4] See W. V. D'Antonio and Julian Samora, "Occupational Stratification in
Four Southwestern Communities: A Study of Ethnic Differential Employment
in Hospitals," *Social Forces*, XLI (October 1962), 17–25. Their findings show
that Spanish-name persons in El Paso were primarily located at the lower
levels of the occupational ladder. However, some 15 per cent of the medical
doctors and 12 per cent of the registered nurses in El Paso were Spanish-
speaking.

TABLE I

GENERAL CHARACTERISTICS OF ADULT
SPANISH-SURNAME AND ANGLO POPULATION,
EL PASO URBAN AREA, 1960*
(In Percentages)

Characteristics	Spanish-surname	Anglo
Education:		
7 Years or less	60.0	7.6
4 Years high school or more	17.0	64.0
Per cent white-collar	29.0	67.0
Owner-occupied dwellings	50.2	58.8
Renter-occupied	49.8	41.2
Percentage of owned homes valued at $15,000+	13.0	41.8
Percentage of rented dwellings whose gross rent was $80.00+	2.7	33.5
Housing deteriorating	22.1	10.1
Housing dilapidated	15.0	2.5
Crowding		
.50 or fewer persons per room	13.1	34.9
1.01 or more persons per room	47.1	10.8

* Source: U.S. Bureau of the Census. *U.S. Censuses of Population and Housing: 1960. Census Tracts.* Final Report PHC(1)-43. U.S. Government Printing Office, Washington, D.C., 1962

unit in which they lived, and the value of their home was somewhat less than that of Anglos. Furthermore, their housing was more likely to be deteriorating and overcrowded.

Labor union activity in El Paso has been typical of southern American cities in the early stages of industrialization. Except in a few skilled and traditional trades, labor unions were rather weak and not very widespread. Among the Anglos, the Railway Brotherhoods were strong and well respected. As a matter of fact, one of their members had been elected mayor of the city in 1949. The building trades also were beginning to develop strength, and here both Anglo and Spanish-name persons were found. Probably the strongest union, the United Mine and Mill Workers of America, was associated with the smelting industry. Organized in the 1920's, the union has continued to retain the loyalty of its membership (largely Mexican) ever since, despite the fact that it was ejected from the Congress of Industrial Organizations in 1950 because of its communist leadership. Two efforts to oust this union, spearheaded by the CIO and other groups, failed miserably during the 1950's.

The El Paso garment industries employed more than 4,000 persons, of whom only about 300 were dues-paying union members. Union leaders complained that it was very difficult to organize the workers, many of whom lived in C. Juarez. Many workers were women who regarded their jobs as temporary. Moreover, it was customary for a regular proportion of these to migrate to Los Angeles as soon as they had accumulated enough savings. Since most workers were earning more money (between $32.00 and $50.00 per week in 1955) than bank clerks in C. Juarez, to cite one example, they saw little need to join the union. The peculiar problem of residing in one nation and working in another raised complex questions about workers' legal rights. As a result of all these factors, union leaders were beginning to pressure the United States government to prohibit the employment in El Paso of persons residing in C. Juarez. This move was strongly and so far successfully resisted by El Paso businessmen.

Government, Politics, and Education

Government and politics, like most organizational activities, were under the active control of the Anglo business community during most of the period of the 1950's. In earlier days, managers and owners of the largest businesses were actively engaged in politics and held municipal offices. In most recent years there has been a tendency, especially evident in the composition of the city council and the county commissioners, to elect persons representing small and medium-size business.[5] This change in the composition of officeholders has not altered local political behavior significantly. The one-party system of the South, the business orientation of officeholders, and the relative absence of ethnically-based political factions resulted in a rather orderly and stable governmental administration.

Until recently the conduct of local government was almost divorced from the ethnic situation. Not only was a large proportion of the Spanish-name population partially disenfranchized by the poll-tax and other devices, but also those who were interested in politics did not have a unified ethnic community to support them. Occasionally, Spanish-name civil servants were employed in the lower levels of municipal administration. Since they were not in policy positions they were generally unable to obtain concessions for the deprived areas of the city. From the beginning, the uncertain legal status of the *Chamizal* probably inhibited adequate development of city services in that area. During and after the New Deal, public housing was developed and a program of general rehabilitation of the south side was begun. Spurred by problems of rapid urban growth and aided by an expanding economy, the city government has in recent years launched a systematic program to improve all areas of the city.

In general, El Paso politics has not been characterized by ideological factions. Administrations have generally pursued the ideal of "an efficient business-like government." As west Texans, who had worked out a *modus vivendi* with the Spanish-name population in some ways similar to the New Mexico pattern,

[5] As observed also by Robert O. Schulze, "The Role of Economic Dominants in Community Power Structure," *American Sociological Review*, XXIII (February 1958), 3–9.

they prided themselves as not being prejudiced and "bringing the Mexicans along as fast as they are able to develop."

This is evident in the pattern of educational development in the community. Both the Board of Education and educational administrators have begun to face directly the peculiar educational problems which confront a border community. During this period El Paso's six high schools were generally considered good by regional standards. They were all differentially caught up with the difficult problem of educating an ethnically heterogeneous student body. For example, two of the schools were populated almost exclusively by children who were recent arrivals from Mexico or whose parents were first-generation arrivals. In many cases, trying to teach them English posed as great a problem as trying to indoctrinate them into American ways.

The problem was equally trying on the primary school level. The assistant superintendent of schools reported, when we first began the study in 1954, that approximately 70 per cent of the total student enrollment of 31,000 had Spanish surnames. Since more than 90 per cent of these began their formal education with no knowledge of English, special language programs had to be developed for them. This was particularly arduous in schools where there were large proportions of children of Anglo parents. The cultural toleration of school administrators was evidenced by the fact that they inaugurated Spanish classes in the primary grades in schools dominated by Anglo-Americans. This program was intended to overcome partially the inability of the Anglo sector to understand Spanish in a community where half of the population could speak Spanish.

Since the early part of the twentieth century, by special arrangement, Juarez children whose parents were Mexican citizens were allowed to attend El Paso schools. There were 203 children so enrolled in the public schools in 1955 paying a special tuition of twenty dollars each per month. Undoubtedly there were also other Juarez children attending the El Paso schools who "lived" with relatives in El Paso. El Paso also had a Catholic elementary school population of 6,000, three parochial and several private high schools, and Texas Western College for higher education. Small numbers of students from C. Juarez attended all of these schools.

Religion

Although religious statistics were not available for the city, it can be estimated that about 60 per cent of the population was Catholic. A small Jewish congregation, probably less than 2 per cent of the population, was also present. About four fifths of the non-Spanish-name population was Protestant and they represented a wide range of denominations. Economically, the Protestants roughly constituted the upper half of the community. The highest status denominations were Presbyterian, Episcopalian and Methodist. A well-to-do Jewish colony had been established in El Paso for several generations. Jewish businessmen were well respected and were elected to high offices in the business community.

In general, the Protestant community was complacent about the local religious situation. A large proportion of the nominal Protestants, especially those in lower economic strata, remained unchurched. Limited energy was put into a missionary program among Spanish-name people in both communities.

The Catholic bishop estimated that 80 per cent of his "flock" had Spanish surnames. Anglo-Catholics were generally of middle-class backgrounds. The Church recognized that it had two major local tasks: to provide the congregations with spiritual instruction, and to facilitate their assimilation into American society. However, its resources were limited in the face of the magnitude of the problem. The high mobility and low economic status of the Spanish-name population hindered systematic church contacts and the raising of funds for religious, educational, and welfare purposes. Moreover, few of the clergy were Spanish-speaking, and they were completely isolated from the clergy in C. Juarez. Almost no religious contacts for liaison purposes existed across the border at this time.

Welfare

Meeting the health and welfare problems of the people has always been a formidable task for local agencies. A few of these problems have been: the serious health hazards in the over-crowded areas of the city and the *Chamizal*, the heavy welfare case loads in periods of economic depression, the presence of a large and impoverished transient population of uncertain legal status,[6] the sporadic lack of economic opportunity for native Spanish-name persons, juvenile delinquency, inadequate hospital facilities, and related problems resulting from cultural pluralism. The city has never had sufficient material resources or a sufficient number of trained and interested persons to meet these problems. Neither has it had a centrally directed program of action which co-ordinated the many efforts of the voluntary private associations with governmental, educational, and religious. Only recently has the United Fund begun to provide some co-ordination beyond that of fund raising. Among the Spanish-name population, the League of United Latin American Citizens (LULAC) was the major spokesman for the Spanish-name population during this decade, but its influence was limited.

Voluntary Associations and Mass Communication

Like all large American cities, El Paso has a welter of private voluntary associations, with varying degrees of community con-

---

[6] A particularly troublesome problem involved Juarez women who came to El Paso to give birth. The El Paso General Hospital could not refuse them service, even though they were not American citizens. Among other things, giving birth in El Paso made the child eligible for American citizenship.

sciousness. The Chamber of Commerce, the Junior Chamber, and service clubs like Rotary, Lions, Kiwanis, and others, were almost completely Anglo in membership. Despite the fact that El Paso is a large metropolis, members of these organizations display a civic pride more characteristic of smaller cities which want to grow. Local patriotism climaxes annually with the Sun Carnival, a period of festivity after Christmas which is capped by the Sun Bowl football game.

The Spanish-name community has developed relatively few voluntary organizations, LULAC being the most prominent among them.[7] This not only reflects its generally low socio-economic level, but also its relatively low level of internal social integration. The differential degree of organizational density of the Anglo and Spanish-name sub-communities has consequences for their relative abilities to mobilize people to resolve community issues.

El Paso had two daily newspapers, separately owned and operated. *The El Paso Times* was, in general, more conservative and attracted more of the upper-middle and upper-status groups while *The El Paso Herald Post* appealed somewhat more to the lower and middle-status groups. Although both papers were Democratic politically, the *Post's* peppery editor took the critic's role, and on various occasions relished roasting the municipal administration and certain "blue-nosed" groups. His paper was generally regarded as being more interested in and sympathetic to the Spanish-name population. However, neither paper systematically reported local news of specific interest to the Spanish-name community. Neither did they devote much space (less than 1 per cent) to Mexican news.

Three Spanish-language newspapers, one of which was pub-

[7] LULAC, the League of United Latin American Citizens, has branches throughout the Southwest. It has served primarily as a social club although some of its leaders want it to take a more militant stance on economic and political issues.

lished in El Paso, provided news of the activities of the El Paso
Spanish-name population, of C. Juarez, and of Mexico. These
papers also reported general El Paso news. In addition, five
radio stations and two TV stations provided local news. Spanish-
speaking residents of El Paso were also able to tune in the radio
stations located in C. Juarez.

C. JUAREZ

The post-Columbian history of this community began in
1659 when Father García de San Francisco de Zúñiga came as
a missionary to the Rio Grande Valley, then inhabited by small,
dispersed bands of Indians. He and two assistants laid the
foundations for the mission of Nuestra Señora de Guadelupe,
which was formally dedicated in 1668. For almost two centuries
the only permanent settlement in this area was on the southwest
or Mexican side of the river. The United States-Mexican War
of 1846–1848 was almost bloodless in this area because of the
tact used by leaders on both sides. The Treaty of Hidalgo in
1848 stipulated that Mexicans on the northeast side of the river
could have one year to choose whether they would move to
Mexico or become citizens of the United States with all the
rights thereof. In 1865 Benito Juárez, the great Mexican patriot,
made the old city of El Paso del Norte his headquarters in
the struggle against Maximillian and the French.

The city was given its present name in 1888 to honor Benito
Juárez and to end the growing confusion in names between
itself and its Texas neighbor. Like its northern neighbor, C.
Juarez has grown tremendously in the last two decades. From a
level of approximately 55,000 in 1940, the population had
increased to 131,000 in 1950 and close to 300,000 in 1960.

Ecology and Economy

Since El Paso and C. Juarez are highly interdependent economically, they may, in one sense, be thought of as a single

ecological community. Yet their peculiar social and cultural systems make for strikingly different internal ecological patterns. C. Juarez is a much more densely populated city than El Paso, its physical appearance is poorer, and its pattern of land use is less orderly.

The image which most Americans have of a Mexican border city is of a central business district comprised of taverns and tourist shops, beyond which are the houses of prostitution and the slums. Indeed, this stereotype seemed to be verified when, at the time this survey began, one first entered C. Juarez from the Santa Fe Bridge (see Figure 4). The narrow crowded streets were lined with souvenir shops and filled with street hawkers peddling their wares. But beyond this there was a "central" business district which catered to the native population. It was a thriving area similar to those found in interior Mexican cities, containing the stores, shops, banks, and services needed to serve a growing population.

Beyond the business area, stretching east and west parallel to the river, were found middle-class homes and apartments which had a rather drab and uniform appearance. Interspersed among these one might see some of the most luxurious and ostentatious dwellings found in the entire region. Also located in this area were local shopping districts, schools, and some offices. The streets were paved, well lit, cleaned, and patrolled.

Beyond this mainly residential area, the land use suddenly became mixed and deteriorated. Factories, warehouses, adobe houses, vacant lots, and new dwellings were scattered without apparent pattern. The paving deteriorated or became nonexistent, city services decreased or became nonexistent, and dirt and dust were everywhere. This extremely dense area did not gradually thin out as in the United States, but ceased rather suddenly. Although the total built-up area of the city was about one fourth of El Paso, it contained almost the same number of inhabitants.

On either side of the built-up part of C. Juarez, a curious ecological inversion occurred when compared to El Paso. Stretching southeast near the river on relatively low ground opposite an El Paso fringe district were found the country club and a new upper-class suburban residential development.[8] On the opposite side of the city, running northwest on higher ground were found some of the worst slums of the city. This was an incredibly jumbled area with the good and poor adobe dwellings built on eroding ravines next to washed-out and unpaved roads. Tar paper shacks, a modern school, tumbling and rusting tin structures, garages, and stores were built without pattern. Only limited city services extended to this area. Despite the proximity of the city reservoir, no homes contained running water.

The tragic ecological pattern of the city reflected the inability of the city and Mexico itself to solve its basic economic problems. So overpopulated was the city for its economic base that one wondered how the large population could survive. The outstanding feature of the local economy was its dependence on another country and city and its inability to develop a dynamic and self-sufficient industrial base. Yet the very presence of the flourishing economy of El Paso served both as a barrier and a stimulant to business activity.

Without the border the local economy would be similar to that of other Mexican cities farther in the interior. This semi-arid region generally supported cattle raising, cotton growing, and associated small industries. These activities were indeed found and well developed locally. A meat-packing plant, stockyards, two cottonseed oil plants and related facilities were

[8] It was in this area also that the Mexican government established its National Border Program in 1961. Under the direction of Antonio J. Bermúdez of C. Juarez, the program is designed to stimulate the economy, raise the standard of living, and, in general, make Mexico's border cities more attractive to tourists.

located in C. Juarez. However, these enterprises probably did not employ more than a thousand workers. The "independent" economic base of the city also included an iron foundry, a textile mill, a brick and allied products plant, and several small factories. As a market center for a large hinterland of northern Mexico, C. Juarez also contained wholesale, retail, banking and other services of considerable size and importance. Combined, these enterprises employed less than three thousand workers.

Beyond this point the economy of the city was built on its border status. As the major port of entry for Mexico and the United States, it contained a network of railroads and highways referred to above. These and associated facilities employed workers in warehouses, immigration offices, offices regulating international commerce, banks, clearing houses, and so on. The location of an army post and other governmental offices was also related to the border status of the city. The bulk of the "legitimate" local workers (30 per cent) were employed in these activities.

The remaining major segment of the economy was geared largely to the tourist trade and to the economy of El Paso. A brewery and two distilleries, which hired several hundred workers, attempted to assuage the thirst of thousands of tourists and local El Paso clients. Almost four hundred bars and an equal number of restaurants and souvenir shops hired thousands of workers (about 35 per cent of the labor force), who serviced the tourists who poured across the border to see a bit of "Ol' Mexico," buy some leather goods or jewelry, and visit a restaurant or night club. Apparently this situation has existed for a long time, for the historian Peixotto said of his visit there in 1916 that C. Juarez "was a thriving enough Mexican town, deriving a rather large if illicit revenue from gambling joints, a cockpit, a bull ring, and a jockey club."[9] Today the city has

[9] Peixotto, *op. cit.*, p. 95.

two handsome bull rings, a prospective new race track, and a somewhat more polished look of respectability.

Today, as formerly, the military personnel located in El Paso is especially prominent among the tourists who find C. Juarez to be a major recreational attraction. Local bankers estimated that the greater part of the tourists' dollars went into the so-called vices, i. e., prostitution, narcotics, and lewd or bawdy shows where cheap liquor was sold at exorbitant prices. The importance of the tourist business to the local economy was evidenced by the fact that the Juarez municipal budget for 1958 was twenty-one million pesos (less than two million dollars), and almost one third of the municipal income was raised from licenses to operate liquor stores, bars and other establishments which catered to tourists.[10]

The Juarez economy also depended for dollars on the fact that one sixth (15,700 persons) of its labor force has been regularly employed in El Paso in recent years. All of the wages earned were not spent in Mexico, however. These workers and the great majority of Juarenses spent a large part of their earnings in El Paso. Local clothing retailers estimated that about 80 per cent of all dry goods and clothing bought by Juarenses were purchased in El Paso.[11]

The Juarez Municipal Department of Economic and Tourist Development published statistics which showed that in 1959 the per capita average expenditure of all Juarez residents in

[10] The National Border Project appears to be aimed, in part, at lessening the city's dependence on these "undesirable" aspects of tourism.

[11] Unless otherwise indicated, all statements on border economic conditions represent the combined judgments of the financiers and business leaders of the two cities. See also *The Monthly Business Review,* XXXVI, No. 7, n.d., published by the Federal Reserve Bank of Dallas. This is a special issue devoted to El Paso, Texas, and includes important data on goods shipped into and out of Mexico via C. Juarez. There is also a recent publication (1961) by the Mexican Border Program (Calle Manuel Ma. Contreras 133, Mexico 5, D. F.) devoted to C. Juarez, containing the most up-to-date material available.

El Paso was $172.00, spent mainly on food and clothing.[12] As one Juarez banker explained, "Practically all Juarez wears U. S. clothing; of course, we get tourist trade, so we are able to spend there too." Liquor has long been one of the most popular items of tourist purchase. During the month of December 1958, for example, 247,800 bottles of liquor, worth 2,478,000 pesos (approximately $200,000) were bought by Americans in C. Juarez.[13] This was an increase of some 20,000 bottles over 1956.

Unlike the situation in El Paso, occupational and business groups in C. Juarez were unionized at all levels. Moreover, their organizations had direct relevance for the local political situation. Labor unions were found among bootblacks, taxi drivers, waiters, factory workers and school teachers. While the manifest ties of some of these unions to the PRI party were obscure, they were nonetheless present. As in El Paso, the Chamber of Commerce, Rotary, Kiwanis, and other service clubs spoke for a certain group of businessmen who formed a highly integrated social system. They were, for the most part, in the "independent" sector of the local economy: banking, manufacturing, and local marketing. The hundreds of bar, restaurant, and small shopowners were in another organization under the protective eye of one of the branches of PRI.

Government and Politics

Three features of Mexican governmental structure must be understood to appreciate the local political situation. First,

---

[12] *El Fronterizo,* April 15, 1959.

[13] These figures were obtained from data in the U. S. Customs Office in El Paso. The state of Texas charges a tax of about 33 cents for every quart bottle of liquor which is brought into El Paso, and liquor sales were computed on the basis of available tax records (see *El Fronterizo,* April 12, 1959). According to figures released by the Juarez Department of Economic and Tourism Development, during the year 1958, 39,381,736 persons and 7,852,931 vehicles crossed the two international bridges between El Paso and C. Juarez (*El Fronterizo,* April 24, 1959). By the end of 1962, almost 60 million persons were crossing this border annually, representing 26 per cent of all United States-Mexico border crossings.

although local governments have a semblance of autonomy, they are controlled by a highly centralized governmental and party system.[14] Second, the Mexican people generally expect that the government will resolve all local problems—industrial, welfare, education, recreational, and cultural. Third, although free political expression is constitutionally guaranteed, the PRI has been in control since the Revolution.

This party has developed a complex parastructure involving a network of labor, farmer, consumer, educational, professional, cultural, recreational, and patriotic organizations. Its main support has come from organized labor, the small farmer, and the small businessman. Perhaps most impressive politically have been the achievement of an orderly succession to the presidency and the removal of the military from predominant influence on political life. The party rather than any single individual is the dominating force in Mexican politics today. The party also lives with an antibusiness, antipatronal, antichurch, and anti-United States rhetoric. More recently, such polemics have been rather muted. Under PRI leadership the nation has made some impressive economic and social gains. Although rising levels of living, agrarian reform, and rapid industrialization still remain party objectives, a number of serious obstacles delay their early realization. These include a rapidly increasing population, lack of capital, lack of resources, antiquated tradition-oriented bureaucracies, professionally untrained and poorly paid civil servants.

Most of the problems which exist on the national level apply to C. Juarez. One party rule has existed in the city until recently. In the most recent elections, however, the Party of National Action (Partido Accion Nacional) (PAN) has begun to show strength. Its leadership has come primarily from business and professional groups in the city, and its voting support

[14] Leonard Cárdenas, Jr., discusses this point in detail in "The Municipality in Northern Mexico," in *Southwestern Studies*, I, No. 1 (Spring 1963). He states, in part, that "the Mexican municipio is, in effect, a decentralized agency of the state for administration purposes . . ." (p. 18).

has come from white-collar workers, serious churchgoers, some small businessmen and employees of the PAN activists. A stable two-party system may be emerging in the city and along the border, even if not yet in the nation as a whole.[15]

The PAN attacked the local government as being corrupt, inefficient, overly-concerned with state and national politics, antibusiness, and neglectful of local problems. PAN saw the most serious problems as an unbalanced economy, unemployment, lack of educational facilities, unsystematic urban development, an antiquated tax system, and widespread vice. PAN proposed to install a business-like government, free from central party controls, and dedicated to solve local community problems. However, while both parties claimed to be aware of these problems, neither seemed to have practical solutions to resolve them.

[15] For a more complete discussion of this situation see the following: William P. Tucker, *The Mexican Government Today* (Minneapolis: University of Minnesota Press, 1957), especially Chapters 4, 25, and 26; L. Vincent Padgett, "Mexico's One Party System: A Re-Evaluation," *The American Political Science Review*, II (December 1957), 995–1008; and Robert E. Scott, *Mexican Government in Transition* (Urbana: University of Illinois Press, 1959), pp. 182–186, and 237–241. The Party of National Action is in some ways similar to the Christian Democratic parties of Western Europe, although it has not, up to now, taken on all the formal philosophical aspects of these parties, nor does it enjoy the prestige and stability of the Western European parties, nor even the growing strength of such parties as that of Chile under Eduardo Frei Montalva. The long Church-State struggle in Mexico, which culminated in the bitter persecutions of the 1920's still continues to limit the influence and development of this party. PAN has also suffered from internal dissension between conservatives interested primarily in free elections and nineteenth-century prerogatives, and moderate reformers who realize the need for more social change. The founders of PAN in C. Juarez appeared to be anything but wealthy bankers and docile tools of the clergy. Rather they were small businessmen of humble origin whose major energy was devoted to the formation of a party in opposition to PRI. They, too, wanted a better life for all Mexicans, but didn't think it was possible under one-party government. The PAN has also shown strength in Baja California, and in the Yucatan Peninsula as well as in certain sections of Mexico City. The PAN viewpoint has been expressed publicly since 1939 in a weekly news magazine called *La Nación*.

Education and Welfare

The cleavage between the PRI party and its parastructure and the PAN party and its tangent associations became increasingly widened as our study progressed. PRI became an easy target because it was structurally incapable of meeting the many problems which were under the jurisdiction of the federal and/or state government. For example, the Juarez public educational system was sorely deficient. It lacked teachers, schools, and supplies. As a consequence, an estimated 10 to 15 per cent of the school-age population could not attend school in 1954. The one high school, of recent construction, was badly short of books. The situation continued to deteriorate during the latter part of the decade because of the rapid population increase, despite the building of eight new schools in three years.

By law, the state and federal governments were responsible for education; yet PAN and the independent business and professional leaders in the community expected the local administration to meet the problem. It did not have the resources. Although parochial schools were officially outlawed, the business-professional groups were in the process of building them. The federal government had, in fact, acknowledged in recent years that it could not meet Mexico's school problem, and it did not interfere with private education.

Several small private schools specializing in English and commercial courses sprang up in the city in recent years. The Juarez Agricultural College, also largely dependent on state and federal support, was located on the outskirts of the city. Its resources were very limited but it aided students who were desperately poor but determined to obtain some form of higher education. Many Juarenses cast envious eyes across the border and attempted by legal or illegal means to get their children into the El Paso school system.

As indicated, C. Juarez faced a desperate welfare problem produced by unemployment, underemployment and overpopulation. The ill-health, malnutrition, and poor housing endured by thousands could not be met within the traditional structure of begging, personal charity, and government welfare. The United Fund program of El Paso was not developed in C. Juarez because the political cleavage in the community discouraged the development of a joint private-public welfare structure. Those who could afford it and were willing supported a needy family (often a distant kin or an ex-employee), or contributed to a private charity such as the local Boy's Town, the church, or a service organization.

The magnitude of the welfare problem was clearly summarized in the mayor's final report of October 1959. He estimated that there were then 25,000 persons without stable residence in the city. They had come in search of better living conditions, hoping to find extraordinary job opportunities on the border, either in Mexico or in the United States. Unable to carry out their plans and without the immediate possibility of returning home, they became a problem of serious proportion for the authorities in matters of housing, policing, health, diet, education, and work.[16]

Religion

Most Juarez citizens were at least nominal Catholics. Many Church activities were formally restricted by a number of national laws which were being less rigorously enforced locally in recent years. For example, clergymen appeared in public at times wearing their clerical garb, which was against the law. Although technically illegal, the Church was engaged in a vigorous program of building churches and schools. Businessmen and others had overcome their timidity about publicly displaying their interest and support of religious activities.[17] In

[16] VI *Informe Semestral del Presidente Municipal*, C. Juarez, October 1959 (writers' translation).

[17] The Constitution of 1917 prohibits the Church from owning property, and all priests are automatically disfranchised and required to wear civilian clothes in public.

response to this increased activity and to the expanding population, the Juarez region was raised to the level of a diocese with its own bishop in 1957. Yet religious authorities felt that they lacked buildings and personnel to carry out their functions properly. There were less than twenty priests in the region in 1955 to serve the religious needs of the growing population, and the number of priests had not increased appreciably by 1960.

Obviously a large proportion of the population was unchurched. Some of the PRI leaders were aggressive Masons and retained their traditional hostility toward the Church. Several Protestant churches were located in the city and they seemed to have a solidary following. The small Jewish colony apparently conducted most of its religious activities in El Paso.

Voluntary Associations

Organizational density in C. Juarez was somewhat lower than in El Paso because the former city had a larger proportion of its population in lower economic levels who belonged to no organization. Yet a large number of "voluntary organizations" were found in C. Juarez and these seemed to be closely tied to the two political currents. White-collar, professional, and business persons belonged to the same number and type of occupational and civic organizations on the national, state, and local level as their American counterparts. C. Juarez supported a larger number of "cultural" organizations than El Paso. Literary, musical, historical, and art groups were patronized by the contending political groups because they did not want to participate in the same organizations.

Mass Communication

C. Juarez had two daily newspapers owned by the same national chain. For a short time one of these papers took the role of the "loyal opposition" toward the local government. After a series of local crises, it reaffirmed the national policy of support or noncriticism. Local polemics, therefore, were restricted to the several small but widely read weeklies which were published by the labor unions and opposing political groups. The city also boasted a locally operated television station and three radio stations, one of which was among the most powerful in the Southwest and was heard throughout Texas, New Mexico, parts of Arizona, and vast areas of Mexico.

We have attempted to present a brief sketch of the ecology, institutional patterns, and problems confronting El Paso and C. Juarez. Table II presents summary data for some of the important characteristics of the two cities. While the populations of both cities grew at a more or less equal pace during the 1950's, there was little else in which they were equal. Even the first generation Spanish-speaking workers in El Paso were better off than their Juarez relatives. El Paso had more of its youth in

TABLE II

CHARACTERISTICS OF EL PASO AND C. JUAREZ
POPULATIONS: 1960

	El Paso	C. Juarez
Number of inhabitants	276,687	262,119
Per cent 14–17 years old in school	85.9	31
Median years of schooling, population 25 years old or older	11.1	4
Per capita annual income (1959 estimates)	$1,920	$640
Labor Force	91,400	95,000
Per cent unemployed	6	15

Sources: United States Census of Population, 1960; Mexico VIII Censo General de Poblacion 1960; Bulletin of the Mexican Border Program on Ciudad Juarez, 1961.* The latter publication contains a detailed discussion on the economics of the two cities, and prospects for future growth and development.

* Estimates based on 1950 census data. The population for El Paso in 1950 was 130,485 and for C. Juarez 131,308.

schools at all age levels, and its adult population was more highly educated. It had less unemployment, despite the fact that it employed one sixth of the total Juarez labor force. The per capita annual income of the El Pasoan was three times as high as that of his neighbor in C. Juarez. As several Mexican friends used to ask: "Why should an almost dry riverbed make such a big difference?"

INTER-COMMUNITY AFFAIRS

National political boundaries may serve as focal points for tension and conflict between nations. The United States and Mexico have had a number of disputes or disagreements in the past, especially on matters dealing with political boundaries. Among these were the War of 1846–1848, the unresolved problem (prior to 1963) of the Chamizal area of El Paso which was claimed by Mexico,[18] the raid into New Mexico by Pancho Villa

[18] For a typical statement on El Chamizal from the Mexican viewpoint, see the article by Lic. Clemente Bolio, in *El Correo de C. Juarez*, August 9, 1962. Lic. Bolio was the president of the Regional Committee of the Chihuahua Society of Historical Studies; he argued succinctly that justice required that the 1911 Arbitration Award be honored. For a complete description and analysis of the Chamizal case, see *The International Boundary Commission United States and Mexico* (Austin: The University of Texas Press, 1941), pp. 132–174. The Chamizal consists of some 600 acres of land between the present channel of the Rio Grande on the south and the obliterated channel of 1852-1853. It had been under United States and Texas jurisdiction since 1853. When the case of ownership was submitted to arbitration in 1911, 6,000 of El Paso's 40,000 population were living in the Chamizal. However, only some 3,500 persons were affected by the agreement reached in July 1963.
The Mexican claim has been that the river took an abrupt and sudden change between 1864 and 1873 causing it to cut a new channel. They also claimed that under the treaties of 1848 and 1852, all of the land lying south of the old channel still belonged to Mexico. The treaties had stipulated that the midpoint of the river should remain the boundary between the two countries, and that gradual and slow changes caused by erosion and accretion of soil would bring about legitimate changes in the boundary. However, if changes in the river bed were caused by avulsion or rapid change, such a change would not constitute a change in the boundary. The Chamizal dispute remained for so long unresolved, in part because the parties were not able to

in 1915, and the subsequent pursuit of Villa into Mexico by General Pershing. These disputes tended to heighten the cultural and ethnic distinctions between the nations, and generally encouraged strong prejudices on both sides.

Under other circumstances, political boundaries may provide nations the opportunity for contacts which can reduce tension and conflict. A *modus operandi* may arise in border areas which makes it possible for different peoples to work together toward common economic and social goals both for the immediate area and for their respective nations. Border areas are sometimes the locale of important international contacts or events and they may come to symbolize international friendship and mutual admiration. Two cases in point were the meeting between Presidents Taft and Díaz at C. Juarez and El Paso in 1909, and the meeting between Presidents Camacho and Roosevelt at Monterrey, Mexico, in 1943. These events stimulated a host of other activities, which were designed to reduce sources of hostility and conflict.

In the case of El Paso and C. Juarez, the international contacts of the communities' leaders were important not only because they set the tone for general relations between the two communities, but also because they comprised the stage for

agree on whether or not the change which brought the Chamizal into existence was slow and gradual or avulsive. It has been agreed that the changes which occurred between 1852 and 1864 were slow and gradual, and the Arbitration Commission of 1911, by a two to one vote, declared that the changes between 1864 and 1873 were sudden and avulsive. The United States formally rejected the decision on the grounds that (a) the facts regarding these changes were not demonstrated, and (b) that the Commission had failed to define clearly the course of the river in 1864. The United States also declared that the award was so uncertain and indefinite that it could not be complied with. In July 1963 the American government formally acknowledged that the Chamizal belonged to Mexico and made plans to transfer the land. Figure 2 shows the land in dispute as well as the proposed new boundary. The city of El Paso published a pamphlet to commemorate the Chamizal settlement. Maps and figures in this chapter are taken from this pamphlet.

FIGURE 2. *Chamizal boundary agreement. (Solid line indicates Rio Grande River boundary; dotted line represents the new river channel and international boundary.) Courtesy of El Paso Department of Planning.*

decision-making in an international context. For these reasons it was important to know how much and what kinds of contacts existed among the business and political leaders of the two communities in 1955.

Business Contacts

During the first visit to the border we interviewed thirty-eight business and nineteen political influentials in El Paso and thirty-seven and twenty-two respectively in C. Juarez. Four out of five Juarez business leaders reported that they had business contacts with El Pasoans, while three out of five El Pasoans indicated they had similar contacts with people in C. Juarez. One fifth of the Juarez leaders said that the two cities were "mutually interdependent economically," one third felt that

El Paso was economically dependent on C. Juarez, and the remaining held an opposing view. The El Pasoans on the other hand unanimously felt that in business contacts, C. Juarez was more dependent on the El Paso economy. Whatever the actual case, businessmen in both cities had to be concerned about their international relations, and did their utmost to avoid political activity injurious to their interests. A tightening or a change in customs regulations or immigration policies on either side would affect the industrialists in El Paso who employed large numbers of Juarenses; the merchants in El Paso who also employed Juarenses and who needed their trade; the Mexican retailers who wanted tourist trade and minimum duty on goods admitted into the United States; the Mexican brokers who handled the import of American goods; and the bankers who were constantly concerned about having a favorable dollar balance in the Mexican economy.

The following incident illustrates the impact which a change in national policy could have on the economy of the two border communities. In the spring of 1954 the Mexican government devalued the Mexican peso in relation to the American dollar from 8.4 to 1.0 to 12.5 to 1.0. The repercussions of this devaluation were strongly felt in the border area for the next year or so. The following quotations offer some evidence of the complexity of the problem and of the variety of attitudes surrounding it. An El Paso banker commented:

> We just went through a devaluation of the peso that was pretty severe. . . . Locally, for several weeks after devaluation almost nothing came across. After a month or so trade began again.

In October, another banker linked devaluation with the import-export problem in the following terms:

> There has been no bank activity since the devaluation in April; it caught all of us unawares. Before this devaluation there was an active import-export trade. . . . Whereas a Mexican used to take three bags

of merchandise home on the streetcar, today he carries only one. No luxuries are permitted in Mexico from the U. S. either. As a result, there is more, rather than less economic nationalism in Mexico today. They're trying to become self-sufficient economically. This is a rough way to do it.

Another El Paso influential summarized the situation:

About 3,500 items are now made in Mexico, protected by tariff, so practically all imports of these items have stopped. This has brought about a change in Juarez-El Paso relationships. Mexican nationalism is the cause of this restricted trade. The effort to make Juarez aware of Mexico's growing industry has resulted in the Juarez Exposition, opening soon. It is estimated that of every tourist dollar spent in Juarez, eighty cents returned to El Paso during the war and peak postwar years of trade. This is no longer true. Devaluation of the peso has hurt El Paso business even further, while Juarez business has increased with national restrictions. On the other hand, El Pasoans are not spending as much in Juarez now due to a falling off of the quality of food and drink in Juarez restaurants.

We asked a variety of El Paso merchants how trade restrictions and peso devaluation had affected their business.

A downtown haberdasher indicated that he had suffered a drop of 40 per cent in his trade. An army surplus store owner revealed that a drop of 30 per cent in his trade following the devaluation made him realize how dependent he was on Mexican trade.

A chain foodstore manager had a different view of the situation:

There has been some drop in business, but not enough to worry about. The strength of our business comes from the factories in the area which hire Mexican labor. They buy here with their American-earned money. But there is not as much business with Mexican pesos.

One of the most influential businessmen in El Paso appeared to be resigned to the growth of Mexican business nationalism:

Mexico today has a problem which has been growing for the past few years; they have a right to do what will help them. In their *Buy Mexico* campaign they have caused us a business loss. Small business has been hurt even more, and they (the small businessmen) have asked the Chamber of Commerce to try to get restrictions eased, while they recognize Mexico's right to do as they will. There is the feeling of some in El Paso that Mexico should reciprocate the duty-free allowances which the U.S. permits to U.S. tourists.

No unanimity was expressed by the Juarez influentials on what the peso devaluation and the *Buy Mexican* programs meant. Their attitudes were, however, often at variance with those expressed by El Pasoans. An influential Juarez banker said:

> The U.S. could have done much to gain Mexican friendship by not allowing the peso devaluation. It could have offered help in getting investments, which is what we need. . . . Tourist trade is of the first importance. There is much fault on both sides. There is too much easy money exploitation by some Juarez merchants seeking a quick fortune. But there is fault too in El Paso on the advice they give to tourists: 'Don't take your car to Juarez'; 'Be careful! They'll rob you'; 'Watch out for vice.'
>
> *Buy Mexico* is good for Mexico, but there are things which it will not pay Mexico to produce. Mexican industry must be light. We'll have to go on buying much from the U.S. . . . We are no less patriotic here. Buying in El Paso is a personal convenience, not a lack of patriotism.
>
> There has been a great increase in tourist trade following devaluation. People have started coming here to buy things. Local people now think twice about buying in El Paso. Wages have gone up in proportion to devaluation.

Not all Juarez influentials were wholehearted supporters of the *Buy Mexico* program. The following comments by a municipal official reflected the internal cleavage:

> *Buy Mexico* will work only for those who can't afford to buy in the U.S. Quality is the difference. Patriotism is no issue. . . . The advantage to Juarez of its border situation is more business activity through tourism and working in El Paso. Those earning American money own their own homes, cars, and other vestments of economic well-being. They live better economically than many [Mexicans] in higher social

positions. . . . This struggle of *Buy Mexico* is useless; the law of supply
and demand will win out. People will buy the cheapest and best. The
Mexicans must lower their prices and raise quality. The Juarez
businessman buys cheap in the interior and sells high here.

In summary, peso devaluation, a strongly nationalistic *Buy
Mexico* campaign, tourism, duty-free allotments, and Juarenses
working in El Paso stores and in factories, were all important
considerations which made businessmen on both sides of the
border realize that their relations had to be regularized.

Working toward this end, leaders of the two Chambers of
Commerce established in 1952 a special International Committee. The committee was charged with the responsibility of
resolving problems of mutual concern and improving the
economy of both communities. This committee apparently was
instrumental in helping C. Juarez arrange its first National
Industrial Exposition in October 1954. It also undertook to
foster better international understanding by honoring American
and Mexican groups which visited the communities. For
example, when the newspaperwomen of Texas held their
Annual Convention in El Paso in November 1954, a special
luncheon was given in their honor by the Juarez Chamber of
Commerce. The executive board of the El Paso Chamber was
also present at this affair.

Most of the leaders candidly admitted that the activity of
the International Committee of the Chambers of Commerce
had been more social than economic in the early years. However, they recognized the potential economic importance of
this committee in the long run. That it could be effective was
aptly demonstrated by the part which it played in the Juarez
Industrial Exposition referred to above. The exposition was
actually economically undesirable from the point of view of the
El Paso businessmen since its principal aim was to encourage
Mexicans to buy Mexican. Nevertheless, the El Paso Chamber
of Commerce, through its committee members, gave substantial

help to the sponsors of the exposition. The officials of the El Paso Chamber were honored guests at the ceremonies opening the exposition. When several of these officials were asked whether the exposition might affect their markets adversely, they agreed that it might but hastened to add that they could not stop the Mexicans from carrying out their plans. They felt that in the long run both communities would benefit from such co-operation. This attitude was well summarized by a Chamber of Commerce official:

> We have to get along with them, you know. They are our neighbors. We are kind of emissaries of the U.S. here. If we don't get along with them, then the U.S. doesn't get along, and that is not good for the country. So we go to it to get along. It's our duty.

All of the service clubs (Rotary, Lions, Kiwanis) in both cities had special committees to handle international banquets, luncheons and other ceremonials. Many businessmen made it a point to lunch occasionally at "their service club" in the neighboring city. Although the value of these kinds of contacts was difficult to gauge, most informants agreed they were a good thing, if for no other reason than that they "give us a chance to know each other better." The following comments by an American, made in an informal grouping of Mexicans and Americans just prior to a Rotary luncheon in C. Juarez, typifies the kinds of conversations that took place:

> Solve that one [the economic problem facing the two cities] and all others will resolve themselves; and you won't have political instability and its related headaches. Only when the economy of Juarez comes to approximate that of El Paso will healthy relations exist. The great difference in the economies also has the psychological effect of producing an inferiority complex in the Mexican. Add to this the poor image which most Anglos have of Mexicans [due to their contacts only with wetback maids and gardeners and braceros] and you have a real problem. The paseños just don't know many of the cultured people of Juarez, who in many cases are more highly cultured than they are.

He went on to praise Rotary because it helped bring Mexicans and Americans together.[19]

In summary, it appears that although economic relationships between the people of the two cities occurred at various levels, for example, employer-employee, buyer-seller, tourist-native, most of the personal contacts among the business leaders were in the formal voluntary associations and the activities they sponsored. Businessmen in both cities recognized some degree of economic interdependence, but they did not try to build intimate and personal relationships upon business ones. A more systematic analysis of the nature and amount of these contacts will be made later in the chapter.

Political Contacts

Most of the business activities referred to above could not have taken place without the positive sanctions of the governments at several levels. On the federal level, immigration and customs officials learned over the years to reduce friction within areas of their control. One of the oldest international agencies on the border is the Water Boundaries Commission, which has sought for years to distribute scarce waters of the Rio Grande equitably. On the municipal level, the mayors of both cities were in constant contact to meet the common problems faced by the police, fire, health, and other departments. The municipal governments have established their own international relations committees to resolve these problems. As one mayor of C. Juarez put it:

> Within the framework of national dignity my policy has been to work closely with El Paso authorities. . . . In police questions we are one

[19] Almost half of the population of El Paso was of Spanish-name background. Most of these people had friends and relatives residing in C. Juarez whom they visited regularly. The least amount of contact probably occurred between the Anglos of El Paso and the average Juarez citizen. There was also minimal contact between Anglos and Spanish-name persons in El Paso itself.

area here. If anybody commits a crime here and goes to El Paso and El Paso wouldn't help, we would be stuck. We work hard on these mutual problems. Our health departments also get together. In the campaign against flies, mosquitos, and venereal disease both cities co-operate.

Officials in both cities agreed that during recent years the relations between the cities had generally been cordial, although at times frictions and tensions did arise. In recent years the strains were more often induced by outside forces than persons residing in either of the communities. United States Senator William Langer's visit to the border in 1954 was one such case. As one Juarez political influential reported it:

> A few weeks ago, something happened with Senator Langer which I didn't like. We have been working closely with the El Paso police, and dope smuggling has been clamped down [the FBI in El Paso has been working with us and instructing our detectives in their methods]. I was surprised when Langer came here and blamed everything on us. I was also surprised when Jones said to Langer that there were no peddlers in El Paso because it was so easy to get dope in Juarez.

The problems of narcotics, vice, and prostitution control brought the two cities together, but they always remained a potential source of irritation and friction. Although Juarenses criticized themselves a great deal on this problem even to Americans, they were loath to hear Americans pontificate on the subject. One El Paso influential insisted that the vice problem in Juarez wasn't entirely the fault of the Mexicans:

> The girls aren't there for the benefit of the Mexicans. They are there for the Americans, especially for the soldiers. And the same goes for the bars and night clubs. Texas has a law prohibiting the sale of hard liquor in bars and public places [i.e., for drinking on the premises], so the Americans all go to Juarez.

The local governments and their committees constantly worked to minimize legislation at the state or national levels which would adversely affect the relationships between the two cities. In recent years, for example, the Mexican government passed laws aimed to restrict the flow of duty-free American goods into the country. These laws had particularly adverse effect on the furniture and appliance businesses in El Paso. Liquor and gasoline lobbies in Texas have tried for years to get the state to levy heavy state taxes on the import of these products into Texas. Both cities, of course, feared changes in policy regarding the border working permits which made it possible for Juarenses to work in El Paso.

Many face-to-face contacts among the political influentials took place on ceremonial occasions, such as Pan American Day, the Fourth of July, the Sixteenth of September, and Sun Carnival Week. On such occasions the officials of one city were the guests of the host city, and were often asked to speak. Banquets honoring military officials stationed locally and visiting dignitaries also brought the officials together.

The above observations suggest the variety and complexity of the contacts found among the political and business leaders of the two cities. A detailed analysis[20] of the nature and amount of contacts among the different leaders revealed distinct differences. On a variety of indices, the Juarez businessmen had significantly more contact with El Pasoans and United States society in general than any other group of leaders. Certain individual political leaders in both cities had extremely high cross-national contacts. However, a large majority of Juarez

[20] The interview schedule in 1955 included a nine-item index of international contacts. The amount of contact of the business and political leaders in the two cities was compared. The chi-square test of association showed that differences in contact between the Juarez business leaders and the other three groups were statistically significant at the .01 level. That is, the probability of these differences occurring by chance alone was less than one in 100. This strongly supports our contention that the social forces operating on the Juarez businessmen were significantly different from those operating on the other three groups.

businessmen spoke English well, had received some education in El Paso or other United States schools, and carried on extensive business relations with Americans. They had more personal friends in the other country and visited them more frequently than any other group. They visited El Paso on the average of once a week, and were more likely than El Pasoans or Juarez political leaders to include Americans among their best friends.

Several factors may account for the differences in cross-cultural contacts. In the first place, political systems are primarily concerned with boundary maintenance, so that the focus of their activities, at least at the local level, tends to be internal. The peculiar conditions of border life encouraged some governmental officials in both systems to extend their contacts across the border. However, this pattern was not characteristic of most governmental and political leaders.

For the businessmen the situation was somewhat different. Historically, business has been and continues to be universalistic in its orientations. It pays little attention to man-made boundaries, governmental restrictions, or *Buy Mexico* campaigns. El Paso businessmen were keenly aware of their dependence on Mexican customers. They believed that customers would be naturally attracted to El Paso if the governments did not place "unnatural" barriers in the way. However, they did recognize that although Juarez trade was important, they could get along without it.

Juarez businessmen had more international contacts than other groups for a number of reasons. In the first place, the Mexican Revolution forced many of their families into temporary exile in the United States. Consequently they went to American schools where they learned English, and something about Anglo-Saxon culture and values. Secondly, Mexican business has in recent years been patterned after American and Western European business. The proximity of American business across the border served as a model which could be closely observed. Third, there were economic reasons for contact with American business. Juarez businessmen indicated that much of the goods they needed could be obtained more readily and less expensively from El Paso than from the interior of Mexico. Therefore, they found it hard to resist the temptation to order high quality and abundant supplies from El Paso. Last, the border provided them with an unusual opportunity to observe at close hand a successful "free enterprise" system in operation. While they desired this system for themselves, they also felt a growing loyalty to Mexican economic policies. This led to ambivalent attitudes and contradictory behavior. This condition was exemplified by a Juarez businessman who said, "Everybody prefers free trade. A free zone would help the frontier, but (it would) not be good for Mexico, and so as a Mexican I oppose it."

The question may be raised whether the cleavage between the business and political influentials in Mexico might be aggravated by this high degree of contact which Mexican businessmen had with El Paso. Aggravations may be exacerbated when businessmen are in a position daily to compare their lot with businessmen across the river who are enjoying institutional arrangements which they feel are denied them.

We have attempted in this chapter to present a brief history and description of these two communities. From their very beginning they have been closely related both economically and socially. Yet as part of larger national systems they have had different political and economic fortunes. Interdependence in a context of economic and other types of inequalities has produced an ambivalence among the business and political leaders of both communities which has sometimes led to conflict. Yet over the years their relationships have been institutionalized and conflict has been reduced.

The relations among the business and political leaders of the two communities today are quite complex. Generally speaking, the two Mexican groups had more contacts in the United States than their American counterparts had in Mexico. Among the Mexicans the businessmen appeared to have more contacts and a greater variety of contacts than the governmental and political leaders.

The symptoms of nationalism, which are so endemic in Latin America today, were prevalent along the border when we first began the research. Yet this nationalism did not automatically lead to conflict and hostility. It is true that some businessmen resented the peso devaluation and the *Buy Mexico* campaign because of the adverse effect on their business, and that some Mexicans resented the aggressive business tactics of some El Paso merchants. But on the whole, leaders on both sides of the border viewed these situations as normal problems which arise when two nations are so close to one another. They were determined not to let such problems lead to conflict. The *modus vivendi* worked out by the municipal governments, the regularized relations between the business communities, and the friendships established across the border constituted the bedrock of confidence which was needed to resolve such international issues as are described in Chapter 8.

Before examining problem-solving in an international context we need to know something more of the structure of influence and the decision-making processes within each city. The next chapter describes the influentials in business and politics in the two communities and how they were identified.

CHAPTER 3

Identification of Business and Political Influentials

ONE OF THE LONG-RANGE problems in the border research was to study the role which influential persons in El Paso and C. Juarez played in technological and/or organizational interchange between the nations. We felt in 1954 that a requisite for studying this problem was knowledge of the structure of influence within and between business and government because these institutions would be heavily involved in international interchanges. How influential people in these two sectors perceived the power structure within their communities and in the community across the border would undoubtedly affect their behavior. It would also be important to know the amount and type of contacts then taking place between the influential persons of these communities.

In pursuing the study of influentials we were not primarily concerned with the internal administrative problems or the general authoritative relationships within the institutions. Neither did we intend to make a systematic census nor record protocols of decision-making in the two communities. However, we were concerned with community decisions involving the economic and governmental institutions. At that time, we were under the influence of Floyd Hunter and we adapted some of his techniques for locating influentials, after making certain modifications to suit our purposes. We felt that these modifications would shed more light on the inter-institutional relationships within and between the cities. Such information later proved useful in studying general decisions within and between the communities.

To begin the study of influence, we decided to interview the people who held the highest formal or authoritative positions in the business and governmental organizations of the two cities. These included mayors and former mayors, city councilmen, judges, appointed city and federal officials, and top executives of finance, commerce, and industry. In addition, we also decided to interview high administrative officials in education, religion, labor unions, the mass-media of communications, leading professionals and other presumed knowledgeables. The purpose of these interviews was to obtain as intimate a picture as possible of the normal routinized authority relationships within the institutions. We assumed that the officials we interviewed would have an intimate and accurate knowledge of the decisions which affected their institutions, and that they would know the people who had greatest influence within their institutional sectors and people who had influence in matters involving relationships with other institutions. We also considered the possibility that our respondents might themselves be highly influential in their institutions and in community decisions involving their institutions.

In seeking to identify the influentials we made a number of assumptions: (1) that a small number of persons (less than one hundred) were crucial in decision-making within the institutions of the community; (2) that major community decisions were primarily in the hands of business and political leaders; (3) that people of influence would be known to knowledgeable persons and that they would have some success in making decisions within their sectors and possibly in the broader community; (4) that we could study both El Paso and C. Juarez with the same methods even though the cities were in different countries and represented differing sociocultural systems; and (5) that the best people to ask about who had influence were those who occupied high positions in business and government, on the grounds that they were the ones who had to make formal decisions or implement the decisions reached by others.

These assumptions were not completely untested. Our exploratory interviews with heads of all the institutions suggested that the most influential persons in community decision-making tended to be businessmen or political leaders. The interviews also revealed that the heads of the largest business and governmental bureaus were either very knowledgeable about the local power structure, or could direct us to people who were very knowledgeable about local power arrangements, or were themselves highly influential. Thus we used these respondents as primary sources of knowledge about both local and international issues and as sources of knowledge about persons who had the reputation for greatest influence or power.

The task pursued during and after the exploratory interviews was to identify the persons who were reputed to be the most influential in business and/or politics in their respective communities. In the interviews with them and others we sought in 1955 to arrive at their perception about the power situation in the business and political sectors of El Paso and C. Juarez, and about the structure of community power in general.[1]

---

[1] For a recent study employing methodology in many ways similar to ours, see M. Elaine Burgess, *Negro Leadership in a Southern City* (Chapel Hill: University of North Carolina Press, 1961), especially Chapters 4 and 5. For a full range of criticisms about the use of these techniques, see the *American Sociological Review*, XXVIII (December 1962), 848–854.

IDENTIFYING BUSINESS AND POLITICAL INFLUENTIALS

In the Appendix the method employed to identify influentials is described in detail. Here it is sufficient to indicate that we asked all institutional heads to name a dozen people who they felt had the greatest amount of personal influence and power in the governmental and political area. Then we began to interview the people named, and received from them names of influentials in the two institutional sectors.

Seventy-three El Pasoans out of the eighty-nine whom we formally interviewed provided us such names. In C. Juarez, seventy-one provided names. The names (fictitious) of the business and political influentials in both cities and how the judges from these sectors and knowledgeables[2] voted for them appear in Tables III, IV, V and VI. Although more persons were nominated in El Paso than in C. Juarez, about the same total number received three or more votes in both cities.[3] The greater number of nominations in El Paso may reflect its larger and more diversified business structure, and its more complex legal-political structure. The voting also points to greater clarity in the perceived location of influence in C. Juarez, both in business and in politics, because a higher proportion of those receiving votes in C. Juarez received three or more votes.

Irrespective of the institutional identity of the judges and knowledgeables, they were more likely to select twelve busi-

[2] By "knowledgeables" we mean those persons in positions of some importance in community organizations, such as general manager of the Chamber of Commerce, City Clerk, newspaper reporter, who were not perceived to be influentials.

[3] The problem of deciding what degree of consensus is necessary among the judges to decide that a person is an influential is still unresolved. We decided beforehand to call "influential" all those who received at least three votes from the different judges. The clustering of votes actually revealed that the majority in every one of the four sectors (two from each city) received only one or two votes. The utility of the technique must lie in the close relationship between the high vote-receivers and those found to be decision-makers in a broad range of community issues. We will consider this point in a later chapter.

TABLE III

EL PASO BUSINESS INFLUENTIALS RANKED ACCORDING TO NUMBER OF VOTES RECEIVED, 1955

Votes From Judges

Name	(1) Political N-17	(2) Business N-32	(3) Knowledge-ables N-20	(4) Total Votes N-69	(5) Votes From Sociometric Leaders N-12
William Cofield	10	27	7	44	7
Fred Alger	9	27	8	44	7
Allen Bartlett	8	23	11	42	7
H. J. Popsley	7	21	10	38	7
Bill Bell	5	12	4	21	6
Sam Chappell	5	13	1	19	3
Joe Webster	4	9	4	17	1
Mike Kerrin	6	7	3	16	2
Steve Ladowski	1	11	4	16	3
James Lynn	1	7	6	14	2
Jack Brown	3	9	2	14	4
Vince Elson	3	9	2	14	3
Al Jones	4	7	3	14	2
Hal Boyton	5	6	2	13	
Frank Sterling	2	10	1	13	
Charles Stephans	1	7	5	13	
Howard Banks	2	8	2	12	
Phil Beardsley	4	5	2	11	
Edward Broon	1	4	5	10	
Dan Hicks	3	3	3	9	
John Burns	2	3	3	8	
Ed Sneedby	1	5	2	8	
Sam Popsley	2	2	4	8	
Walt Doyle	1	5	2	8	
Ferd Ramírez	2	4	1	8	

Note: *The remaining influentials received votes as follows:*
Three tied with 7 votes
Ten tied with 6 votes
Four tied with 5 votes
Five tied with 4 votes
Four tied with 3 votes

ness influentials than twelve political influentials. The vote
received by the top twelve persons, hereafter referred to as the
"key influentials" or "sociometric leaders," is instructive in this
regard. In both cities the business influentials received substantially more votes than did the politicos (political influentials): 329 and 250 for the Juarez and El Paso businessmen

TABLE IV
EL PASO POLITICAL INFLUENTIALS RANKED
ACCORDING TO NUMBER OF VOTES RECEIVED, 1955

Votes From Judges

Name	(1) Political N-16	(2) Business N-28	(3) Knowledge-ables N-18	(4) Total Votes N-62	(5) Votes From Sociometric Leaders N-12
Edward Broon	13	15	10	38	8
Albert Stillman	11	17	9	37	4
James Lynn	6	4	9	19	2
Juan Rivera	3	8	8	19	2
Ferd Ramírez	4	11	3	18	4
John Burns	3	5	6	14	3
Ray Battle	6	2	4	12	1
William Cofield	4	0	5	9	2
Fred Hackett	1	2	6	9	0
Dan Hicks	2	6	0	8	1
Fred Alger	4	1	3	8	2
Phil Beardsley	4	3	1	8	3
Thomas Parton	3	1	3	7	
Harold Nall	4	1	2	7	
José Jiménez	2	2	2	6	

Note: *The remaining influentials received votes as follows:*
Two tied with 5 votes
Six tied with 4 votes
Seven tied with 3 votes

TABLE V

C. JUAREZ BUSINESS INFLUENTIALS RANKED
ACCORDING TO NUMBER OF VOTES RECEIVED, 1955

Votes From Judges

Name	(1) Political N-17	(2) Business N-33	(3) Knowledge-ables N-21	(4) Total Votes N-71	(5) Votes From Sociometric Leaders N-12
Pablo Navárez	7	26	15	48	7
Jaime García	10	19	15	44	4
Cristóbal Villareal	7	23	14	44	6
Juan Banco	12	17	10	39	4
Miguel Aguirre	7	19	8	34	5
Francisco Porvenir	2	19	13	34	7
Alfredo González	7	11	8	25	2
Felipe Morales	6	12	6	24	5
Jesús Blanco	3	13	5	21	4
Rafael Gómez	2	12	7	21	7
Enrique Hernández	2	13	4	19	5
Ramón Torres	1	15	2	18	4
Luis Viejo	3	10	14	17	
Alfonso Miramar	3	9	3	15	
Manuel Flores	1	14	0	15	
David Castillo	6	4	5	15	
Rodrigo Leal	1	8	6	15	
Alfonso Palmer	2	10	3	15	
Pablo Telles	3	4	7	14	
Manuel O'Higgins	3	6	5	14	
Fernando Steel	5	5	3	13	
Renato Herrera	5	3	4	12	
René Poblete	1	9	1	11	

Note: *The remaining influentials received votes as follows:*
    One with 9 votes
    Two tied with 8 votes
    Two tied with 7 votes
    Five tied with 6 votes
    Four tied with 5 votes
    Four tied with 4 votes
    Four tied with 3 votes

TABLE VI

C. JUAREZ POLITICAL INFLUENTIALS RANKED
ACCORDING TO NUMBER OF VOTES RECEIVED, 1955

Votes From Judges

Name	(1) Political N-20	(2) Business N-31	(3) Knowledge- ables N-17	(4) Total Votes N-68	(5) Votes From Sociometric Leaders N-10
Clemente Pérez	17	30	16	63	6
Raúl Días	14	14	9	37	4
Antonio Flores	11	8	12	31	5
Juan Seguro	7	14	6	27	4
Gen. Carlos Medina	8	12	5	25	5
Pablo Miranda	10	7	7	24	5
Gov. Alfredo Montones	5	14	5	24	3
Vicente Galdós H.	6	7	7	20	4
Jaime Prado	7	4	2	13	3
Luis Muñoz	3	4	4	11	1
Alberto Rico	1	4	5	10	
Miguel Fernández	3	4	3	10	
Raúl Mora	6	3	1	10	
Esteban Terrazas	6	4	0	10	
David García M.	5	1	4	10	
Gen. Tomás Romero	4	4	2	10	
Domingo Castro	1	8	1	10	

Note: *The remaining influentials received votes as follows:*
Three tied with 8 votes
One with 7 votes
Two tied with 6 votes
Seven tied with 4 votes
Five tied with 3 votes

respectively, and 248 and 181 for their political counterparts. Yet the mayors of the two cities were among those who received most votes. The mayor of C. Juarez received almost unanimous support as a key political influential, while the El Paso mayor was nominated as a key influential by 60 per cent of the judges.

The pattern of voting was similar within each city, but different between cities. Thus, the data reveal that there was more agreement in C. Juarez than in El Paso about who were the influentials. Half of the Juarez influentials received ten or more votes, compared to less than two fifths of the El Pasoans. In both cities and in both institutional sectors, the key influentials received a majority of all votes cast in their categories. Even among themselves the key influentials agreed on the identity of the top six and the next six influentials. The upper half of the key influentials in business and politics in El Paso received more than twice the votes of those in the lower half from the key influentials themselves (column 5 in Tables III and IV). The tendency was apparent also among the Juarez key influentials, although the upper and lower halves were less sharply demarcated (see column 5 of Tables V and VI).

Patterns of Influence

A number of expectations on the perception of influence were anticipated. The more crystallized the influence system the more the key influentials of each sector should agree on the influentials. The businessmen should be expected to exhibit greater agreement than the politicos on who the business influentials are, and similarly, the political influentials should agree more consistently than the businessmen on the identity of the political influentials. Finally, the influentials in each city should be able to identify fewer influentials in the other city than in their own. In general, the above expectations were borne out.

For reasons that will be made explicit later we expected to find more crystallization (agreement on influentials) in the voting patterns of C. Juarez than El Paso. Judging from the voting behavior of the key influentials, crystallization was highest among the Juarez businessmen and lowest among the El Paso politicos. The key Juarez business influentials voted for each other an average of five times, the Juarez politicos and the El Paso businessmen averaged four mutual votes, while the El Paso politicos averaged only 2.7 mutual votes. Crystallization was also revealed by the fact that the key Juarez business influentials cast a total of sixty votes for each other, and only fifty-six for all other Juarez businessmen. Similar patterns were found in the other three categories.

As suggested above, we expected judges to display greater agreement on the identity of influentials within their own institutional sector. In Tables III, IV, V, VI the nominations for influentials are separated into three categories, on the basis of whether the judge was a political or economic influential or whether he was a knowledgeable.[4] Comparing the votes of the three categories, we found in general that influentials received proportionately more votes from judges within their institutional sector. This was most true of the business influentials. If a simple monolithic influence system had existed in either city, and if it were accurately perceived, we should have expected more agreement among the judges from any sector on the identity of influentials in both business and politics. While some persons did receive strong support as both business and political influentials, the judges distinguished these as separate influence areas. Furthermore, they seemed more certain about the situation in their own spheres.

Identifying Influentials Across the Border

Judges in both cities were asked the general question, "Who are some of the most influential persons in the community life

[4] If an individual received three or more votes in both business and politics, he was placed in the category in which he received the larger number of votes. It is noteworthy that in every case in which such voting occurred, the individual always received more votes for the category that corresponded with his occupation at the time. Thus, for example, the mayor of El Paso in 1954-1955, who was also a leading businessman, received four times as many votes as a political influential than as a business influential.

TABLE VII

NOMINATIONS FOR INFLUENTIALS IN EL PASO AND
C. JUAREZ AS GIVEN BY JUDGES IN THE OPPOSITE CITY

	El Paso	C. Juarez
Number of nominees	80	36
Number of persons receiving 10 or more votes	3	4
Number of persons receiving 3 or more votes	16	7
Number of political influentials selected	7	2
Number of business influentials selected	9	5
Average number of votes per influential	8	11.5
Number of judges	49 (Juarenses)	43 (Paseños)

of the other city?" Table VII summarizes the results. Two political influentials in El Paso and one in C. Juarez received ten or more votes. These included Broon and Pérez, the two mayors. Every influential selected by three or more judges in the neighboring city was also selected as an influential within his own city. For both cities, one in every five names nominated received three or more votes. This voting pattern adds further, if limited, support to the perception of a greater diffusion of perceived influence in El Paso as compared with C. Juarez. The El Pasoans gave three or more votes to only seven Juarez influentials, and gave them an average of 11.5 votes each. On the other hand, the Juarez judges gave three or more votes to sixteen El Pasoans, but gave them an average of only eight votes apiece. These findings demonstrate that those judges who ventured to identify influentials in the other city tended to support the image of influence which we obtained within each city.

To summarize, although the judges perceived influence to be rather unevenly distributed in business and politics in El

Paso and C. Juarez, they tended to give the majority of their votes to a small group at the top of each influence category. Mexicans seemed to agree more on their influentials than the Americans, and the businessmen displayed greater consensus than the politicos. Moreover business and politics were generally perceived to be independent spheres of influence, although there was some notable overlapping. We may now turn our attention more directly to the influentials. Who were they? What positions did they occupy in the institutional spheres of their cities? What were some of their salient social characteristics?

The Business Influentials in El Paso and C. Juarez

Table VIII provides data on the occupations and positions held by the business influentials of the two cities. The types of enterprises and positions which they held were rather similar for both cities. Industrialists and retail merchants were most highly represented, followed by bankers and wholesalers in

TABLE VIII
ECONOMIC AFFILIATION OF BUSINESS INFLUENTIALS

Affiliation	El Paso	C. Juarez
Banking	6	5
Manufacturing	15	16
Retailing	13	14
Wholesale	5	5
Utilities	2	3
Communications	3	1
Total	44	44

Note: *Seven El Paso businessmen were excluded from this list in 1955 because they received more votes as political influentials and were classified as such. Three businessmen from C. Juarez were excluded for the same reason.*

almost equal numbers. However, caution must be observed in interpreting the similarities. The business influentials in El Paso commanded corporate enterprises that employed as many as 1,500 people and had annual payrolls of over three million dollars. One corporation had over one billion dollars in assets, and nineteen companies had assessed valuations ranging from one million to over fifteen million dollars. There was no business of comparable size, earnings, or worth in C. Juarez. While most enterprises there were incorporated, they generally consisted of husband, wife, their children, and perhaps one or two close relatives. Over two fifths of the El Paso influentials were associated with enterprises which employed between 200 and 1,500 persons. In contrast, nine tenths of the Juarez businessmen employed fewer than fifty persons.

The influentials of the two cities also differed in the extent and nature of their business activities. Most of the El Paso business influentials had only one occupation. The majority held stocks and six were chairmen of boards of other companies in addition to their own enterprises.

On the other hand, the Juarez influentials had almost three times as many "other" business interests as their El Paso counterparts. Many were simultaneously the president or owners of two or three businesses. Perhaps this pattern of multiple business interests may be accounted for by the fact that business activity in the city had not yet achieved a very high degree of complexity and diversity. The Juarez businessman was owner as well as manager of relatively small enterprises. If successful in one venture, he would have capital to invest in another. With capital in short supply in C. Juarez and Mexico, and with business opportunities broadening, the tendency was to diversify business interests rather than to reinvest everything in one enterprise. The executive in El Paso had a much more complex role to perform, often as an executive of an enterprise which he did not own. This difference between the two business groups is illuminated by the fact that three fourths of the El Pasoans were presidents or vice-presidents as opposed to one seventh of the Juarenses, the great majority of the latter being "owners or partners."

Despite these differences, the fact that bankers, industrialists and retail and wholesale merchants were chosen in almost equal proportions in both cities may point to a growing convergence in certain values held by the businessmen and an emerging similarity in the business structures of the two communities. That industrialists and bankers dominated the lists of key influentials in both cities is further manifestation of this emerging similarity. In neither city did an absentee owner make the list of key influentials. Particularly in El Paso, the executives of nationally-owned corporations received only moderate support as business influentials.

It may be of interest to compare the two groups of business influentials further. The El Paso businessmen were considerably younger and had had more formal education than their Juarez counterparts. About half of both groups had been born outside their respective states. Although well over half of both

TABLE IX

CHARACTERISTICS OF INFLUENTIALS IN TWO BORDER CITIES, 1955*

| Characteristics | El Paso | | C. Juarez | |
	Business N-38	Political N-19	Business N-37	Political N-22
	(1)	(2)	(3)	(4)
Age-mean years	51.7	49.4	55.6	49.0
Education-median years	16.0	16.6	12.6	11.4
Born outside the state	50%	47%	50%	64%
Fathers in white-collar occupations	78%	80%	69%	55%

* Includes only those influentials from whom complete information was obtained.

groups were reared in white-collar families, there is some evidence that the Juarez businessmen had experienced a little more upward social mobility. Table IX summarizes the findings.

Similar patterns in the membership of voluntary associations were also found for the businessmen of the two cities. Columns 1 and 3 of Table X show that both groups belonged to the local Chamber of Commerce and either Rotary, Kiwanis or Lions. The Juarez businessmen averaged four association memberships to three for their El Paso counterparts. The two cities' representatives were equally active in community welfare organizations. However while the Juarez businessmen were considerably more active in church-related organizations they were considerably less active in political party activities. Nine

TABLE X

PERCENTAGE DISTRIBUTION OF BUSINESS AND POLITICAL INFLUENTIALS WHO WERE MEMBERS OF SELECTED LOCAL ORGANIZATIONS IN TWO BORDER CITIES, 1955*

Types of Organizations	El Paso Influentials		C. Juarez Influentials	
	Business N-38	Political N-19	Business N-37	Political N-22
	(1)	(2)	(3)	(4)
Chamber of Commerce	95	70	90	9
Service Clubs	76	73	62	14
Church Organizations	21	21	57	10
Masonic Lodges	21	10	—	30
International Committees	18	21	14	—
Community Welfare Associations	34	21	33	5
Asociación Cívica (Civic Association)	—	—	30	—
Political Party Affiliation	68	80	10	95
Mean Number of Organizational Memberships	3.0	3.7	4.1	2.7

* Includes only those from whom complete information was obtained.

tenths claimed no party affiliation, while two thirds of the El Paso business influentials indicated they were "Democrats for Eisenhower."

We have already noted the similarity in social status and social origin (as reflected in father's occupation) of the businessmen in the two cities. In El Paso, all of them, regardless of their origins, were wealthy. They lived in the best residential areas of the city and belonged to the exclusive clubs.[5] Almost half of the business influentials were holding the same position that their fathers had held before them. Most had secured a college education and had gradually "worked their way up" in their parents' firms. On the other hand, there was a small group of about 15 per cent who had experienced considerable upward mobility. They were reared in homes of limited means where the father was typically a tenant farmer or a manual laborer. Illustrative of this kind of mobility was the case of Allen Bartlett, a bank president, who was selected as a key business influential. He had worked his way up in the classic American tradition, an accomplishment which he and others pointed to with great pride.

Despite the changes wrought by the Mexican Revolution of 1910, a similar pattern was found among the Juarez businessmen. About half revealed that they came from upper-class families who were temporarily declassed by the Revolution. About one third succeeded in reaching occupations similar to those held by their fathers prior to the Revolution. As in El Paso, some 15 per cent had little formal education, came from families of limited circumstances, began their occupational careers as manual laborers, and gradually rose to their current positions.

[5] For a comparison between the mobility patterns of these leaders and those of the United States in general, see Bernard Barber, *Social Stratification* (New York: Harcourt, Brace and World, 1957), Chapters 13-16. Our findings support those summarized by Barber: "Most social mobility is quite gradual. However, a small minority, consisting of a few per cent of the total population, move up, and probably down as well, in a very large degree" (p. 468).

A final point may be made about these influentials. The key business influentials in both cities were, without exception, men whose business interests were primarily local. To be sure there were business influentials in both cities who owned or managed large enterprises which had large external markets. They often spent much time away from the city or were considered "transient" managers. In no case were these men named key or sociometric leaders, despite the size and economic importance of their enterprises. Whatever else business influentials were, they were men who had lived in the area a long time and had made community affairs a primary personal commitment.

Political Influentials

Perhaps the major structural similarity between the political systems of El Paso and C. Juarez was the presence of essentially one-party systems. This fact has limited implications because local politics in C. Juarez, as in all Mexican cities, is an integral part of national politics. State and federal involvement in local affairs is handled both through official governmental channels and through the PRI party. To be a political influential and to occupy public office, one had to be a member of PRI. But this was not enough. The typical road to gaining political influence or governmental office was first to be an active member of one of PRI's many subgroups, then to gain greater influence in the local PRI organization and gain the attention of state and national party officers, and then to be nominated for a governmental or party office.

El Paso, on the other hand, was relatively free of state and federal government intervention in the determination of local party organization and leadership. In fact, many of the influentials were proud of the fact that as of 1955 the community did not have a broad-based political party machine. Thus, the road to political influence and public office was a matter of impressing a few local business and political leaders. These structural dissimilarities in the roads to political influence need to be kept in mind when comparing the political influentials of the two cities.

The most striking difference between the two communities in the composition of political influentials was that the executive branch of government contributed the lion's share of the politicos in C. Juarez while the judicial and executive branches contributed an equal share of influentials in El Paso (see Table XI). In C. Juarez all major executive officeholders, elected as well as appointed, were chosen as influentials. With only three exceptions they all received ten or more votes. Among these were the city treasurer, and the state and federal tax collectors. Commenting on the importance of these offices and officials one official said: "They'll all be rich before they get out of office." Whether true or not, it pointed to the problem of the *mordida* (the bite or bribe) in Mexico. Several businessmen explained in detail how agents from one of the treasury offices could and did subtly and successfully shake them down. Some businessmen openly admitted that they carried two sets of accounts and records, one for themselves and one for the tax collectors. One of the latter, commenting on the pervasiveness of the *mordida* and the difficulty of trying to combat it, acknowledged that he had recently turned down a "gift" of 500 pesos (approximately $40.00) from a Juarez taxpayer who appeared surprised at his refusal. The *mordida* did in fact appear to be quasi-legitimate. Several businessmen confessed that they preferred to pay the *mordida* than to submit to a careful inspection of their books, even if they had nothing to hide. They also felt that as long as most government officials were underpaid the system had to continue.[6]

[6] This does not imply that there were no honest politicians or government officials in C. Juarez, or no crooked ones in El Paso. In C. Juarez, several political influentials were specifically pointed out as honest men and above reproach, but many businessmen felt that the majority of officeholders used the office to enrich themselves.

TABLE XI

OCCUPATIONS OF POLITICAL INFLUENTIALS
IN TWO BORDER CITIES, 1955

Occupation and
Branch of Government

Executive

El Paso	*C. Juarez*
Mayor* (Businessman)	Mayor* (Government)
Ex-mayor* (Businessman)	Governor* (Lawyer)
Ex-federal Official* (Government)	Ex-mayor* (Businessman)
County Clerk* (Government)	Mayor pro-tem* (Small Business-
County Judge* (Lawyer)	man)
Ex-mayor (Railroad Engineer)	Public Works Chief* (Government)
Ex-federal Official (Government)	City Clerk* (Lawyer)
General-Military Command (Gov-	Police Chief* (Government)
ernment)	City Treasurer* (Government)
Mayor Elect (Businessman)	State Tax Collector* (Government)
	Federal Tax Collector* (Govern-
	ment)
	Federal Customs Official (Govern-
	ment)
	Chief of Immigration* (Govern-
	ment)
	General-Military Command (Gov-
	ernment)
	Federal Medical Position (Physi-
	cian)
	State Traffic Commission* (Busi-
	nessman)
	Ex-mayor* (Businessman)
	Ex-mayor (Businessman)
	Ex-mayor (Businessman)
Sub-total 9	Sub-total 18

Legislative

City Councilman (Businessman)	Senator, Federal* (Government)
	Federal Deputy (Government-La-
	bor)
	City Council (Professional)
	City Council (Farmer, Ejido
	Leader)

		City Council (Labor Leader)	
		City Council (Labor Leader)	
Sub-total	1	Sub-total	6

Judiciary

Federal Judge* (Government)		District Judge (Lawyer)	
Judge (Government-Lawyer)			
Judge (Government-Lawyer)			
Judge (Government-Lawyer)			
District Attorney (Government-Lawyer)			
Ex-district Attorney (Lawyer)			
County Sheriff (Semi-professional)			
Sub-total	7	Sub-total	1

Non-Governmental		*Other PRI Personnel*	
Businessman*		Labor Leader, CTM*	
Lawyers (6)		LMOP, Secretary General*	
Catholic Bishop		Labor Leader, CROC	
Businessman		LMOP, Small Business	
Sub-total	9	Sub-total	4

		Opposition Leader	
		Businessman	
		Sub-total	1
Grand Totals	26	Grand Totals	30

Note: *Indicates that the individual received ten or more votes. Person's major occupational career pattern is shown in parenthesis. Four El Paso and five Juarez leaders are excluded from this list and listed previously as business influentials, because they had received more votes in the latter category. None of them were occupying political office at the time.*

In contrast to the above, persons in El Paso, holding such offices as treasurer, internal revenue chief, and city clerk were never mentioned as being influential. These offices were so highly bureaucratized and narrowly circumscribed that their incumbents were not able to use them for personal gain. Neither were they perceived to be policymakers at the broad community level.

The mayors of both cities received the most votes as influential politicos. A typical comment from a Juarez knowledgeable was, "The mayor is the only one with influence in local politics. The rest don't count; they are merely his stooges." Others listed both the mayor and the governor as the most influential in community political affairs, while some of the businessmen argued that the mayor was merely a tool of the governor, as was the case in all Mexican cities.

Although the voting for the Juarez mayor approached unanimity, his influence was said to be conditional upon occupying the office. Thus, while he held office, Pérez could derive power from it which he could use either to his own personal advantage, or to making major community decisions, or both. Mayor Pérez was an agronomist by profession. He was a congenial, handsome, well-built athletic man in his late thirties when he was elected. All sides considered him to be well-intentioned. Unafraid to discuss Mexican politics openly, he appeared to be well-informed on the complex problems involved in developing a democratic political system. As a native of the city, he had availed himself of the opportunity to receive part of his formal education in El Paso. Mayor Pérez spoke English well and was well liked by El Paso influentials, who credited him with helping to improve inter-city relations. He openly admired many features of American life. Nevertheless, he was completely dedicated to Mexico and to PRI. He had been a long-time party member and had held several local offices including the presidency of the local party. He was selected for mayor by the governor when the latter's first choice was roundly rejected by the local officialdom.

Mayor Pérez appeared to have power only to the extent that

the governor was not interested in the local situation.[7] As will
be seen later, the governor did become heavily involved in
local affairs and forced the mayor to take actions which brought
about an open split between business and government at the
local level. During the latter part of his administration Pérez
was under heavy attack by the businessmen and professionals
of the Civic Association, and even by a local newspaper usually
sympathetic to the administration. Some local PRI officials felt
that the mayor should have opposed the governor more reso-
lutely. Failure to do so led many to believe that, "Once he
leaves office, he's dead politically." While Mayor Pérez may
not have had the qualities necessary for continued political
influence, this was not true of other former mayors during the
1940's and 1950's.

Although a few people made similar observations about the
future of El Paso's mayor, most insisted that Mayor Broon
would continue to be influential in the city for years to come,
and could, in fact, have easily won another term in office in
1955 if he had chosen to run again. These judgments were supported by pointing to his accomplishments in office, his domination of the political scene in recent years, his popularity with
the Spanish-surname people for whom he had carried out many
public works projects, and his unusual success as a businessman.

Returning to the analysis of the composition of political influentials, Table XI shows that those in the legislative branches
of government were not frequently selected as influentials in
either city. Legislators who were selected as influentials were
probably nominated for the influence they held in other associations. For example, the two aldermen in C. Juarez who made
the influential list were also labor and agrarian officials and

[7] The problem of local elections and local autonomy is a central one in comparing these two political systems. The question of state and federal PRI
control of local elections was raised publicly by a group of mayors in 1959.
The municipalities are demanding more independence in the selection of local
public officials. So far at least, they have not received it.

automatically minor leaders in PRI. The one councilman to
be selected in El Paso, Mr. Jiménez, was up to that time the
first and only Spanish-surname person in the city council.
Thus, the influence of these three legislators was a function of
their perceived influence as vote-getters and representatives
of important interest groups.

Table XI also reveals some striking differences in the importance of lawyers in El Paso and labor leaders in C. Juarez. This
observation must be interpreted in light of the fact that in El
Paso the lawyers were among the key influentials, while labor
leaders in C. Juarez were lower influentials. The difference in
the roles played by the lawyers in the two cities is highlighted
by scrutinizing the occupational backgrounds of the politicians.
More than half of El Paso's twenty-six politicos were lawyers,
and all of them had practiced law privately. Several represented
the largest business enterprises in the city. In contrast, only
three of C. Juarez' thirty politicos were lawyers. The political
situation for lawyers in Mexico was explained by one political
influential in this way:

> Lawyers, and professionals in general, have become involved in
> local politics; but in reality, only very few of them are prepared for
> it. The majority become involved because they have some friend in
> the state or federal government and they think that he can help them
> obtain a job. The professionals have not yet developed sufficiently to
> understand that becoming involved in politics, whether local, state, or
> federal, must be on a high plane with the purpose of trying to improve
> the living conditions of the people. Our professionals tend exclusively
> to obtain either a job which will make it possible for them to work
> the classic *mordida*, or a concession to exploit some particular business.

Such a comment was never made about El Paso or American
lawyers. Indeed, lawyers were accepted as an integral part of
the political system. The labyrinth of laws, interpretations, and
precedents which characterize American political life calls for
the heavy involvement of lawyers. Thus it is not too surprising
to find a much greater representation of judges among the

political influentials in El Paso as compared to C. Juarez. Commenting on this condition, some Juarez business influentials and politicos contended that "the judiciary in Mexico is nothing but a tool of the executive branch of government."

One in three political influentials in El Paso was a businessman, while less than one in four was such in C. Juarez. One fourth of the Juarez politicos were labor leaders but none appeared in El Paso. Strikingly, career governmental officials (men whose careers hinged upon their affiliation with PRI) formed the largest single category of politicos in C. Juarez (one in three), while only one in five of the El Paso politicos were in this category. Moreover the tenure of these latter governmental workers was not as clearly linked to their allegiance to other party influentials. In general the politicos in C. Juarez represented the groups which PRI felt should have influence, namely, small business, government, professionals, agriculture and organized labor.

In contrast, labor was not represented among the El Paso influentials and none of them ever spoke of labor as an interest group which ought to be represented. Apart from the railroad brotherhoods, labor was poorly organized in the city. The CIO had been recently unsuccessful in its attempts to oust the Mine and Mill Workers Union from the smelter plants. Its organizational efforts in other industries had also met with little success. Businessmen were content to deal with local unions whatever their stripe if they did not become politically insistent.

One may not conclude that the weakness of organized labor in El Paso and the absence of a two-party system left all the political power to businessmen and lawyers. The large minority of Spanish-name persons of Mexican background in the city was becoming a political force to contend with. Leaders in the Anglo and Spanish-name population did occasionally study the need for "Latino" representation in the government. An attempt to channel political action of the "Latinos" in 1951 was the placing of a Spanish-name person on the city council, and José Jiménez was elected on a slate headed by Mayor Broon. As one influential put it: "It is generally agreed that one of the city councilmen ought to be a Spanish-name person." However, steps were also taken in the primaries to run Spanish-name persons against each other to prevent vote-splitting.

In 1955, three of the political influentials were Spanish-name persons; two of them held public office, one at the city and one at the county level. The third had been very active in international relations for many years. Thus a peculiar reversal was evident in the two communities. In El Paso the working classes, made up predominantly of Spanish-name persons, were under-represented among the politicos, while in C. Juarez the big businessmen were underrepresented.

Further differences between the two groups may be observed in Tables IX and X which present data on their general social characteristics, and associational memberships. Most of the El Paso politicos belonged to the Chamber of Commerce and the Service Clubs, while this was a rarity among Juarez political influentials. Other than the subgroups within PRI, the political influentials were most likely to be members of the Masonic Lodge, which itself has had a strong political orientation throughout Mexican history.

The two sets of politicos differed little in average age. However, the El Pasoans had more formal education (reflecting their legal training) and were somewhat more likely to have been natives of their community. A greater proportion of them were reared in families whose fathers were white-collar workers.

A comparison of the mobility patterns further elucidates the differences between the politicos of the two communities. While less than 15 per cent of the El Pasoans were reared in business-professional families, the politicos as a whole moved upward moderately from white-collar backgrounds to professional status. Most had obtained a college education, and had achieved moderate financial security. While not wealthy by business standards, many did share the style of life and the participational patterns of the country-club set.

The mobility patterns of the Juarez politicos were clearly influenced by the Mexican Revolution. Although one third of them experienced considerable upward mobility, the current status of others exhibited much ambiguity. As local officials and influentials, they enjoyed certain prerogatives of office (e.g., ceremonial dining) which gave them social access to high status persons like El Paso officials and generals of the United States Army. Yet many were regarded and regarded themselves as working-class people. Two examples illustrate the point. Miguel Urtado, elected to the National Chamber of Deputies, had been a mechanic, an army captain, a low echelon government official and an officer of a labor union. Urtado primarily thought of himself as a labor union leader and skilled worker. Again, Alderman José Puente had been a baker and a waiter, and then an official in the union of restaurant workers. This mobility reflects PRI's policy of granting labor unions political power and public office at the local, state and national levels. PRI's policy seemed to be that the amount of power awarded to a particular interest group within the party should reflect the strength of that interest group within the community. The mayor's office generally went to the strongest group, which in C. Juarez was a professional-small business coalition.

The social mobility which PRI policy made possible for interest-group leaders created unanticipated status and power problems especially on the border. While upward mobility to high office was possible, the constitution specifically forbids re-election to the same office. Thus the problems of maintenance of status and power arise. The constant turnover of officials leads to a surplus of candidates for office who have tasted higher status and power and want them as a steady diet.

Therefore an official or ex-official must either maneuver for a new office, use the office for personal gain, or risk losing status and power. For those seeking political careers, this situation stimulates competition for the attention of party leaders and blind subservience to them. For incumbents who tire of the political game, the office may be used to play the *mordida* game, so that enough money can be accumulated to launch a legitimate business.

INTERPRETATION AND CONCLUSIONS

Power is more easily analyzed within the political than within the business sector of a community. In government there is a sanctioned and hierarchical distribution of authoritative power vested in specific offices. In democratic systems, laws usually define the limits of authority and the means to make decisions. However, officials vary in personal qualities and these will affect their ability to control decision-making. These attributes constitute influence. The ability to command cannot exist apart from influence, for some latitude is always present in making decisions. It is also possible for people to influence governmental and community decisions without having formal authority. Businessmen who have no formal political authority may, in fact, have more influence over governmental decisions than the elected officials.

If authority and influence coincide in the governmental sphere, we should expect only governmental officials to be political influentials. This was not the picture given by our respondents in the two communities, although it was more closely approximated in C. Juarez than in El Paso. However, we cannot conclude that the Mexican city had the more responsive democratic system. There, political and community influence was perceived to be largely an extension of the authority vested in the public office. This extension encompassed areas not included in the municipal code. Actually, the Mexican municipal code does not vary significantly from the American in defining the limits of public authority. This means that in Mexico, the process of institutionalizing government by rules rather than by men has been slow and uncertain despite the Revolution of 1910. Although the rules are codified, they are not considered to be universally binding, obligatory and limiting. This situation has made it possible for those in authority to derive personal influence in both governmental and non-governmental areas of life.

This did not appear to be the case for El Paso. Bureaucracy had advanced there to such a degree that holding of public office did not necessarily lead to extending personal influence beyond the governmental arena. The official was not expected to enrich himself in office, nor was it even incumbent on him to initiate new community programs on his own. Businessmen seemed to be much more influential in the political system of El Paso than Juarez, and fewer officeholders were selected as political influentials. The composition of politicos in C. Juarez points to the high centralization of power in Mexico, which has been amply documented in the literature.[8] Power proceeds downward from the president to the governors of the several states, and through them, to municipal leaders. The executive branch has been the main source of power, while the judicial and legislative branches have acted more as legitimating bodies than independent sources of power. The Juarez political list mirrored this closely, for almost all of the high executive officials were selected as key influentials. In contrast, local legislative and judicial leaders received little support as influentials.

A problem closely related to this discussion is that of personalism in Latin American governments. Tannenbaum, Wise, and others have stressed the importance of the leader or the *caudillo*

[8] For example, in William P. Tucker, *Mexican Government Today* (Minneapolis: University of Minnesota Press, 1957); and Robert Scott, *Mexican Government in Transition* (Urbana: University of Illinois Press, 1959).

in Mexican politics.[9] Our findings suggest that some modification of this *caudillo* theme is needed. Whatever the merits of the theme historically, it now appears that the occupancy of a particular office is a prime requisite for power in Mexico, and this office is secured through PRI. To occupy office is to have both authority and influence, and these diminish as one descends the political ladder. From the point of view of the individual, the office limits both his power and influence. For example, lines of people formed three or four times weekly outside particular governmental offices quietly waiting for help. They clearly recognized the locus of power.

To be sure, the individual officeholder could take personal relationships into account when he distributed appointive offices under his control. Thus, in the state of Chihuahua and in other states, the governor traditionally gave important state and municipal positions to his relatives and close friends. It is doubtful that he could do this once out of office. This is more illustrative of nepotism than caudilloism, although the latter is not dead in Mexico.

The situation in the United States is not so simple. Recent community studies have documented a variety of evidence on the relation of authority and influence. In some cases, authority and influence are not located at the same political address. Public officeholders wait to be told by businessmen what to do.[10] More recently, evidence has appeared that politicians may

[9] See Frank Tannenbaum, "Personal Government in Mexico," *Foreign Affairs*, XXVII, No. 1 (October 1948), 44–57; and George Wise, *Caudillo, A Portrait of Antonio Guzman Blanco* (New York: Columbia University Press, 1951).

[10] For this view and a commentary on it, see Hunter, *op. cit.;* Delbert C. Miller, "Industry and Community Power Structure," *American Journal of Sociology*, LXIV (November 1958), 299–310; Robert Agger, "Power Attributions in the Local Community," *Social Forces*, XXXIV (May 1956), 322–331; Peter H. Rossi, "Community Decision Making," *Administrative Science Quarterly*, I (March 1957), 440–441; and C. W. Mills, "The Middle Classes in Middle Sized Cities," *American Sociological Review*, XI (October 1946), 520–529.

indeed have initiative and autonomy in political decision-making.[11] In the case of El Paso, the former pattern was strongly suggested. This may have been due, in part, to the fact that the political sector was under the surveillance of an informally organized party structure dominated by businessmen. However, political influentials were chosen, not because of their party activities, but because of the positions they held in business and because of their personal influence in government and the community. They had influence because they were spokesmen for an interest outside of government, e.g., business, ethnic groups, or because of their formidable technical capacities and knowledge.

The problem of describing and analyzing the power of the business community is made difficult by the absence of a legitimized formal authority pattern embracing all businesses. Nevertheless, it appeared that some stratification principles were operating in both communities because bankers were highly rated as were certain industrialists and the largest retail and wholesale merchants. Control of wealth in one form or another seemed to be a major factor of business influence in both cities, although it was not always decisive.

In the process of identifying the reputed business and political influentials of the two cities, we became increasingly aware of the problems relating to institutional integration in the two cities. The social origins and present activities of the four groups of influentials were different enough to suggest that other factors were operating to create institutional integration

[11] See particularly, Robert Dahl, *Who Governs?* (New Haven: Yale University Press, 1961). Robert Presthus suggests that economic and political decision-makers get involved and are most effective in different kinds of issues. See his *Men at the Top* (New York: Oxford University Press, 1964), pp. 406–407. Likewise, M. Kent Jennings has shown that political leaders are not necessarily subservient to businessmen in community decision-making. See *Community Influentials* (New York: The Free Press, 1964).

or cleavages. Moreover, the problem of institutional relations was seen to have significance for decision-making processes. In the following chapter integration and cleavage among influentials will be examined further. Later chapters will pursue the relevance of institutional co-ordination in issue resolution.

CHAPTER 4

Integration and Cleavage Among Business and Political Influentials

ONE OF THE MOST controversial problems in contemporary research on community decision-making and leadership has centered around the question of the extent to which a small, organized elite rules the community. The early findings of the Lynds in *Middletown* and Hunter's later findings in Regional City led many people to believe that a monolithic power structure characterizes the American community.[1] According to such an interpretation, one particular sector, most probably business, dominates the community, and its influentials and their follow-

[1] Whether Floyd Hunter meant to imply this monolithic model is not clear in his book, *Community Power Structure* (Chapel Hill: University of North Carolina Press, 1953). He discusses cliques, coalitions and factions, as well as general business domination. For an attempt to clarify the problem, see W. V. D'Antonio, H. J. Ehrlich and E. C. Erickson, "Further Notes on the Study of Community Power," in *American Sociological Review*, XXVII (December 1962), 848–854.

ers resolve community problems within an integrated set of values and attitudes. Usually the small group of decision-makers are united on all major issues because they share common values and economic fates.

While acknowledging that this pattern has existed and may still exist in many American communities, most political sociologists feel that current research reveals the presence of several other patterns. Thus, Rossi, Form and Miller, among many others, have delineated several power models based on their research.[2] These models vary from the one-man rule to a situation where there is a high degree of fragmentation of power, with no single person or group in control of community decisions. The most outspoken exponent of the latter model has been Professor Robert A. Dahl of Yale, who suggests from his study of New Haven that influentials have narrowly restricted spheres of community influence, closely identified with their particular occupations. From this situation a pluralism emerges in the community in which power is diffused among many different groups, although in any single group only a small number of persons are active and influential.[3]

The monolithic model, in its extreme form, posits that opposition and conflict are absent in the community. The power elite in such a community possesses a common set of values and attitudes arising out of their interests which they apply unilaterally to the community. In the extreme fragmented or pluralistic power model, no one interest is all-powerful because there is no necessary agreement on what constitutes community problems and, where consensus exists, varying positions are

[2] See Peter H. Rossi, "Theory and Method in the Study of Power in the Local Community" (mimeographed, 1960), pp. 37–39; William H. Form and D. C. Miller, *Industry, Labor and Community* (New York: Harper, 1960), Chapter II, pp. 18–55.

[3] See Robert Dahl, *Who Governs?* (New Haven: Yale University Press, 1961).

taken on the direction to be employed to solve such problems. A wide gamut of situations is possible in these pluralistic patterns, ranging from institutional autonomy in decisions affecting one sector to persistent conflict on all matters affecting any institutional sector.

Hypotheses of business domination of El Paso and political domination of C. Juarez may be thought of as hypotheses of monolithic power. Several questions may be posed to test such hypotheses. In what sense and to what degree did the influentials of the two cities form a more or less socially and politically integrated unit within their communities? To what extent did the business and political influentials think alike, develop common institutional concerns and come together socially? Or put differently, to what extent did they think differently about their occupational worlds, remain by themselves, and build up separate spheres of influence?

This chapter attempts to answer some of these questions by comparing the business and political influentials of the two communities for the following: social characteristics and voluntary associational membership, attitudes toward business and politics, approach to community problems, and extent of overlap in institutional identification.[4]

Social Characteristics and Voluntary Association Membership

As a first measure of integration it was hypothesized that there would be greater similarity in the social characteristics and voluntary association memberships among the El Paso business and political influentials than among their Juarez counterparts. Data on such social characteristics as age, place of birth, social origins, father's occupation, and education, are

[4] For a parallel discussion in the American context, see Robert Presthus, *Men at the Top* (New York: Oxford University Press, 1964), pp. 175–203.

in Table IX, and were discussed in the previous chapter. The findings generally supported the expectation that greater differences existed among the Juarez than El Paso influentials. Regardless of whether the El Pasoan was a business or political influential, he was likely to be about fifty years old, to have come from a white-collar background and have finished college, and to be a "Democrat for Ike."

Among the Juarez influentials considerable differences were revealed. The Juarez businessmen were more than six years older on the average than the politicos, had more formal education, were more likely to have been reared in families whose fathers were white-collar workers, were more oriented toward the Church, and they evaded political identifications. The politicos were more likely to have been born out of state, belong to fewer voluntary associations, to be members of PRI, and not be oriented toward formal religion.

Table X documents the organizational participation of the four "groups." It shows that the proportion of business and political influentials who were members of various El Paso organizations were relatively equal. The sector leaders not only came together at meetings of the Chamber of Commerce, Rotary, Kiwanis and Lions, but they worked together in community welfare associations, international committees, and to some extent, in church-related organizations.

A different pattern emerged for C. Juarez. The Chamber of Commerce was almost as exclusively the preserve of the business influentials, as PRI was of the politicos. The businessmen were more than likely to be members of service clubs, predominantly Rotary, while no politico was a member of Rotary, although a few were members of Lions. Again, organizations related to the Catholic Church and private community welfare were run almost exclusively by the Juarez businessmen, to the exclusion of PRI members. About one third of the politicos claimed membership in one of the Masonic Lodges, while none of the businessmen were members.[5] The political influentials, most of whom were members of PRI, were usually involved in one of the three major sectors of the party: the Agrarian, the Labor, or the Popular. Most of them were officers of the sector organizations and/or officers of subgroups within one of the sectors. Thus, the major focus of their associational life was within one of these groups.

A group of business influentials, led by Francisco Porvenir and Rodrigo Leal, had formed the Civic Association following the elections of 1952. About a dozen of the business influentials constituted the active core of this organization.[6] Such men as Navárez, Porvenir, Morales, Blanco, Torres and Leal were not only active in the Association but also in the Chamber of Commerce and church-related organizations such as the Boy's Town.

In summary, the data clearly support the observation that the El Paso influentials constituted a rather closely knit group in terms of social characteristics and associational activities, while

[5] Several businessmen asserted that to get ahead in Mexican politics one had to belong to one of the Masonic lodges. While Masons have played a notable role in Mexican political history—e.g., President Benito Juárez was a Mason—Masonic lodges appear to be less influential today than formerly. Two out of three businessmen claimed regular attendance at Sunday Mass while only one in four politicos made a similar claim. The politicos expressed more or less open hostility toward the Church. One of them said, "I believe in God but not in man. Although I was reared in the Catholic tradition, I have taken refuge in Masonry." Several politicos claimed that the clergy were interfering in politics, especially by warning the people against PRI, even to the extent of "using the confessional" to do so. Despite rapprochement between some high Church officials and the Mexican government in recent years, Church-State relations continue to pose vexing problems which do not appear resolvable in the near future.

[6] The alleged purpose of the organization was to help bring good government to C. Juarez. Its leaders claimed that they were trying to educate the masses to an understanding of their civic responsibilities. Because of the overlap in leadership between the Association and the Chamber of Commerce, local politicos claimed that the businessmen were "illegitimately" engaging in politics.

a clear-cut cleavage split the business and political influentials of C. Juarez.

COMPARATIVE PERSPECTIVES ON BUSINESS AND POLITICS

Common membership patterns should reflect consensus on institutional values and should facilitate similar behavior in terms of those values. Obversely, variations in organizational memberships should reflect ideological and behavioral diversity. To test this hypothesis, all of the respondents were asked fifty questions in the interviews, half of them dealing with business values and practices and half with political values and practices.[7] The respondents were asked to compare certain business and political principles and practices of the two countries, and to evaluate them. The typical form of the question was: Does the Mexican businessman tend to inherit his business position more or less often than the American businessman? Why do you take this position? Does the American politician work more closely with businessmen than the Mexican? Why do you feel this way? A summary of the images held by the four groups about Mexican and American business and political principles and practices is presented in Tables XII and XIII.

As expected, the business and political influentials of El Paso shared much the same outlook on the fifty questions. Only four times did their responses diverge significantly: on a question regarding the business reinvestment practices and on three political questions. On the other questions they responded in similar proportions. The pattern for the Juarez influentials was in the opposite direction, although it was not as extreme as expected. On thirteen questions, eleven involving political principles and practices, the differences between the two

[7] The chi-sq. test of association was used to determine whether the differences between groups were significant. Whenever the statistical probability of their occurring by chance was .05 or less, we accepted them as significantly different.

TABLE XII

SUMMARY OF IMAGES OF AMERICAN AND MEXICAN BUSINESS HELD BY AMERICAN AND MEXICAN INFLUENTIALS

American Businessman	*Mexican Businessman*
1. Only lack of ambition keeps worker from becoming a businessman.	Average working man has little chance of becoming a businessman.
2. No clear-cut attitude of class-consciousness between employer and employee; class lines blurred.	Sharp awareness of social class differences between employer and employee.
3. Religion is basic to his business conduct.	Religion and business do not mix for a variety of reasons.
4. Is very definitely civic-minded, i.e., concerned with community and welfare problems.	Is not very civic-minded; charity toward others is a personal matter.
5. Prefers broad stockholdings, has achieved rather than inherited his position, and conducts his business with impartial treatment to all alike.	Prefers family ownership to "public" stockholdings. Inherits rather than achieves his position, and family-personal ties loom large in business.
6. Education for business is superior, with proper emphasis on ethics. However, he has definite "cultural" shortcomings.	Education for business inadequate; not prepared ethically for business life; education gives him a broad "cultural" background.
7. Expects reasonable profits through high unit production and reinvestment, spurred by keen competition.	Seeks unjustly high profits, satisfied with limited market, little reinvestment, little or no competition in Mexico.
8. Prefers less governmental interference on the national level; is proud of the happy marriage of business-government in El Paso.	Businessmen do not get along well with government officials either nationally or locally, because government cannot be trusted.
9. Sees labor as competitor for business profits, but is somewhat afraid of labor's growing power.	Labor is more an enemy than a competitor, a tool of government having undue power over business.

Note: *The images summarized in this and the following Table represent the perceptions of the majority of the four groups.*

TABLE XIII

SUMMARY OF IMAGES OF AMERICAN AND MEXICAN POLITICS HELD BY AMERICAN AND MEXICAN INFLUENTIALS

American Politics	Mexican Politics
1. Politicians are drawn from all social classes; political bossism is a feature only of certain large cities.	Politicians are generally drawn from lower class; generally characterized as *caciques* or *caudillos* (political bosses).
2. Politicians are not above graft and corruption on individual basis, but as a group they are not corrupt.	Graft and corruption pervade the entire political system; the *mordida* has been institutionalized.
3. The politician is sensitive to the demands of the clergyman, and does not hesitate to affirm his faith in public. American clergy have healthy influence on political life.	Politicians are opposed to mixing of politics and religion in their own life. Militantly opposed to any effort by the clergy to influence Mexican political life.
4. Government and business are happily married; government regulation of business is just, extending itself only where essential for public welfare.	Rift between government and business is deep in Mexico; government ownership and regulation of business is strongly questioned except by Mexican politicos.
5. Political ideals for which most of the rest of the world are still striving are everyday realities in the United States. These include free speech, free press, freedom of religion, open and honest elections, equal justice before the law, protection of property, and protection of labor.	Governmental officials are very proud of accomplishments of the Mexican Revolution with regard to free speech, free press, etc. Others see politicians as mouthing high sounding phrases unrelated to the realities of Mexican life.

groups were significant. On most of the other questions they tended to diverge to a greater extent than did their El Paso counterparts.

A detailed analysis of the responses to some questions illustrates the differences between the influentials in the two cities. We asked whether there was more or less opportunity in the United States as compared with Mexico for a worker to rise to the ranks of the businessman. Although all the El Pasoans agreed that the Mexicans had less opportunity than the Americans, a strong difference of opinions was manifested among the two Mexican groups. Almost half of the politicos insisted that the Mexicans had equal or greater opportunity to get ahead, while only one fifth of the businessmen concurred. The majority of the latter insisted that government interference and inefficiency made this almost impossible in Mexico. Undoubtedly the Juarez politicos were responding to the question in terms of their revolutionary ideology which emphasizes equality of opportunity for all. The businessmen, on the other hand, expressed a perspective characteristic of laissez-faire ideology which stresses freedom from governmental control as a requisite for mobility.

Since cleavage in the area of political ideology was most pronounced, more detailed analysis is required. Respondents were asked to compare United States and Mexican society in four areas: (1) the degree to which seven democratic ideals were more nearly realized; (2) the comparative representativeness of the two governments; (3) the amount of graft and corruption in the governments; (4) business-government relations both locally and nationally.

In the first area the following question was asked: "On this card are listed a number of ideals commonly associated with a democratic society. Let us assume that both the United States and Mexico enjoy these ideals to some degree. In which country is each ideal more closely realized?" The ideals were Free Speech, Freedom of Religion, Free Press, Open and Honest Elections, Protection of Property Rights, Protection of the Rights of Labor, and Equal Justice for all. Both El Paso groups agreed that the Americans had more nearly realized these ideals than the Mexicans. The Mexicans diverged sharply on four of the seven ideals. For example, in the matter of open and honest elections, five out of six Juarez businessmen said that the United States was superior, while a majority of the politicos felt that achievement was about the same in both countries. In general, the political influentials felt that Mexico had caught up with the United States in the achievement of these ideals, while the businessmen were critical of the accomplishments of the Mexican Revolution and tended to view the United States as still ahead. The contrasting views are illustrated by these comments from a politician and banker respectively:

> These ideals were always desired, but were made effective by the Revolution. The constitution and the laws we live by are a direct result of the Revolution, as has been the elimination of social injustices.

> The Revolution was an important event which brought unity to Mexico; but I'm not sure that it was necessary. Our progress is probably a result of the world progress of the last forty years, a natural phenomenon.

This general pattern of similar responses for El Paso influentials and deviating responses for the two Mexican groups persisted in questions about the social origins of governmental officials in two countries. Almost all political and business influentials in El Paso felt that American governmental officials were derived from all the social classes. Most of the Mexican politicos attributed the identical pattern to Mexico, but the businessmen were evenly divided on the question.

The El Pasoans believed that their city and nation were generally free of graft, corruption, and political bossism. Again, the Mexican groups diverged, with the businessmen tending to charge widespread corruption and bossism, while the politicos tended to minimize them as things of the past. One politico admitted that, "Of course, we have petty men, always looking for their *mordida*, but the president is honest and fights hard against evil. I can only say that here in Mexico it (corruption) has diminished greatly." Regarding political bossism, a Juarez manufacturer exclaimed: "It's a political machine in Mexico. The bosses all depend on the central machine. There is nothing so powerful in the United States. Your two-party system prevents this."

An attempt was made to ascertain the degree of integration or cleavage between business and government by directly asking the four groups to evaluate business-government relations on the local and national levels, the degree of governmental regulation of business, and the amount of government ownership of enterprises in each country. The El Pasoans strongly agreed that business and government got along better both locally and nationally in the United States. An El Paso manufacturer says: "I don't know about all cities, but in El Paso the relations are excellent. . . . Without a doubt we are a shining example of a profound and dignified existence of good government, and respected by business above all."

The two groups also concurred that there was too much governmental regulation and ownership of business in Mexico. Since American businessmen complain of any kind of governmental regulation (except subsidies), it is not surprising to find them differing from the El Paso politicos on questions regarding this situation in the United States. As expected, the political influentials defended the degree of present governmental regulation and ownership as proper and necessary. In view of the fact that the businessmen felt that business and government got along very well, their disagreement with the politicos on these questions attests to their belief in the "conventional wisdom" of free, private enterprise.

The Juarenses continued the pattern described earlier. The businessmen evaluated general business-government relations in the United States as much superior to the Mexican ("We wish we had the privileges which the businessmen in El Paso

have"), and especially with respect to governmental regulation and ownership. A Juarez banker summed up the institutional structure in the following words:

> Our governments don't think they are servants. They think the people
> are their servants. They are always trying to rob us, and so we retaliate
> by looking for every chance to gyp them. In El Paso you can be both
> businessman and a politician; here there is a line of demarcation
> between the two. If the people waited for the government to help
> them, they'd starve.

Expectedly, the Juarez politicos perceived the situation differently. They thought that business-government relations were
about the same in both countries, that government regulation
and ownership of business in Mexico was proper and just, as
it also was in the United States. When the Juarez political influentials addressed themselves to their conflict with business,
they explained it in the following way:

> Our Chamber of Commerce is made up of the rich of the city. They
> have gotten themselves involved in politics where they don't belong.
> They charge the government with being guilty of the high cost of
> living here, but it is they themselves that are guilty of charging the
> high prices, and we know that, and we have been fighting them. They
> don't co-operate with the government at all like they should.

> They [business and government] have never been united here, and
> now because of politics they are more separated than ever. The lack
> of co-operation is due to two things: (1) personal egoism on the part
> of the businessmen, and (2) the fact that they know that their tax
> money will not be used for proper purposes. So the fault is only partly
> that of the businessmen.

The picture that emerges out of the responses to these questions about business and politics may now be summarized. The
El Paso influentials, regardless of occupational identification,
shared a common outlook. They agreed on the practices which
were being followed by business and government in the United
States, and they were proud of the accomplishments of both.
They were particularly pleased with the close co-operation

existing between the two sectors locally, and felt that their
situation was superior in every way to the situation across the
border. The perceptions of the two influential groups in C.
Juarez were diverse. They tended to agree about and approve
of the relations between business and government in the United
States. The political influentials felt that, although the relations
between the two institutions nationally and locally differed
from those in the United States, they were nonetheless just and
fair because of the peculiar conditions in Mexico. They also felt
a sense of equality with the United States in the achievements
of political liberties fostered by the Mexican Revolution. The
business influentials, on the other hand, looked longingly and
approvingly at American business-government relations. With
this type of ideological commitment and with the alleged
repressive governmental control and corruption, they launched
the *Asociación Cívica* to achieve a measure of what they saw
across the border.

COMMUNITY PROBLEMS

When institutional influentials have similar social backgrounds, similar participational patterns, and common views on
their institutional relations, they should be expected to have
similar views about community problems and what ought to
be done about them. Thus, we hypothesized that the business
and political influentials in El Paso would exhibit greater agreement than the Juarez influentials on the identification of the
main community issues and of the organizations involved in
resolving the issues.

The four groups were asked to name the most pressing problems facing their respective cities. They all concurred that finding sufficient water for farming, domestic, and industrial needs
was the most pressing problem. El Paso influentials generally
agreed on the priority of the remaining problems in the following order of importance: traffic control, new industry, educa-

tional expansion, stimulation of the economy, and delinquency control. They also agreed that local government and business associations were most actively engaged in co-operative attacks on these problems. The prevailing position was that community agencies had agreed on problems and were co-operatively working toward their solution without opposition. No organization was singled out as derelict in its community responsibilities.

With one major exception, the Juarez influentials also identified the same local problems. The need to expand public utilities and educational services was considered second only in importance to finding an adequate water supply for the city. However, one half of the businessmen felt that better local government was a major issue. They argued consistently that corruption in government was a long-standing problem in Mexico which prevented the country from having a healthier business climate. In fact, they insisted that such problems as education, traffic control, improved sanitation, and slum clearance would never be resolved until the men in the Mexican government, from the president down to the mayor, were changed. As might be anticipated, the politicos dismissed these charges as "mere politics."

Disagreements were also evident in response to the question seeking to identify the organizations working to solve local problems. Four fifths of the associations named by businessmen were under their control; namely, the Chamber of Commerce, service clubs, *Asociación Cívica*, and associations related to the Church. Two thirds of the businessmen identified government-dominated groups, including the government itself, as not doing their part to resolve local problems.

Typically, the politicos tended to minimize the cleavage. They named both government and business-dominated groups equally as organizations capable of helping to solve major community problems. Moreover, they were generally unwilling to identify or accuse certain local groups as failing in their com-

munity obligations. They dismissed the complaints of the Civic
Association as the grumblings of a few self-seeking individuals,
and referred to businessmen who did not belong to the Civic
Association (because they preferred to remain neutral) to validate their position.

In sum, the El Paso business and political influentials shared
a common perspective about community problems and how
they should be solved. The Juarez influentials tended to agree
on community problems, but not on the groups which were
working to resolve them. While the business influentials wanted
to maximize cleavages, the politicos minimized them.

INSTITUTIONAL OVERLAP AMONG THE INFLUENTIALS

If El Paso had a more or less monolithic business influence
structure, one would expect business influentials to also be
named as political influentials. On the other hand, if business
and politics were two different spheres of influence and decision-making, influentials in one sector would not be chosen as
influentials in the other. Similar logic should apply to C. Juarez.
If the Revolutionary Party were in complete control of Mexican
community life, one would expect a monolithic power structure
in which the political influentials would be perceived as wield-
ing major economic power. Again, if business and politics had
separate spheres of influence, there should be no overlap on
the lists of influentials.

Table XIV reveals that the boundaries between business and
politics were perhaps more clearly marked in C. Juarez than in
El Paso. Among the business influentials of both cities, four out
of five were identified only as such. No one in either city who
was primarily identified as a politico was also identified as a
business influential. In this sense at least, business appeared
to be an independent sector not dominated by the political or
governmental sector in either city.

Four out of five of the Juarez political influentials were not

TABLE XIV

INSTITUTIONAL IDENTIFICATION OF BUSINESS AND POLITICAL INFLUENTIALS IN TWO BORDER CITIES

Influentials	El Paso Number	C. Juarez Number
Business only *	40	38
Business and political	11	7
Political only	19	28
Total	70	73

* Seven of these 40 El Paso businessmen were nominated less than three times as political influentials. One El Paso political influential received less than three votes as a business influential. In C. Juarez two businessmen received less than three votes as political influentials, while two political influentials received less than three votes as business influentials.

identified as having influence in business, as opposed to three out of five El Paso politicos. Let us examine this in more detail.

Among the top twenty-five business influentials in El Paso, eleven received three or more votes as political influentials, and eight of these eleven emerged as political key influentials.[8] Among the lesser politicos—those in the lower half of the list— only two qualified as business influentials. Of the eight key politicos who were also business influentials, only one was holding public office at the time of the study. Thus, while the businessmen made up less than 40 per cent of the political influentials, they comprised two thirds of their key or socio- metric influentials. This, at least, is probative evidence of busi- ness domination in community decision-making.

In C. Juarez there was less overlap between the two institu- tional sectors. Seven Mexican businessmen received three or more votes as both business and political influentials, but only

[8] Two of three mayors since 1947 were businessmen, and the mayor-elect in 1955 was a businessman.

one (Luis Muñoz, who was then mayor pro tem) was a key political influential, and only Alberto Rico, a former mayor, ranked among the top half of the politicos. Porvenir and Leal, key business influentials, received most of their votes as political influentials from neutral businessmen who wouldn't openly support them and the Civic Association, but admired their "foolhardy efforts to engage PRI in open conflict."

There was no evidence that PRI or any of its local leaders were dominating the business influence structure of the city. Neither was there much evidence that business dominated Juarez political life. This situation did not result from a lack of desire on the part of businessmen to have political influence.

Neither city had a unified, integrated monolithic influence or power structure. Nevertheless, it was clear that El Paso came closer to such a situation than C. Juarez. In the latter city there appeared to be a bifurcation of business and political power, although some businessmen were organizing to have more influence in the political sector.

This chapter pursued the question whether the relations among the political and business influentials identified by the reputational technique pointed also to variations in their backgrounds, behavior, and institutional values and evaluations. Such variations or uniformities will be useful to interpret their behavior during the community decision-making process. Four areas were examined: social backgrounds, patterns of associational participation, assessments of business and political values and practices, and identification of community problems and the groups working to resolve them.

In all of these areas, there seemed to be more similarities among the business and political influentials of El Paso than those of C. Juarez. Both sets of American influentials intermingled freely in the Chamber of Commerce and the service clubs; they identified the same community problems and the groups resolving them; they concurred on their value assessments of business and politics, and they approved of business involvement in local government. The influentials of C. Juarez differed in their social origins, participational patterns, evaluations of the achievement of politics and business, and the identification of community problems.

On the basis of these data, the appearance of a monolithic power arrangement would appear more possible in El Paso than C. Juarez. However, institutional integration in the community can point to societal integration as well as to a monolithic power structure. Final conclusions on which situation exists must await observations on the tenure or circulation of influentials, the social composition of persons and groups involved in community decision-making, and the ability of major interest groups in the community to influence decisions affecting their welfare. Each of these areas will be studied in later chapters, but now we shall turn to the first of these, namely, tenure of community influentials.

CHAPTER 5

Stability and Change in
Influence: 1955-1958

INTRODUCTION

ALTHOUGH THE PRIMARY RESEARCH objectives in 1955 had been to identify the "most influential" persons in business and politics, and learn something about their backgrounds and activities, we were not insensitive to the major issues which were arising and being resolved during this time in the two cities. For example, we followed with keen interest the critical municipal elections and their aftermath in El Paso in 1955. We also studied very closely the various activities of the Juarez Civic Association. Just as we left the border in the summer of 1955, the Civic Association-PAN candidate for the federal congress won a surprising victory. Even more surprising was the sudden "resignation" of the governor of Chihuahua in August 1955. In the following year, Francisco Porvenir and Rodrigo Leal, leaders of the Chamber of Commerce and the Civic Association, and business partners for almost twenty years, ran against each other for mayor of C. Juarez, on the PRI and PAN tickets respectively. Finally, in 1957 Juan Rivera became El Paso's first Spanish-surname mayor. These events are described in detail in Chapters 6 and 7.

In 1958 we decided to return to the border to explore in more detail the relationship between the reputation for influence and actual influence in community decision-making. To pursue the comparative design further we hoped to study similar issues in the two communities with a parallel design. These issues are analyzed in later chapters. Here we shall be concerned with the question of the extent to which the reputed influentials found in the first study would still be considered influential in 1958, and, if changes occurred, what they would signify.

Two devices were used to obtain information on reputational influence in 1958. First a slate of names of "the most influential persons in the community" was sought from reliable judges. Henceforth, they shall be called general community influentials.[1] Second, respondents were asked for a list of names of persons who would be most capable of assuring the success of a specific community project, namely, building a new hospital. With this material the question of reputation of influence may be examined in two ways. The 1958 general influentials may be compared to the 1955 lists of influentials, and the names of the ideal hospital committee may be compared with those on the 1955 and 1958 general influentials list. In this way the tenure of influentials and the reliability of the reputational technique can be probed. Later, the relationships between reputed influence and actual influence will be explored.

The Longevity of Influence: El Paso

Seven of our most knowledgeable informants were asked to select the names of general community influentials in 1958. Of the forty-nine named, we interviewed thirty-one and an addi-

---

[1] See section on methodology in the Appendix for techniques used in locating influentials in 1958.

tional twenty knowledgeables. All were asked to select ten "key influentials" from the prepared list of forty-nine names. The results are found in Table XV. Of the forty-nine general influentials, only four failed to receive votes as key influentials. One of these, Ray Battle, a key political influential in 1955, was retiring from public office in 1958, and the judges were dubious that he could continue to be active. Seven persons were added to the general list of influentials in 1958 who were not influentials in either sector in 1955. None of these seven was selected as a key influential in 1958.

Exactly one dozen persons received ten or more votes as key influentials in 1958. Cofield, Alger, Bartlett, Webster and Elson had been key influentials of business in 1955. Stillman

TABLE XV

GENERAL INFLUENTIALS IN EL PASO, 1958, ARRANGED
ACCORDING TO NUMBER OF VOTES RECEIVED AS
KEY INFLUENTIALS; AND SHOWING THEIR
INFLUENCE POSITION IN 1955

Name	1958 Votes	Influence Position in 1955
Wm. Cofield	25	KI in B and P
Fred Alger	25	KI in B and P
Allen Bartlett	19	KI in B
Judge Stillman	17	KI in P
Charles Stephans	17	I in B and P
Juan Rivera	15	KI in P
Joe Webster	14	KI in B
Phil Beardsley	14	KI in P; also I in B
Thomas Parton	12	I in B and P
Neil Bradley	11	I in B and P
Vince Elson	11	KI in B
Joe Lynd	10	I in B
John Burns	9	KI in P; also I in B
Frank Bowers	9	

Name	1958 Votes	Influence Position in 1955
Al Jones	9	KI in B
Edward Broon	6	KI in P; also I in B
Bill Marshall	6	I in P
James Lynn	6	KI in B and P
Tom Banfel	5	I in B
Norb Smith	5	I in P
Bill Bell	4	KI in B
F. Wheatley	3	I in B
Mat Wilson	3	I in B
Jack Brown	3	KI in B
Ned Bryan	3	
Harold Nall	2	I in P
Mrs. R. Birman	2	
Charles Miller	2	I in P
Elmer Cook	2	I in P
Mat Todd	2	
Ray Franks	2	I in P
H. J. Popsley	2	KI in B
Dr. Phillip Byrd	2	
Ed Sneedby	2	I in B
S. Rekless	1	I in B
Mike Kerrin	1	KI in B
Howard Banks	1	I in B
Hal Boyton	1	I in B
Wm. Doyle	1	I in B
Phillip Harman	1	I in B
José Jiménez	1	I in P
Dan Hicks	1	KI in P; also I in B
Bishop Schwann	1	I in P
Frank Sterling	1	I in B
Sam Chappel	1	KI in B
Mart Rollins	0	I in B
Mike Reilly	0	
Ray Battle	0	KI in P
Dave Merton	0	

Abbreviations: **KI** = *Key Influential*
    I = *Influential*
    B = *Business*
    P = *Politics*

and Rivera, both key politicos in 1955, were still holding public office in 1958. Perhaps most significant of all, ten of the eleven persons who had been business and political influentials in 1955 were selected as general influentials in 1958, and six of them as key influentials. Table XVI summarizes some of the more salient aspects of the voting pattern.

TABLE XVI
GENERAL INFLUENTIALS IN 1958 WHO WERE
INFLUENTIALS IN 1955

Business and Politics	Business only	Politics only	Total
10	20	12	42

KEY INFLUENTIALS IN 1958 WHO WERE
KEY INFLUENTIALS IN 1955

Business and Politics	Business only	Politics only	Total
2	3	3	8

Several questions arise: Were businessmen or political influentials more likely to be selected as key influentials in 1958? What happened to the sociometric business leaders of 1955? What happened to the key politicos of 1955?[2]

In 1955, seventy persons had been named business and/or political influentials in El Paso. For one reason or another, twenty-eight (eight political and twenty business influentials) were not mentioned as having general influence in 1958. Death and retirement accounted for about half of the dropouts. No political influential still holding public office was dropped. Among the political influentials dropped, only Fred Ramírez, who had retired, had been a key politico in 1955. The business-

[2] The terms "Sociometric Leaders" and "Key Influentials" are used interchangeably.

men who were still active in business but dropped from the list were said not to be interested in general community affairs. Eight of the twelve key influentials in 1958 were businessmen and identified as business influentials in 1955. It seems, then, that businessmen were more likely than politicians to remain as key influentials in 1958.

The key business influentials of 1955 were, without exception, still listed as general influentials in 1958. In fact, five were still key influentials. The others received varying degrees of support depending on their activities. For example, H. J. Popsley had been one of the highest vote-getters in 1955, but received little support as a key influential in 1958. Although he served on important committees, he seldom initiated action on his own, although he presumably could if he had wanted to. James Lynn had been named a key influential in both sectors in 1955, but was perceived to be "not doing very much lately" in 1958.

The same pattern seemed to hold when the list of 1955 political influentials was examined. Five were selected as key influentials in 1958. Hackett and Ramírez had retired from public life, and Ray Battle and Dan Hicks, while on the list of general influentials, received little support as key influentials because they also were said to be near to retirement. Edward Broon, the mayor in 1954–1955, was said to be biding his time.

It may be concluded that the judges did generally discriminate between persons whom they perceived to have general community influence and those whose influence was limited to one sector such as business.[3] They also seemed to be aware of who was retiring, who had lost political influence, and who was on the upswing. Businessmen were more likely than politicians or professionals to be selected as general influentials, but public officials were not ignored. Thus, seven incumbents

[3] All questions were asked of thirty-one top influentials plus knowledgeables, and others actually involved in current issues.

and the Democratic Party leader were listed. Lawyers continued to play a prominent role, and labor was still not represented. The Spanish-name minority was represented only by Rivera, who had moved up from county clerk to mayor between 1955 and 1958, and Jiménez, who, though no longer in office, was still considered to have a political following. The most notable addition to the list of general influentials was a woman, Mrs. Birman, who was said by several judges to have political aspirations, and perhaps sufficient resources to attain elective office. (In 1961 she came within a thousand votes of being elected the mayor of El Paso.) The most notable change that seemed to take place between 1955 and 1958 was the upward movement of the newspaper editors into the ranks of the key influentials.

The role of the clergy continued to be difficult to assess. Most judges asserted that there was not a genuine influential among them. Nevertheless, Bishop Schwann received some support, as he had in 1955. The judges generally felt that the sentiments of the clergy were expressed through such key influentials as Alger, Elson and Lynd.

The Ideal Hospital Project Committee, 1958

One of the issues studied in detail was the way in which El Paso and C. Juarez went about solving the need for expanded hospital facilities. Before discussing the issue in the interview, we asked the following question:

Suppose that a major hospital project were before the community, one that required decision by a group of leaders whom nearly all would accept. If you were completely free to choose, which people would you choose to make up this group—regardless of whether or not you know them personally?

No names were suggested to the respondents, and we asked for an eight-man committee. The names of seventy persons were given, but only twenty received three or more votes.

Sixteen of these twenty had been listed as business and/or political influentials in 1955. Table XVII shows that Alger, Bartlett, Cofield and Beardsley received almost half of all the votes obtained by the top twenty. With very few exceptions,

TABLE XVII

TOP TWENTY CHOICES FOR THE "IDEAL HOSPITAL COMMITTEE" IN EL PASO IN 1958, NUMBER OF VOTES RECEIVED, AND WHETHER OR NOT THE INDIVIDUAL HAD BEEN SELECTED AS INFLUENTIAL IN 1955 OR 1958

Ideal Hospital Committee	Votes Received	Type of Influential in 1955	General or key Influential in 1958
Fred Alger	17	KI in B and P	KI
Allen Bartlett	12	KI in B	KI
Wm. Cofield	11	KI in B and P	KI
Phil Beardsley	10	KI in P and I in B	KI
Dr. Raymond Martin	9	—	—
Juan Rivera	8	KI in P	KI
Vince Elson	7	KI in B	KI
Ed. Sneedby	6	I in B	GI
Dr. Phillip Byrd	6	—	GI
H. J. Popsley	5	KI in B	GI
Fred Mallory	4	I in B	—
Mrs. R. Birman	3	—	GI
Neil Bradley	3	I in B and P	KI
Joe Lynd	3	I in B	KI
F. Wheatley	3	I in B	KI
Charles Stephans	3	I in B and P	KI
Joe Webster	3	KI in B	KI
John Burns	3	I in B and P	GI
Tom Banfel	3	I in B	KI
Hal Niles	3	—	—

Abbreviations: *KI = Key Influential*
GI = General Influential
B = Business
P = Politics

the respondents turned to the men who had been selected as business and/or political influentials three years previously. Two of the important exceptions were Doctors Martin and Byrd, who were at the time playing a prominent role in the hospital project. Mrs. Birman was also among the top twenty, and she, too, had been active in promoting the current hospital project.

In occupational terms, those in banking and finance received the largest proportion of votes, about one out of every four. One eighth of the votes were received by executives in retail trade or the construction industry. Local government officials received only 5 per cent of the votes, while medical doctors, who presumably had a strong interest in the project, received only 15 per cent of the votes cast. When influentials were asked why physicians were not selected in larger numbers, they replied that a successful project needed men with organizational skill, men with knowledge about fund drives and construction, and men with influence to put people and groups to work. Men like Alger, Bartlett, Elson, and Beardsley were such men. They needed one or two physicians for technical and symbolic purposes, but the job was ideally suited to the men of business.

When the composition of the Hospital Project Committee is compared with the general influentials of 1958, a close relationship is apparent. Only two members among the top twenty in the hospital project list were not among the general community influentials. In fact, ten out of the twelve general key influentials were also selected for the hospital committee. Only Stillman and Parton were not chosen.[4] The pattern that clearly emerges is that those who were given strong support as "ideal decision-makers" in a specific issue (the hospital project), also received strong support as general community influentials in

[4] The new General Community Hospital which was approved by the voters in November 1958 was named in honor of Judge Stillman.

1958.[5] These men had also received strong support as business and/or political influentials in 1955. The respondents, whatever their occupation and institutional identification, seemed to be choosing their "ideal decision-makers" from among persons whom they believed to be the actual and general decision-makers in the community.

The Longevity of Influence: C. Juarez

Fifty-one persons were selected as top influentials in C. Juarez in 1958. Twenty-one of them were interviewed—along with four others—and all were asked to select ten "key influentials" in the community from the prepared list.[6] The results appear in Table XVIII. Only eight influentials of 1955 received no votes as key influentials in 1958. Three of them had been political influentials who no longer held office and were not allied with the new administration, one was a member of the new administration, and four were businessmen who were "tending to their business." Eleven new persons became influentials in 1958, and two of these were found among the key influentials. One had been active elsewhere in the state in 1955, and the second was a bishop. Between 1955 and 1958 C. Juarez had become a full-fledged religious diocese. Bishop Mendoza had come to the city determined to make religion a relevant part of community life. As a result, whether people supported him or not, they came to recognize him as an influential person. The other nine additions to the list were followers either of PRI or of PAN.

[5] The respondent did not select an ideal hospital committee and then immediately proceed to examine the list of fifty names and select the ten most influential. Between these two questions he was asked to name the key issues then before the community, the roles of certain other persons and groups in these issues, and his own involvement.

[6] The interviewed included eight members of PAN, eight neutrals and nine members of PRI. Only the Panistas formed a single, integrated group.

TABLE XVIII

GENERAL INFLUENTIALS IN C. JUAREZ, 1958, ARRANGED
ACCORDING TO NUMBER OF VOTES RECEIVED AS
KEY INFLUENTIALS; AND SHOWING THEIR
INFLUENCE POSITION IN 1955

Name	1958 Votes	Influence Position in 1955
Francisco Porvenir	20	KI in B; also I in P
Ramón Torres	16	KI in B
Domingo Castro	15	KI in P
Pablo Navárez	14	KI in B
Jaime García	13	KI in B
Rodrigo Leal	11	I in B and P
Jorge González	11	KI in B
Jesús Blanco	11	KI in B
Luis Viejo	10	KI in B
Miguel Aguirre	9	KI in B
Bishop Rafael Mendoza	9	—
Alberto Rico	9	KI in P; also I in B
Alfredo Urbina	9	—
René Poblete	7	I in B
Manuel O'Higgins	7	I in B
César González B.	7	—
Juan Banco	7	KI in B
Rafael López	6	I in B
Jaime Prado	6	KI in P
Fernando Steel	6	I in B
Enrique Hernández	6	KI in B
Hernán Sánchez	5	—
Cristobal Villareal	4	KI in B
Benito Campeón	3	—
Dr. Francisco Amarillo	3	—
Juan García M.	3	I in B
Pedro Rodríguez	3	—
David Castillo M.	3	I in B and P
Rafael Gómez	3	KI in B
Miguel Delgado	2	I in P
José Mijares	2	I in B
Clemente Pérez	2	KI in P
Pablo Juárez	2	—

Name	1958 Votes	Influence Position in 1955
Oscar Herrera	2	—
Raimundo Soto	2	I in B
Manuel Flores	1	I in B
Eduardo Orozco	1	I in B
Esteban Terrazas	1	KI in P
Dr. Felipe Mundo	1	—
Salvador Torres	1	I in P
Renato Herrera	1	I in B and P
Alfonso Palmer	1	I in B
Antonio Chávez	1	I in B
Vicente Galdós	0	KI in P
Luis Muñoz	0	KI in P
Carlos Ramos	0	I in P
Alfonso Miramar	0	I in B
David Romero	0	—
Rómulo Murguía	0	I in P
David Sisneros	0	I in B
Pablo Telles	0	I in B

Abbreviations: *KI* = *Key Influential*
  I = *Influential*
  B = *Business*
  P = *Politics*

TABLE XIX

GENERAL INFLUENTIALS IN 1958 WHO WERE INFLUENTIALS IN 1955

Business and Politics	Business only	Politics only	Total
5	25	10	40

KEY INFLUENTIALS IN 1958 WHO WERE KEY INFLUENTIALS IN 1955

Business and Politics	Business only	Politics only	Total
0	8	2	10

Table XIX shows the relationship between the voting patterns of 1955 and 1958. Again, we will attempt to answer three questions about these lists: Were business or political influentials (as defined in 1955) more likely than others to be selected as general influentials in 1958? What happened to the key business influentials of 1955? What happened to the key politicos of 1955?

Seventy-three persons had been selected as business or political influentials in 1955. Thirty-three of them failed to make the list of general influentials in 1958. As can be seen from Table XIX, the greatest casualty occurred among the political influentials of 1955. Nineteen of them had literally dropped from sight as of 1958 as compared to fourteen business influentials. Perhaps more important was the movement into the ranks of key influentials in 1958. In terms of their traditional occupational identification, businessmen were more likely than politicians to be selected as general and key influentials in 1958. Actually, only four key influentials of 1958 were businessmen who were *not involved in politics* in one way or another. These men, all of whom were key business influentials in 1955, continued to receive strong support even though they were officially neutral in the bitter political battle that had been raging for almost four years. Their support stemmed from the fact that they made large contributions to charitable organizations, they served on noncontroversial committees, and the industries they owned were perceived to be vital to the community's economic life. Both sides accepted their neutrality.

The other key influentials of 1958 were either members of PRI or of PAN. The PRI leaders included Mayor Porvenir, Governor Castro, Pablo Navárez, Alberto Rico, and Alfredo Urbina. These men constituted at best a loose coalition, with Porvenir and Navárez on one side, the governor and Urbina on the other, and Rico independent. Torres, Leal and Blanco were the now active Panistas, and all had unsuccessfully sought office between 1955 and 1958. They formed a united, close-knit leadership within PAN. While they had not succeeded in winning public office, they had made, at least temporarily, a viable, two-party system operative in C. Juarez.

From the above analysis, four distinct groupings can be identified in the general influence list of 1958. There were the new men of power in PRI led by Mayor Porvenir; the old-line PRI factions, including former Mayors Rico, Pérez, and Delgado; the Panistas led by Torres, Leal and Blanco; and the businessmen who tried to avoid political entanglements and generally accommodated with the ongoing administration. García, Gonzáles, Viejo, and Aguirre were the outstanding figures in this neutralist camp. Major support as key influentials went to those heavily involved in the struggle to control city government. The politicos of 1955 were more likely than the business influentials to suffer loss of influence, mainly because they had lost out, at least temporarily, in the local struggle to control PRI.

Only one key business influential of 1955 lost his position in 1958. The others were now openly engaged in politics. The same cannot be said for the key political influentials. What happened to them? Four of them had left the state, three to take federal appointments; six others had left the city, and only Castro and Rico had not lost status.

Among the lesser political influentials, labor leaders like Puente, Martínez, Robles, and Urtado were out of public office and no longer heads of their unions. In short, those who lost political office and were unable to maneuver their way to a new office simply lost their influence. This was especially true of those whose social status was insecure, like the labor leaders. Only political influentials who were former mayors, and one or two who continued to hold important party posts, were named general influentials in 1958. Former Mayor Pérez, if he was not "dead, politically," as had been predicted in 1955, had definitely suffered a loss of influence within PRI.

The question may be raised whether so many political influ-

entials would have "dropped from sight" had we derived separate lists of influence for business and politics as we did in
1955. Probably few more would have been retained. The data
showed that the police chief, the city treasurer, the federal
deputy, and the secretary-general of PRI's Popular sector, plus
two medical doctors serving in the administration qualified as
general influentials. But the data also suggested that Porvenir
was bringing about at least a temporary reorganization of the
PRI structure. He was clearly in control of the local party and,
on the surface at least, had abolished the *mordida* to the extent
that even those opposed to PRI made few references to it. Yet
they felt that the election of Porvenir had not brought an end
to the problems about which they had complained in 1955.

Clearly something had happened, at least temporarily, to the
old political structure. Influence was beginning to take on the
more conventional meaning of ability to affect the general
community-decision process. Labor union leaders and representatives of other PRI groupings did not usually qualify as
general community influentials because they were not able to
exert their influence in the traditional manner. To them Porvenir
was an outsider, an intruder who ignored the proper balance of
things. They remained loyal to the party only because there
was no viable alternative.

In 1958 the opposition alleged fewer times that the mayor
was a tool of the governor, and that the governor was the only
real influential in the city. In fact, they generally admitted that
Porvenir had achieved considerable autonomy, even while
recognizing the inevitable influence of the governor in municipal affairs. Followers of Porvenir and neutrals noted this fact
with approval, while opponents argued that Porvenir was beat-
ing his head against a stone wall, and that autonomy would
result in less financial aid from the governor or the president.
The Panistas claimed that Porvenir's joining PRI was like
putting a drop of water into a bottle of black ink.

The general influence structure of C. Juarez in 1958 also pointed to closer ties between business and politics. This was inevitable since some of the city's leading businessmen were now running the government. The fact that Porvenir was able to retain his post as head of the International Committee of the Chamber of Commerce revealed that he had strong support within the Chamber's executive board. But a significant segment of the business community had broken with him. In fact, the Civic Association had split almost evenly, half supporting Porvenir and the other half supporting Leal. This rupture was also reflected in the changing attitude toward party identification. In 1955, fully 90 per cent of the businessmen claimed no political party identification. In 1958 this figure had dropped to less than 30 per cent, as the businessmen lined up behind Porvenir and Leal in PRI and PAN respectively.

One may not conclude that the rapprochement of business with government signified that the government was responding systematically to business interests. It is true that the Chamber of Commerce operated in a somewhat more friendly environment, and that some reforms in fiscal policies were being inaugurated. But Porvenir was ambitious to produce a memorable administration, and that could not be done without money. To raise money he was dependent on political organs which have their own dynamics. The questions a businessman in politics faces include a taxation policy toward business, a question which Porvenir had to face. How he did this is examined in a later chapter. Certainly, businessmen were not agreed on the question of the role of the businessman in politics as the following two quotations indicate:

> Businessmen should not get involved in politics directly. We need people who are going to devote their whole lives to politics, so that they will know well how to function.

> Take the case of Ramón Torres, for example; a fine person, a brilliant industrialist, honest, sincere, but he made a mistake by

entering politics because he didn't know how to act, or all the strange kinds of things that he would get involved in. He just doesn't know how to be a politician. Two things can happen to a businessman:

1—he becomes a politician and enriches himself at the expense of the people;

2—he doesn't play politics and then gets ruined by the politicians and his business also suffers.

A more optimistic view was expressed by the former mayor, Alberto Rico.

I saw the local government as a business, big business, and I ran it as such. I got the best businessmen in town to help me out and every month I had all the books audited so that I could be sure that everything was being run honestly, especially the public works. You know, the professional politicians just don't fit into modern government; they don't know how to run the government. That is the trouble with Mexico. They put people into big jobs who are friends of theirs, even when the men don't have any qualifications for that job at all, and most of them don't. Well, I know better and that's why I did more in three years for the city than the rest of them did in their whole life.

The Ideal Hospital Project Committee, 1958

For almost a decade C. Juarez had been constructing a new General Hospital. We decided to study this issue in detail and the means of resolving it. As in El Paso, we asked judges to select a committee of eight persons whom they believed could ensure the success of such a project in the community. Obviously, this task had a different reality significance in the two communities. That is, the question embraces a method of community operation which is conventional in the United States, but "community" projects in the private sphere are rarer in countries having strong centralized governments and countries split by ideological issues. Nonetheless, the same method of selecting judges was used in the two cities.

In trying to evaluate the nominations to the ideal hospital committee made by the C. Juarez judges, it should be borne

TABLE XX

TOP TWENTY CHOICES FOR THE "IDEAL HOSPITAL
COMMITTEE" IN C. JUAREZ IN 1958, NUMBER OF
VOTES RECEIVED, AND WHETHER OR NOT
THE INDIVIDUAL HAD BEEN SELECTED
AS INFLUENTIAL IN 1955 OR 1958

Ideal Hospital Committee	Votes Received	Type of Influential in 1955	General or key Influential in 1958
Ramón Torres	7	KI in B	GI
Rodrigo Leal	7	I in B and P	GI
Manuel O'Higgins	7	BI	GI
Luis Viejo	7	KI in B	KI
Fernando Steel	6	BI	GI
Dr. Oscar Lara M.	6	—	—
Dr. Arturo Suárez F.	6	—	—
Miguel Aguirre	6	KI in B	KI
Enrique Hernández	6	KI in B	GI
Pablo Navárez	5	KI in B	KI
Dr. Francisco Amarillo	5	—	GI
Jesús Blanco	5	KI in B	KI
Jorge González	5	KI in B	KI
Hernan Sánchez	5	—	GI
Francisco Porvenir	4	KI in B and I in P	KI
Dr. Juan Sánchez	4	—	—
René Poblete	4	BI	GI
Ernest Franks	3	—	—
Dr. Pablo Juárez	3	—	GI
José Mijares	3	BI	GI

Abbreviations: KI = Key Influential
GI = General Influential
B = Business
P = Politics

in mind that the judges included nine PRI members, eight
PAN members, and eight neutrals, and that medical doctors
allied to all three groups were interviewed. It would seem
improbable that any narrow closed circle of selections limited

to one segment could occur. Also, it is well to remember that
the judges nominated members to the ideal hospital committee
before they were presented with a list of top influentials and
before issues were discussed. Seventy-one persons were nominated, but only twenty received three or more votes (see Table
XX). Thirteen of these twenty had been business and/or
political influentials in 1955. All thirteen were primarily businessmen in 1955; only Leal and Porvenir had also received
strong support as political influentials.

Five medical doctors received strong support for this committee. Only one other noninfluential (Ernest Franks) made
the list. He was a young American-Mexican who had been
referred to in 1955 as an up-and-coming young man. He had
tried to remain neutral in the political wars by maintaining
strong ties both to Porvenir and to Leal.

Sixteen of these twenty hospital committee choices were
selected as general influentials in 1958. Thirteen persons
appeared on all three lists. That Panistas and neutrals should
receive stronger support than Porvenir for the hospital committee is somewhat puzzling. He had supporters in PRI and among
the neutrals interviewed. In addition, he had worked hard
between 1955 and 1956 to get the General Hospital in operation
and had made its opening a pledge of his administration. Perhaps the fact that he was in public office at the time reminded
the antigovernment judges of the frustrations government
encounters in sponsoring the building of a hospital. At any
rate, the top nine selections included three PRI, three PAN
and three neutrals. Undoubtedly this is partially an artifact of
the nomination technique which was used.

Businessmen received strongest support as hospital committee members (112). Within this category manufacturing and
utilities received the highest number of votes (41), and bankers received only 12 votes. Physicians received 27 votes and
lawyers 14. Government officials, both elected and appointed,

received a total of only nine votes, and four of these went to Mayor Porvenir.

An analysis of the voting of those holding public office revealed that even they felt that a hospital project could best succeed under the sponsorship of the business and professional people. However, they quickly added that under present circumstances in Mexico "It would be foolhardy to undertake it (a public hospital project) without government approval, sanction and patronage." An industrialist said that, assuming the committee could be free of government control:

> I'd follow the same process you use in the States, get at least one banker and other top businessmen from different fields. You wear out one group one time and then use another group another time.

As a group, influentials strongly affirmed the view that businessmen and professionals were most qualified to organize a hospital drive requiring public support. At the same time they recognized that such a project could not succeed in C. Juarez without government sanction. The El Pasoans had also selected a committee dominated by business and professional people, but they never felt that government co-operation was problematic. These differing institutional arrangements reflect institutional co-ordination in El Paso and institutional segmentation or opposition in C. Juarez.

A Comparative Analysis

Both El Paso and C. Juarez underwent significant structural changes in their political systems between 1955 and 1958, and these were clearly reflected in the lists of general influentials which were obtained in 1958. For the first time in El Paso's history a Spanish-name person was elected to the highest political office. While Sr. Porvenir in C. Juarez was not the first businessman to hold the office of mayor, he was the first of a new breed, able to gain control of PRI without having served the party long and faithfully.

In both cities most of the men who were key influentials were primarily businessmen. The implications of this fact must be carefully considered in any attempt to understand local decision-making. Certainly in Mexico and probably also in the United States, career politicians may be expected to have different social orientations than career businessmen. It may be assumed, therefore, that when businessmen gain political power, this will have important consequences on community decision-making. This problem will be explored in more detail in the concluding chapter. We may now summarize our findings.

1. *Business and political influence patterns.* The most notable observation is that those who were perceived to have inter-institutional influence (in business and politics) in 1955 were most likely to be selected as general influentials in 1958. If an individual had been selected only as a political influential in 1955, he was more likely to be named a general influential in 1958 in El Paso than in C. Juarez. This may be due in part to the greater interpenetration of institutions in El Paso. In C. Juarez political influence depended on the ability to hold public office and/or on holding important offices within PRI. Since re-election to the same office was prohibited in Mexico, a high turnover in offices was the norm, so only a few could maintain influence by moving from office to office. In El Paso the possibility of longer tenure in office plus the fact that influence was not tied unilaterally to party loyalty, made possible longer tenure of influence. Perhaps influence could not be built as quickly in El Paso as in C. Juarez, but influence, once attained, could be expected to endure longer.

A different pattern is suggested for the businessmen in 1955. While half of the El Paso business influentials were named general influentials in 1958, over 60 per cent of the Juarez businessmen made the general influential list of 1958. Perhaps this is simply a reflection of the fact that relatively more Juarenses were actively engaged in community decision-making. Many of the El Paso business influentials were simply influential in business and not in the wider community. While they might have been concerned about the way Rivera would run the city, they were generally satisfied with how local government was run and they felt that they had adequate representation in it.

A closer examination of the voting for influentials may be illuminating. Mayor Broon received strong support both as a political and business influential in 1955, even though his tenure of office was completed during the course of the study. In 1958 he was still considered a general influential, although he had lost some support. About half of the interviewing was completed in 1955 when Larkins had taken office. Yet he received minimum support as a political influential. In 1957 Rivera defeated him for office and Larkin was not among the general influentials in 1958.

On the other hand, Harold Nall, a political influential in 1955, had just been elected as county judge in 1958, with the support of both newspapers and Mayor Rivera. Yet he received little support as a key influential. People still had some reservations about him, just as they had about Larkins in 1955. They waited to see what Nall would do in office before deciding whether he was a key influential.

Distinctive patterns in the votes for influentials occurred in C. Juarez. The leading office holders almost automatically received the largest number of votes. In 1955 the support for Mayor Pérez had been almost unanimous; in 1958 a similar pattern was manifested for Mayor Porvenir. The same was true of the voting for Governor Montones in 1955 and Governor Castro in 1958. As of 1958, Pérez and Montones had lost almost all of their support while Castro and Porvenir had moved up.

It appears that in both cities those whom we asked to judge influence did not automatically call an individual influential because he held an important office in politics or in business. Rather they tended to evaluate performance, expected performance, and the resources the person had and how he used them.[7]

2. Ideal Hospital Committee. In both cities the judges believed that the best way to launch a successful hospital building drive was to put the drive in the hands of businessmen. One or two doctors should be involved, but government involvement should be minimized. This judgment was made on the basis that businessmen had successfully handled similar or related projects previously.

3. Integration and cleavage of institutional sectors. Some El Paso influentials admitted that they had opposed the election of Mayor Rivera in 1957, but that they quickly made their peace with him by 1958. The ethnic cleavage was not made to coincide with a business-government cleavage. In fact the election of Rivera marked an important step in the general integration of the Spanish-name population into community life.

The election of Porvenir implied a closer integration between business and government in C. Juarez. Porvenir brought leading business talent into the administration of local government. Although many politically neutral businessmen were more satisfied with government than they had been in years, strong opposition was still maintained by some businessmen led by Leal, Torres, and Blanco. They refused to co-operate with the local government, and Porvenir sought to resolve important local problems without the support of a unified business community.

4. Type of influence structure. The data to this point fail to document the existence of a solidary, unified influence system

[7] For further development of this idea see "The Reputational Technique as a Measure of Community Power: An Evaluation Based on Comparative and Longitudinal Studies," W. V. D'Antonio and E. C. Erickson, *American Sociological Review*, XXVII, No. 3 (June 1962), 362–376.

in either city. El Paso was not completely dominated by business, and neither was C. Juarez dominated by government. Significant changes took place in the influentials nominated in both cities between 1955 and 1958. In both cities groups in political control in 1955 were ousted shortly thereafter. It is true that more businessmen than career politicians were nominated as general influentials, but it is not clear that business monopolized community decision-making. Loose, overlapping coalitions of business and political groups seemed to characterize El Paso, while three factions (old-guard PRI, new PRI, and PAN), plus some neutrals and independents, dominated the C. Juarez scene.

We are now ready to examine the relevance of our knowledge of influentials for actual decision-making that took place in these two cities during the 1950's.

CHAPTER 6

Decision-Making
In El Paso

WHAT PART DID REPUTED influentials play in major community decisions in El Paso and C. Juarez during the 1950's? This question simply asks whether the reputations which people have as influentials have any basis when the actual decision-making process is examined.

There probably is a tendency for people to have monolithic conceptions of community power because they tend to personalize power and authority. Such images had wide currency in each city in 1955. The words of one El Paso influential expressed a dominant view: "Yes, the kingmakers are powerful men, older men who want to keep their monopoly on local affairs in El Paso. They control the council now and the county judge. They have more of a selfish interest than interest in the city, I think." And in C. Juarez, one influential expressed a commonly felt position when he said, "The mayor makes all the decisions here. A businessman would be foolish to take the initiative on his own."

These perceptions will be examined by attempting to answer a series of questions about community decision-making: How do issues arise? Who becomes involved in the social process of decision-making? What is the nature and extent of their involvement? To what extent are reputed influentials and others involved? How are issues resolved? What does the decision-making process reveal about the nature of the integration or cleavage among the local institutions, especially business and politics? The two cities will be compared on a series of similar issues which arose and were resolved during the 1950's. This chapter will describe how these issues were resolved in El Paso, and the following chapter will do the same for C. Juarez. Finally, the initiation and resolution of an international issue involving both communities will be analyzed.

The study of specific issues must be approached with caution, and conclusions must be lightly held. It is difficult to know whether all important issues become sufficiently publicized for the social scientist to become aware of them, so that they may be studied. With respect to those of which he becomes aware, some may be more important or more typical than others. There is no a priori way of deciding which issues are typical, important, or decisive. We feel that the issues we studied were the most important, but only a longer study can answer whether they were typical or decisive. The following issues were studied in El Paso:

Local mayoralty elections—1955, 1957, 1959
A drive for a new private hospital—1952
Introducing the United Fund—1957–1958
Launching a new general hospital—1955–1958

MUNICIPAL ELECTIONS

Traditionally, the major political conflicts in El Paso were resolved within the Democratic Party. As in many other southern cities, the Republican Party was not very active during the

1950's. However, the Democratic Party had not been tightly organized for about twenty-five years, a fact which most influentials accepted with little concern. This structure was not so loose that it permitted all groups to have equal chances to offer candidates for local offices, or that elected officials were free of obligations to particular pressure groups. During the 1950's two leading factions were operating within the party and each had held power in recent years.[1] Both factions were keenly interested in shaping and guiding the political and economic life of the community, and each faction had a newspaper to present its causes to the public. Let us first consider the faction for which *The Post* was the spokesman.

The editor of *The Post* was reputed to be one of the most influential men in the city and was considered something of a maverick. Most of the business influentials opposed but acknowledged his influence. An occasional influential and some small businessmen supported him, but the editor claimed to speak mainly for the "little people," the Spanish-speaking, and several political influentials, such as Fred Hackett. One of them described him as follows:

> *The Post* has a very learned editor who can kill any issue. He is the greatest moving force for good in this community. Some of the most prominent men in town are worried about him.

The strongest political-interest group in El Paso—which was generally opposed by *The Post* and supported by *The Times*—was the City-County Committee (hereinafter referred to as the CCC). It was composed of some two hundred of the leading businessmen and professionals of the city. Their avowed purpose was to identify and support the best qualified persons for local public offices. In the words of one of their leaders:

---

[1] James Lynn, a wealthy industrialist, had been elected mayor in 1947. He was defeated in his bid for re-election in 1949 by Fred Hackett, a railroad locomotive engineer. Hackett in turn was defeated in 1951 by Ed Broon. Broon easily won re-election in 1953.

We seek good candidates, irrespective of their political affiliation. We are not out to further our own ends in this. It [CCC] is led by the best lawyers, those who work for the corporations.

Actually, it was not the entire committee but a small core which was most active in local politics.[2] This core did not always agree on policies. As might be anticipated, several political orientations were found among the two hundred business and professional people who comprised the CCC. Self-styled conservative, liberal, and independent groups existed, but the coalition of the inner core tended toward the conservative. One half of the members of the CCC core were identified in 1955 as business influentials and the other half as political influentials. Three of the politicos were lawyers, who indeed represented the largest financial, industrial and commercial corporations in the city.

THE ELECTION OF 1955 AND THE ROLE OF THE CCC

In January 1955 various groups began seeking candidates for the mayoralty election to be held in the spring. The retiring mayor, Edward Broon, had served two terms which were generally considered to be among the most successful in the city's history. He was an important businessman, a member of the CCC, and he worked with its leaders to find a suitable replacement. George Hawley, a small businessman, was finally selected. Hawley had resided in the city for ten years and had demonstrated his administrative ability in several civic posts varying in importance. The rest of his ticket consisted of the four incumbent councilmen, all small businessmen, including José Jiménez of Spanish-speaking background. The opposition was led by the former Mayor Hackett, a railroad locomotive

[2] This core, composed of about ten of the top business and political influentials, was dubbed "The Kingmakers" by editor Stephans of the opposition newspaper, *The Post*. Some of the "Kingmakers" jokingly used the phrase to refer to themselves, while others vehemently objected to the term.

engineer, whose previous term in office was marked by considerable controversy. Councilmen on his ticket were also small businessmen and they included a person of Spanish-speaking background.

During the time allotted candidates to file for office, the newspapers speculated whether a third candidate, County Clerk Juan Rivera, of Spanish-speaking background, would file. The city had never had a mayor with a Spanish surname, and there was some concern as to what such an eventuality would mean. In fact, Jiménez and Rivera were the first to achieve high city and county offices. Among the Spanish-name leaders, some felt that 1955 was a good time for a qualified person from their group to run, because the ex-mayor "had a poor record," and George Hawley was relatively unknown. They argued that such an eventuality would stimulate most of the Spanish-surname adults to pay their poll taxes, and that this would guarantee election. Other Spanish-name leaders felt that the time was not yet ripe. One of the strongest supporters of the Spanish-name people in El Paso would go no farther than to say, "In time we will have decent Mexican-American officials heading the city." A more pessimistic view was expressed by a prominent Spanish-name leader who said, "I don't think the time will be ripe in my son's time, but in his children's time, yes."

Most of the leaders of the CCC opposed the idea of a Spanish-name mayor on the pragmatic grounds that a qualified candidate was not available.[3] A few admitted that their reservations were based on fear that a model of politics similar to that found in Mexico would invade El Paso. The discussion of the advisability to offer a Spanish name candidate for mayor was terminated when the "eligible" candidate, Juan Rivera, did not choose to run.

[3] Many also expressed the feeling that they didn't want to see El Paso politics become like Mexican politics. They were sure that a person of Mexican descent would govern El Paso much as they perceived Mexico to be governed.

In the campaign that ensued, the two newspapers took opposing sides. *The Post* supported Hackett, the former mayor, as a man of the people. It did its best to discredit the CCC candidate by referring to him as "The Unknown" candidate of the "Kingmakers." *The Times* editorialized the position of the CCC: "The issue in this campaign stands out clear as a bell. Shall we go on with an administration that treats the city of El Paso as a big business that should be run like a business, or beat a retreat to politics-as-usual?"[4] While Editor Stephans was reputed to be one of the most influential persons in El Paso, he was not able to overcome the handicap of a weak candidate, and the candidate supported by the CCC and *The Times* won easily.

The major factors in Hawley's victory are not hard to find. He had the support of the retiring mayor who had been highly successful and who had reportedly done much for the Spanish-speaking people. He also had on his victorious slate José Jiménez, a popular Spanish-name councilman who had served two terms. Finally he had a weak opponent. Hawley's victory was easy, but an unforeseen event caused a temporary crisis. He became ill just before his inauguration day. However, he was sworn in office while still in his hospital bed. Upon the urgent advice of his doctors, he resigned the day after being sworn in. Some days passed before the resignation was officially accepted.

According to the municipal code the city council had to select a mayor in such circumstances. It was free either to choose one of its own members or any citizen who was a registered voter. By a secret ballot vote of 3–1 it chose an alderman as mayor pro tem. Although there was considerable public support for Alderman Jiménez, he made no effort to secure the post. A Democratic Party leader who was a political influential said, "I believe if Jiménez had been anything but Mexican, there would not have been any question about his selection."

[4] *El Paso Times*, March 2, 1955.

Apparently Jiménez felt that various groups would resent a
Mexican-American mayor, and that he would rather be a safe
and sane councilman than mayor under these conditions. Meanwhile, the CCC inner core was worried that the mayor pro tem
might be selected as the permanent mayor. They had not been
advised that the council was going to choose a mayor pro tem,
and for several reasons they objected to the person selected.
The CCC leaders acted promptly. They singled out a successful
young businessman, Frank Larkins, who had previously been
president of the Chamber of Commerce as their candidate, and
urged the council to give him serious consideration.

The influence of the CCC core group may be noted in a
number of situations. While there was still some speculation
and doubt about when the duly elected mayor would make his
resignation official, a councilman received a telephone call from
Thomas J. Parton, a key member of the CCC and a political
influential. Parton expressed anxiety that the council might
act in haste, without consulting some of the civic leaders
most concerned about good local government. The councilman
assured Parton that he intended to consult him and others on
the matter, and continued, "Don't worry, Mr. Parton, we won't
do anything until we know for sure what the Mayor will do."
When Parton assured him that the Mayor was about to make
his resignation official, he replied, "Well, you know more about
it than I do."

The influence of Mr. Parton and his associates is further
documented by the following conversation between a councilman and another political influential:

You know, John, Mr. Parton called a while ago and was a bit worried.
He said: 'Remember, our group put you in there and we have always
backed you up, so we hope you'll give us a chance to express our
views on this problem.' I assured him that we wouldn't do anything
foolish or in a rush.

No, John, Joe is just mayor pro tem. We didn't make him permanent
mayor. . . . Ed wanted him and that's the way it goes. Frankly, and

maybe I shouldn't say this, but I'm for either you or Frank [Larkins]. We have a chance to have a mayor without an election, and I want to see the best man there. I'm going to do lots of heavy thinking about this, and I'm going to call on people like you and Mr. Parton and ask you what you think.

John replied that he thought that Frank Larkins would be an excellent choice. Two or three days later, Frank Larkins was officially chosen by the council as the next mayor of El Paso.

Another participant indicated that most of the work of persuading the council to accept Frank Larkins as mayor was done by John Burns and Thomas Parton, two key spokesmen for the CCC core group.

> I know for a fact that John Burns and Thomas Parton were chiefly instrumental in putting Frank Larkins in as mayor. Three of the councilmen had agreed that if Hawley wasn't able to take office, that Joe Evons (the pro tem mayor) would become the mayor. When . . . [the fourth member of the council] received word of this, he issued a formal statement to the effect that the new mayor should not come from the ranks of the council. Then the informal powers, Mr. Burns and Mr. Parton, got going to promote Mr. Larkins, and Larkins was in. This was a sharp blow to Evons and a real boost to the stock of . . . [the fourth councilman].

Thus, not only did the CCC select the victorious candidate in the Democratic primary and in the April election, but certain of its members played a crucial role in persuading the city council to endorse their choice for a new mayor when the incumbent resigned. The three council members who originally favored Evons as the new mayor could not ignore the pressure from the CCC.

Frank Larkins was sworn in as mayor of El Paso on April 27, 1955. On May 5, Councilman Jiménez proposed that the council reopen the question of permitting the construction of a new shopping center in Mountain View addition. A month earlier this proposal had been defeated, with Jiménez and

Smith voting in favor and Evons and Jones opposing and Mayor Broon casting the tie-breaking vote in the negative. On May 5 the position of Jiménez and Smith was supported by Mayor Larkins, and permission to build the new shopping center was approved by a 3–2 vote. Many observers felt that the mayor's support was a payment of political indebtedness.

The process of selecting a mayor suggests that those in positions of political authority may implicitly or explicitly recognize the "legitimate" influence of bankers, industrialists, merchants and lawyers on political decision-making. The absence of public protest suggests that the public either was not aware of the pressures being exercised or else acquiesced to the judgment of these influentials. No one denied that the influentials were trying to select the man they thought would be best for the city. Even the opposition paper, *The Post*, had few if any alternative suggestions to make.

The failure of the CCC leaders to urge the selection of Mr. Jiménez as mayor may not be construed as simple discrimination. The influentials all agreed that the election of a Spanish-name person as mayor of El Paso was acceptable in principle, and that it should and would happen, but they were not prepared to have it happen in their lifetime.[5] Having inaccurate knowledge of the local social structure, they believed that a "Mexican mayor" would upset the ongoing social system, and that politics "in the Mexican manner" would be the result. Their images of Mexican politics governed their behavior with respect to El Paso politics. They failed to take into account Mr.

[5] The influentials also ignored the fact that a Spanish-name person as mayor would be most desirous to prove himself as a "100 per cent American," and hence would be very sensitive to suggestions from businessmen. Spanish-name persons were keenly aware of their special responsibility in this regard. One of them commented, "If we didn't do a good job, it would not be just another John Smith who had not done a good job as mayor. Ah, no, it would be that José Ramírez, and people with names like Ramírez and Fuentes are just no good in politics. So we have a special duty to ourselves and to our nationality to perform well."

Jiménez' solid small-businessman background, his dependence on their support in the past, and his high regard for their opinions.

In sum, what personal role did influentials play in these important decisions? Only one of the four city councilmen who selected the new mayor was an influential, and the new mayor himself, Frank Larkins, was neither a business nor political influential. However, those who made the crucial decision in the choice of mayor were business and political influentials. They were Burns and Parton, and they, in turn, represented Alger, Webster, Kerrin and the others. Clearly, authority and influence were not located in the same persons, but importantly, both were needed to make decisions and the persons involved were mutually linked by past obligations of a political and nonpolitical sort.

The Year of Crisis: 1957

Many of the fears which influentials expressed that a Spanish-name person might choose to run for mayor of El Paso became a reality in the primary election campaign of the winter of 1957. The county clerk, Mr. Juan Rivera, had considered running for mayor in 1955, but deferred his decision until conditions improved. Rivera had been elected to his county office with both the open and tacit support of many influentials, for they generally recognized his excellent vote-getting ability. He was young, attractive, and had had a distinguished career in the Air Force. They further conceded that he had demonstrated adequate administrative talent as a county clerk. Yet they strongly opposed him as a candidate for mayor. A typical remark was, "We're happy to have him as county clerk, but were he to run for mayor, he'd be beaten badly. He'd find out quickly how unpopular he is!"

In the winter of 1957 the county clerk announced his candidacy for mayor. He was supported by a slate of four "small" businessmen for city council. Stephans and *The Post* publicly supported him in the primary election while the *Times* and the CCC supported the incumbent Larkins and the incumbent city council slate including Mr. Jiménez.

The people of the South Side, who were almost 100 per cent Spanish-surname, turned out in record numbers to pay their poll taxes and to register to vote. They comprised almost a majority of all voters, and they voted solidly in favor of Rivera and his ticket, despite the presence of Mr. Jiménez on the other ticket. The issue was simply one of supporting "one of your kind" for the biggest political job in the city. The campaign received national attention in *Time Magazine* of March 18, 1957. The article stated that "by a margin of 2,754 votes (out of a record 34,883) (Rivera) routed the incumbent mayor, and his "People's slate" won by a landslide in the Democratic primary, which in Texas is really election."

While it is true that the winner of the primary is generally the unopposed candidate in the regular election, that year was an exception. A new opposition appeared which claimed that the victor in the primary was not qualified for the job, and it launched a write-in campaign for its candidate in the general April election. After a hectic campaign the "People's slate" of Juan Rivera won a resounding victory, and El Paso had its first Spanish-name mayor despite the opposition of many of the city's most influential men.

What was the role of the business and political influentials in this election? The great majority of influentials had opposed the election of Rivera as mayor, but he did have the open and vigorous support of *The Post*. The CCC, with the solid backing of most of the businessmen and professionals in the city, could not control the outcome of the decision in this case. Their main tactic had been to prevent Spanish-name persons from becoming candidates by providing social and economic support to others. Mr. Rivera challenged the CCC when he felt he had the appropriate financial and social support. He received the backing of an independent newspaper, obtained sufficient financial aid from various groups, and he was able to find four Anglos with sufficient reputation to run on his slate for the City Council. The only way the CCC could win was to obtain the unanimous support of the Anglo community, and some support from the Spanish-speaking persons loyal to the incumbent councilman, Mr. Jiménez. They succeeded in neither. A sufficient number of Anglos and the overwhelming proportion of Spanish-surname voters recognized the issue as an ethnic one.[6] The results were not unlike those in New England cities where, during the last fifty years, Irish, Italian and Polish groups gradually achieved political control against the resistance of the "Old Yankee" elements.

1958–1959: From Conflict to Harmony

In the summer of 1958 the researchers returned to the border and found that the incumbent mayor had become accepted. As Mr. Burns, a central figure in the CCC, put it: "We didn't think [he] could get elected to the mayor's post. But he surprised [us] all. . . . We have a small group which has tried to get the best man in town to run, and we have generally succeeded, but the last time it didn't work. The mayor had too strong a force in his favor." Mr. Burns further demonstrated the adaptability of the influentials to meet this situation. He indicated that once they found that a Spanish-name person could do the job, they

[6] The 1957 election brought out almost twice as many voters as the 1955 election. The percentage of those registered who actually voted was much higher in 1957 than in any of the four previous elections. Spanish-name leaders estimated that they registered 18,000 Spanish-name persons, persuaded them to pay poll taxes, and got 90 per cent of them to vote. In the heavily Spanish-name South Side precincts, the vote was overwhelmingly for Rivera. For example, in Precincts 11 and 12, the vote was 651 to 43 and 370 to 12, while in Precinct 17, it was 1,242 to 49. In no "Anglo" precinct did Larkins obtain such overwhelming majorities.

"have been very kind to the Mayor. We have taken him to lunch and everything."

Analysis of the editorials and feature articles in *The Times* during 1957–1959 also revealed a gradually changing attitude toward the mayor. Immediately after his inaugural, *The Times* was quick to criticize his every move, to question his policies, and generally harass him. By mid-1958 its mood had changed noticeably, and such editorial criticisms as appeared were muted and tended to be in the nature of advice from an elder statesman. The mayor himself was extremely cautious and careful not to develop programs which were considered extreme. He was sensitive to all sides of every argument, and his chief ambition appeared to be to make a respectable record. Comments from people in diverse walks of life generally were that the mayor was doing a "good job." Although there were occasional charges that Mexican-Americans were getting all the good appointive posts, the evidence failed to corroborate this. For example, the *Directory of Texas City Officials, 1958–1959* listed thirty-one persons as the elected and appointed officials for El Paso. Only the mayor and two others were Spanish-name persons, and the latter two had been in office prior to the incumbent administration. Apparently, the great fear of the influentials, expressed in 1957 by the question, "How can we hold our heads up in the State of Texas when we have a Mexican mayor?" had been dispelled by the summer of 1958.[7]

The 1959 election was in sharp contrast to that of 1957. In January the Democratic Party chairman, an influential who was often mentioned as a possible mayoral candidate, proposed the elimination of the Democratic primary, pointing out that it was up to each local government in Texas to decide whether to hold one. Eliminating the primary would save each candidate a considerable sum, because the cost of running a

[7] The reaction in Mexico was so favorable that the El Paso influentials were quick to perceive the gains in "good neighborliness" and expanded business opportunities.

primary was levied against all filing candidates, who had to pay 20 per cent of the salary of the office for which they were applying. All the former mayors agreed that the primary was a waste of time, money, and energy. However, *The Post* attacked the move as politically motivated to defeat the City administration ticket. *The Times* supported the proposal and indirectly the administration. It editorialized, "It appears certain that [the mayor] will run for re-election without opposition. If there is any opposition ticket being formed . . . [*The Times*] has not been informed of it." The Democratic chairman also expressed satisfaction with the administration, and suggested that, since there probably would not be any opposition, a primary would be a waste of money. The mayor decided to have the city attorney study the legal aspects of the situation.

On January 12 the mayor and his slate, taking all precautions, announced their intentions to run for office and registered to run in the primary election. Shortly after, the Democratic Party decided to hold a primary election and recommended that the people decide in the April election whether primaries should be eliminated. The city council, whose responsibility it was to decide what referenda should be placed on the April election ballot, agreed on the following: (1) a four-year term for mayor and other elected officials, effective 1961; (2) a raise in salary for the mayor and other local officials to bring them in line with county officials; (3) a proposal to eliminate the primary elections. On all of these issues the mayor maintained a disinterested and neutral stand.

On February 4, the mayor, a Catholic, was lauded by the El Paso Ministerial Association. It stated: ". . . [The Community] could have fallen into a divisive competition with various groups pursuing their special interests with little regard for the welfare of the entire community." The mayor was congratulated for having acted always with the welfare of the entire community in mind.

The mayor was the only one of nine city officials to be

nominated in the primaries without opposition. In the April 14 election he and his entire ticket won, and only one councilman received serious opposition. The special referenda pertaining to salary raises and four-year terms were rejected, while the elimination of the city primary was accepted. Since none of the issues aroused organized partisanship, it is difficult to determine who, if anyone, influenced public opinion. An important observation is that the mayor did not take a positive stand on any issue, even though two of them affected him.

Here then, in the space of just four years, a complete reversal in political climate had occurred. Whereas in 1955 a member of an ethnic group felt that the time was not yet ripe for an ethnic to run for mayor, events had so changed by 1957 that he could run and win against even the strongest kind of opposition, and that he could run for re-election in 1959 without any apparent opposition or protest.[8]

A sign of the growing political strength and organization of the Spanish-speaking population and a sign that the Anglo solid front against ethnics running for office had been broken was the 1958 electoral victory of a Spanish-name person over a former city councilman for representative to the State Legislature. The election of County Judge Harold Nall in 1958 foreshadowed changes in political structure fully operating in the 1959 election, for he was elected with the support of both newspapers, the Spanish-surname populations, and some of the leading members of the CCC. Concerning the changing position of the CCC in this election, a veteran political analyst

[8] The issue was summed up as follows by *The Post* on April 7, 1959: ". . . [The Mayor] is to be returned to office without a contest. That is a great contrast to the primary and election of two years ago when he gathered tough opposition because he happened to be a Latin-American. This opposition went anonymously into the general election and tried to beat him with a write-in vote. It failed. Let us hope that the lack of opposition to [the Mayor] means the end of hyphenated Americanism in El Paso."

said, "They were tired of backing a loser, and wanted to back a winner. It's as easy as that."[9]

Elections and the Structure of Power

Elections provide a unique opportunity to evaluate the relative power of influentials and others in key decisions. Political issues and elections in large cities typically involve large numbers of people and several interest groups, so that their relationships become very complex and power becomes somewhat diffused. In such situations business influentials or any coterie of persons who have exerted their power by virtue of their traditionally high status may temporarily cease to control the flow of decisions even when they are allied with political influentials. When the resolution of an issue involves a vote of the citizenry, direct control obviously is taken out of the hands of influentials. They can control such decisions only to the extent that they select the candidates for office or can persuade the city council on how to vote on certain decisions. If, as in 1957, they cannot prevent a popular candidate from running, they face at least a temporary loss of power. This power may be gained by persons or groups not having a reputation for influence or it may shift to other influentials or groups of influentials. The latter is essentially what happened in El Paso in 1957, because the victors were themselves influentials who had marshalled superior resources and increased their status. Their victory demonstrated that there was no single group of influentials in El Paso who monopolized power.

The rapprochement of influentials in 1959 illustrates the ability of business and political leaders in American society to

[9] In this regard, Professor Peter H. Rossi has noted that businessmen are not so much averse to politics, as they are to losing. Successful businessmen seldom lose in the world of business, but the world of politics is much more problematic. After being defeated once or twice by unified minority groups, businessmen must decide either to leave politics or back the sure winners.

adjust quickly to political realities. A major cleavage over an ethnic issue could have had widespread repercussions on the business and social life of the community. That it did not is, in part, due to the mayor, who did not want to deviate from traditional political paths but rather wanted to demonstrate that "Mexican-Americans" could do "as good a job as anyone else in public office." Operationally, this meant that he proceeded cautiously, made use of impartial fact-finding committees, and avoided purely partisan issues. Distrust among Anglo-Americans resulted from their failure to recognize that ethnic-Americans have been absorbing the beliefs, sentiments and values of the dominant culture for years. As is often the case, minority groups may outdo Anglo-Americans in living up to the ideal beliefs and sentiments of the society. The return to a semblance of unity among the influentials in 1959 represented not so much their solidarity as a recognition of the political solidarity of the Spanish-name population in the city and the belief that this population would not depart radically from traditional political ideologies and practices.

Influentials in Nonelectoral Matters

A multitude of factors is involved in the selection of persons as influentials. We propose to examine some of these factors in the context of nongovernmental issues. Three persons stood out above all others in El Paso during our study of decision-making. Who were these three men and why were they called influential?

Mr. Cofield was a highly successful businessman. Although a member of the CCC, he sometimes disagreed with them on policy matters and chose his own course. For example, he made "independent" contributions to the political campaigns of candidates he considered worthy of support. Although it could not be confirmed, he was reported to have contributed to Rivera's campaign in 1957. Whether he did or not, he was capable of this kind of independent action. Cofield avoided publicity and preferred the role of the anonymous philanthropist. However, other business and political influentials in the city were aware of his influence and identified him as one of the top three influentials. Not only did they acknowledge his philanthropy over a twenty-five-year period, but they listened to his opinions on a wide range of matters.

Mr. Stillman was also among the most influential persons in the city. He was not a man of great wealth, for he had devoted his life to public service. As another influential commented: "If he were to speak up on any issue, everyone in El Paso would sit up and listen." Stillman had not chosen to speak out publicly on any issue in recent years. He took the position, which others respected, that as a federal judge it would be unwise for him to make public statements of his thoughts. However, several influentials acknowledged that they sought and received his private counsel. Through these private channels he made it known that he was a friend of the Spanish-surname people and that he did not view with alarm a Spanish-name person running for mayor of El Paso.

The third influential, Mr. Alger, was called by one of his colleagues, "the great leader of this community." In recent years he allegedly achieved the following:

(1) Raised enough money among the business and professional circles of the community in a two-year period to build a 270-bed hospital, of which he was the first board chairman.[10]

(2) Helped obtain the new immigration and customs facilities at the old international bridge connecting El Paso and C. Juarez.

(3) Was largely responsible for bringing a new private secondary school to the city.

[10] Some influentials felt that they should have been consulted more on such policy matters as the amount of money expected from each individual. Others said, "When he wants money for a campaign, he simply says, 'I need $15,000 from you.'"

(4) Promoted the establishment of the United Fund.

Alger was very interested in local politics, and probably was the informal leader of the CCC core group. However, he never became directly involved in local elections, but preferred to have Mr. Burns and Mr. Parton speak for him. Parton was very close to Alger, and many believed that he spoke for Alger.

Alger's role in the establishment of the United Fund illustrates some of the complexities of community decision-making and the difficulties in tracing the channels of influence. It is not a simple task to convince thirty or forty separate agencies that they should *all* pool their fund raising in a single United Fund campaign. El Paso was no exception. The movement to install the United Fund was proposed by Mr. Green, a professional man who was not an influential but a respected minor civic leader. He had hoped it would be possible with a minimum of difficulty to establish the United Fund by purely rational appeals.

Grumblings against the United Fund idea were heard from dissident groups and individuals. The most serious threat came over the matter of participation in United Fund by organizations representing various religious beliefs. Mr. Green was quick to recognize the need for support from community leaders and sought the backing of Mr. Alger. The latter readily perceived the advantages of United Fund to El Paso, and agreed to take complete charge of the campaign. *The Times* and its owner gave enthusiastic support, and Mr. Alger and his "coalition of chieftains" were soon able to harmonize the interests of the several religious groups involved and to overcome easily all lesser difficulties. The editor of *The Herald Post* remained more or less neutral and generally ignored the drive to put United Fund across. United Fund became a reality in El Paso in 1957, with Mr. Alger arranging the important committee appointments.

An examination of the composition of the various committees

of the United Fund showed that care had been taken to include all the important interest groups: business, professional, welfare, labor and religious. The executive committee and its officers were all business influentials. Only two political influentials were found on the five major committees or boards and both of these were successful businessmen. Welfare, labor, religious and ethnic group leaders failed to occupy any top posts in the committees.

United Fund committees typically have as representatives the most prominent and respected members of the community and El Paso followed this pattern. This does not mean, however, that all groups are equally involved in making basic policy decisions. Neither are the people who initiate issues crucial to their solution. They need to involve the most influential persons who have the resources to resolve the issue. Mr. Green brought the United Fund issue to the attention of the "town's leading citizen," Mr. Alger, who accepted the challenge and put the United Fund across. Thus, the initiator had influence because he had access to a key decision-maker who would give "his cause" full consideration.

The pattern by which the new private hospital came into being was similar. Two ministers—one Methodist and one Presbyterian—together with some businessmen initiated the organization to build the new hospital. They asked Mr. Alger to assume direction of the project and thereby assured its success. From these and other cases one concludes that many issues are brought to the attention of key influentials by persons who are not powerful in their own right, but who initiate community projects and know the structure of power well enough to accomplish their goals. In this sense they have indirect influence.

Neither the United Fund nor the hospital projects required participation of government or political influentials. They did require the backing and initiative of Mr. Alger, and the involvement of other influentials and groups to legitimate the projects as community projects. The question may be posed whether Mr. Green, the pastors, or others could have approached any of three or four other influentials (e.g., Mr. Cofield, or Mr. Stillman, the federal judge) and be assured that the projects would have had equal probability of success. Does a city like El Paso have only one man who can resolve such issues or can several influential persons or groups resolve them? This question cannot readily be answered, but it does appear that the establishment of the "activator" role is at least in part a personality matter. Mr. Alger qualified as an activator for he had resources of prestige, wealth, and personal dynamism, and he was willing to use all of them to get projects realized.

Various techniques of exerting influence are discernible in a city the size of El Paso. In this section we have reviewed briefly the styles of three men: Mr. Cofield, who preferred to influence silently by way of private philanthropy; Mr. Stillman, the "elder statesman" whose ideas and counsel were so widely adopted; and Mr. Alger, whose direct involvement in civic activities was well known to all. All of these men brought private resources to bear on community problems in areas which were not within the province of local government and which did not require voting or referenda (e.g., building stadia, recreational centers, and private hospitals). In these activities businessmen had predominant influence, while they had to share influence in municipal elections. In the analysis of the next issue, the establishment of a new general hospital for El Paso, we will find further evidence for modifying the hypothesis of business dominance of community affairs.

EL PASO GENERAL HOSPITAL

The issue arises

During the last decade, El Paso grew very rapidly and the need for more adequate hospital facilities gradually became recognized as a major problem. The situation was somewhat alleviated in 1952 by the building of the new 270-bed hospital under the guidance and inspiration of Mr. Alger. However, this new facility did not meet the needs of the lower socio-economic groups who continued to rely on the outmoded General Hospital. Speaking of the seriousness of the situation, a member of the fact-finding board established to investigate the general hospital facilities said:

> The county is required to provide emergency care, but under a system in effect for years, city and county share the cost. The hospital has deteriorated badly on its cramped budget in recent years and draws only the rag-tag and bobtail of internes, including some from Mexico and other foreign countries.[11] The doctors have been up in arms and began a battle to organize an independent hospital district for El Paso County similar to the school district, with separate taxing powers up to a fixed limit. An election has been set for November 4 (1958), and with both newspapers agitating for it, there probably will be approval. Then comes the question of whether to rehabilitate or go elsewhere and start over again. Many doctors, whose private practice is mostly on the other side of town, prefer having the district build a new hospital closer to other similar facilities. The Medical Society is sparking the campaign to put over the district and is footing the public relations bill. In the meantime, there is a latent opposition from taxpayers who resent the fact that most of those using the hospital are Latins and that many Juarez mothers-to-be rush to this side when their labor sets in and plunk themselves on the hospital doorstep where, of course, they cannot be sent away until the baby is delivered. In that manner, you may remember, they . . . establish the citizenship of the offspring.

As these comments suggest, the hospital issue was a complex one. It was not simply a matter of whether the people agreed with the doctors that better hospital facilities should be made available. There was also the problem of establishing a separate hospital tax district for people who would use it but not pay for it. Although considerable concern was privately expressed

[11] The county judge announced that the University of Texas Medical School did not recognize the hospital as an acceptable place for internship.

with respect to this, not once during the entire hospital campaign in the fall of 1958 did anyone publicly state the issue as one in which the Anglos had to support a charity hospital for Latinos. To be sure, all emergency accident cases had to go to this hospital, regardless of the preference, status, or ability of the patient to pay.[12] To emphasize this, daily ads were run in both newspapers showing a picture of a badly injured person lying in a bed in a badly deteriorated hospital room with the caption, "This Could Be You."[13]

The need for a new General Hospital was not mentioned as a pressing issue during 1954-1955. It became an issue late in 1955, after the State Legislature made it possible for cities and counties to form independent hospital districts. The doctors of the El Paso Medical Society, following the pattern of Dallas and other Texas cities, requested the county judge, Ray Battle, to put the issue of an independent hospital district on the ballot. The General Hospital is under the jurisdiction of the county commissioners' court, composed of the county judge and his four commissioners. Three weeks before the election, the county judge announced that the question of the creation of an independent hospital district had been placed on the ballot. The proposal was defeated by a vote of 2,583 to 1,889. Four major reasons were put forward for its defeat: First, the doctors claimed they had not had sufficient time to organize a campaign directed at the voting public. Second, and closely related, they claimed that the people were not well informed on the issue and so rejected the proposal out of ignorance. Third, the doctors and a number of the influentials alleged that a conflict between the editor of *The Post* and the county judge had been allowed to becloud the main issue. Fourth, the small turnout

[12] This policy has since been modified at the request of the administrator of the Memorial Hospital, so that persons could request to be brought to the latter hospital if they were financially able.

[13] The fact that the son of a well-to-do family had been taken there after an accident was used as an "informal" reminder of the fact that "everyone" used the hospital.

probably reflected the interests of only a minor segment of the population concerned with high property taxes.

The editor was known to favor more and improved hospital facilities for the Spanish-name people of the city. He was also aware that County Judge Battle would have the right to appoint the members of the first board of any new general hospital. Editor Stephans was allegedly so opposed to Judge Battle that he preferred to block temporarily the expansion of the hospital rather than permit the Judge to have so much influence over it. He publicly opposed the project on the grounds that it required an unfair and unnecessary raising of taxes. The entire problem was summarized in these words of a physician who played a key role in the issue both in 1955 and in 1958:

> We didn't have time to organize [in 1955]. [*The Post*] was against it and said it would raise taxes; that killed it. The editor is concerned with personalities more than issues. He didn't like the County Judge two years ago so he raised a cry about taxes, even though the hospital would have benefited the people. Now, he likes the incoming judge so he supports the project.

The drive for new hospital facilities was renewed early in 1958, with the mistakes of the 1955 campaign well in mind. Since County Judge Battle was retiring, the prospects were good that Editor Stephans would not oppose the drive. Informants interviewed before the 1958 election concurred that the County Medical Society and certain physicians had initiated the drive both in 1955 and again in 1958. The data clearly showed that the physicians, stimulated by the complaints of the internes in the General Hospital, were the first to crystallize the problem as a public issue.[14] Half of the general community influentials were personally contacted by physicians on this issue in 1958. Personal phone calls, private

[14] While the county judge and commissioners' court had the legitimate authority to bring the issue before the voting public, the data reveal that the doctors goaded the county officers to act. In this case, the doctors were perceived to have a legitimate interest in an issue which had to be decided by public vote.

luncheons, committee meetings, and informal chance meetings were reported with equal frequency as types of first contact. Less than half of the influentials contacted gave their immediate support to the drive, while the other half decided to remain neutral or do nothing until they received more knowledge about the situation. Key influential Alger let it be known that he favored the project. What the canvassers were after was legitimation of the project because the supporters indicated that little was asked of them other than public assurance to the Medical Society that they favored the new hospital tax district.

Issue resolution. Knowledgeables and community influentials concurred that the medical doctors, newly elected County Judge Harold Nall, the civic organizations (e.g., Rotary, Chamber of Commerce), and the newspapers had done the most to assure a favorable vote for hospital expansion in 1958. The informants were not able to identify anyone working against the hospital campaign, and the majority predicted that the referendum would be approved. No one believed that the proposed hospital district would be rejected, but some thought it would be a close vote. In their accounts of the development of the issue and how it was being resolved, only one influential mentioned the efforts of the various women's organizations. Yet a small group of women, including Mrs. Birman and the leaders of the garden and other clubs, became involved in the hospital campaign. They arranged tours of the old hospital for every major organization in the city and sent out thousands of postal cards urging voters to support the new hospital district. Apparently the general opinion of the influentials was that the issue would be favorably resolved regardless of the activities of the women, and that they merely reflected the majority opinion.

On November 4, 1958, the new hospital district was approved by the voters by a four to one margin. A temporary setback occurred when the election was invalidated over two procedural irregularities. However, the State Legislature passed a special bill with the necessary correction to validate the election. A board of directors, consisting of two physicians and five other citizens (none of them influentials) was selected by the county commissioners' court under the guidance of County Judge Nall. Still to be voted by the property owners was a bond issue of 3.7 million dollars to support the district. On April 14, 1959, in the general election in which Mayor Rivera was re-elected, the property owners voted overwhelmingly to approve the bond issue.[15]

Several crucial factors operating in 1955 were altered to account for the success in 1958.[16] First, clash between the county judge and *The Post* editor was no longer a stumbling block because the new county judge, Harold Nall, was acceptable to both newspapers. Second, the physicians had sufficient time to organize a campaign in co-operation with the county judge which enlisted the support of a wide range of interest groups which cut across all segments of the community. The campaign now emphasized that the hospital district was designed to benefit the entire community. The hospital campaign demonstrated the effectiveness of a program co-ordinating the efforts of governmental figures (the county judge), relevant interest groups (the Medical Society), and the general interest groups such as the newspapers, and civic organizations (Rotary, Lions).[17]

[15] In seeking public support for this bond issue, articles appeared almost daily in both papers; the county judge and the Medical Society took turns informing the people of all the factors involved, and frequent mention was made of the matching funds to be supplied by the federal government through the Hill-Burton Act.

[16] For a paradigm of this kind of conflict see Jessie Bernard, "Parties and Issues in Conflict," *Journal of Conflict Resolution*, I, No. 2 (June 1957), 111-121.

[17] Parenthetically, the new "Hospital District" was approved by the voters in November 1958, and a 3.7 million dollar bond issue to support the district was approved in April 1959. The new General Hospital, named to honor Judge Stillman, did not open its doors until late February 1963. By the time the General Hospital was completed, it had cost nearly six million dollars. In the process it had become one of the most up-to-date hospitals in the Southwest.

Ideal and Real Hospital Projects

In the previous chapter we examined nominations to an ideal hospital project committee. In this chapter we have reviewed how Mr. Alger in 1952 led a fund drive to bring the Memorial Hospital into being. We have traced the campaign to get approval of a General Community Hospital in 1958. The question now arises: Did the ideal hospital committee resemble either or both groups which successfully launched hospital projects?

Alger, Bartlett, Cofield and Beardsley were the men most frequently nominated for the ideal committee. Many of the others who were nominated had helped Alger in the United Fund and Memorial Hospital projects. However, Mayor Rivera, the two medical doctors most active in the General Hospital issue, and the newspaper editors were nominees of the ideal committee. Businessmen received 162 votes, the professions (mainly the medical) received 70 votes, and government personnel, 21. This distribution simply means that, if the judges had a choice, they would prefer to have the businessmen handle the project, with some help from physicians and lawyers. Businessmen were selected because the respondents felt that the hardest part of the project was raising money. They felt that money could not be raised unless people believed the project to be a legitimate one. Consequently, they looked to men who had prestige, wealth, or access to wealth. These men had been successful in "the main show" of American life, making money, and they would be successful, as they had in the past, in raising money for legitimate projects.

But that is not all. The selection of businessmen for the ideal hospital committee reinforces a fundamental American principle, that government should do only those things which the private sector cannot do as well. Private fund-raising techniques for United Fund and private hospitals apparently are preferable to government taxing. The time, energy and enthusiasm which businessmen give to raising money for the United Fund, hospitals and colleges is often equal to that given to defeat tax bills which are designed to provide funds for the same purposes.

In this chapter we have examined a number of community issues to ascertain the role which business and political influentials may have played in them. About seventy persons in 1955 and fifty in 1958 had been named as the most influential members of their community, and as possessing the ability to control decisions in any issue in which they became involved. Let us summarize the findings.

Analysis of local elections during the 1950's in El Paso revealed that most of the business and political influentials were organized in a loose coalition in the CCC, and that they had uncontested political power during the early part of the decade. Later in the decade they were successfully opposed by a smaller group of influentials who were able to come to power because they activated the large number of Spanish-name voters in the city. Recognition of the change in the power situation came in 1959 when the CCC decided to support the candidate it formerly opposed. Thus the deep-seated ethnic split which existed earlier was healed in the harmony campaign of 1959. Only a small number of influentials participated actively in the elections, but all of the main actors were listed as influentials in 1955 and 1958.

The power of the businessmen most closely conformed to the pattern of business dominance suggested by Hunter, Mills, Form, Miller and others,[18] in the establishment of the United Fund and in the project to build a new private hospital. Alger

[18] See Floyd Hunter, *Community Power Structure* (Chapel Hill: University of North Carolina Press, 1953); C. Wright Mills, *The Power Elite* (New York: Oxford University Press, 1956); and William H. Form and Delbert C. Miller, *Industry, Labor and Community* (New York: Harper, 1960).

and his associates were able to exert control when the issue did not require a public referendum, even though public voluntary contributions were expected. These projects were perceived to be capable of resolution—without government participation— via the traditional pattern of the voluntary association. Public support was further assured by the selecting of project directors and committee members so as to represent the widest range of interest groups in the community. Bankers, industrialists and merchants were all needed to assure the financial success of the project but any one of several men could assume leadership. The requirements for leadership seemed to be that the individual must (1) have a prestigious occupation which was not clearly outranked by others in the community; (2) have demonstrated administrative ability; (3) have an interest in community issues; and (4) not be identified as a member of a minority faction.

The resolution of the General Hospital issue further demonstrated that important issues could be resolved with minimal support from the business influentials. However, this decision needed the approval of the public through a referendum. Its successful resolution required the co-operation of a political influential (the county judge), the two newspaper editors (also influentials), and the Medical Society (the legitimate interest group).

The only influentials who were involved in all of the issues studied were the newspaper editors. Since they were often in opposition (one supported the largest ethnic group in opposition to the CCC core group), they were able to give the decision-making process a problematic character. Thus they helped assure that no single solidary, influential group controlled all major decisions. Consequently, several foci of influence appeared in response to certain issues: the business influentials, the CCC, the strong opposition newspaper, and the Spanish-name population. Probably the single individual most responsible for providing alternative choices in the community decision-making was the editor of *The Post*.[19]

Only a small number of influentials in 1955 and 1958 actually participated in community decisions or projects in a major way, but all of the main actors were influentials. Perhaps the primary reason for such limited participation was that most issues were not a threat to any community segment. Although factions or coalitions existed in the city, they were not based upon different economic or political philosophies of handling the community's problems.

[19] With Lipset we have maintained that stable democracy requires some degree of conflict. See S. M. Lipset, *Political Man* (New York: Doubleday, 1960), pp. 9–21, 28ff., 45ff., and 79. This conflict, even in its most orderly form, tends to make of decision-making a multi-staged process. Different actors may appear at different stages, and depending on the nature of the issue, one or another stage, as well as one or another type of actor, may be crucial for the success or failure of a project. The point here is that in El Paso, a maverick editor like Stephans seemed essential to assure that there would be issues about which to contend in the first place. For a trenchant analysis of the multi-staged nature of decision-making, see M. Kent Jennings, *Community Influentials* (New York: The Free Press, 1964).

CHAPTER 7

Decision-Making
In C. Juarez

IT WOULD BE NAIVE to assume that the pattern of decision-making characteristic of a business-oriented American community would be found in other countries. Societies vary in their patterns of institutional relations, in types of issues which arise, and in solutions used to resolve issues. These differences have a bearing on the profile of power found in local communities. Although comparing the power structures of communities found in different societies is fraught with dangers, an attempt must be made to identify the features responsible for their similarities and differences.

The last chapter reviewed the role which El Paso influentials played in municipal elections, a community welfare project, and a General Hospital drive. From the point of view of our research, we were very fortunate to find that C. Juarez was confronting these same problems during the 1950's. This chapter will examine its municipal elections from 1952 to 1959, its private and public welfare campaigns, and its drive to build a new General Hospital.

Below is a brief chronology of the events to be covered:

1952—Clemente Pérez (PRI) elected mayor; opposed by a business-professional coalition.

1952—Civic Association formed by the leaders of the business-professional coalition to build an effective political alternative to PRI.

1954-1955—Welfare programs: aid to flood victims; special funds for extra teachers; school breakfast program. Private aid programs.

1955—Electoral laws changed. Luis Muñoz appointed interim mayor. Francisco Porvenir appointed to head General Hospital Committee.

1956—Francisco Porvenir becomes mayor (PRI), opposed in the election by Rodrigo Leal (PAN). Both men leaders of the Civic Association. Association disintegrates. PAN remains hostile to the administration.

1959—Old line PRI regains municipal control. PAN remains in opposition.

1946-1959—Building the new General Hospital.

MUNICIPAL ELECTIONS

Businessmen in C. Juarez, as in El Paso, were interested in local politics, even though they were usually unsuccessful in attaining their goals. Part of their difficulties stemmed from the general antipathy toward businessmen in state and national politics. Political power in Mexico is highly centralized, and extends downward from the president of the country to the state governors and then to the mayors of the municipalities. Traditionally the president "selects" his governors, and the governors in turn "select" their mayors, who are then officially elected by the people. The Mexican constitutional system is not unlike that of the United States. The party system, however, is somewhat different, being a modification of both the two-party system generally found in the United States and the one-party system as practiced in parts of the Midwest and the South. However, one important difference between the Mexican and American constitutional forms is that in Mexico the federal executive branch of government dominates local government, whereas considerable autonomy is found in American local government. As elsewhere, the executive branch is controlled by the party organization. Now, since the legislative and judicial branches in Mexico are in practice subordinate to the power of the executive, the government and PRI tend to merge. Although some changes have been taking place within this centralized framework which have begun to circumscribe the power of the president and the governors, the general pattern of party domination persists.[1] This trend must be kept in mind while assessing the role of local influentials in decision-making.

The Municipal Elections of 1952 and Their Aftermath.

During the presidential administration of Miguel Alemán, 1946-1952, Alfredo Montones was selected as PRI's candidate for governor of the state of Chihuahua. This conformed to the common practice of selecting governors who were friendly to the president and his administration. The support and friendship of the president assured his election. For a variety of reasons[2] the governor gradually incurred the opposition of

[1] See L. Vincent Padgett, "Mexico's One-Party System: A Re-Evaluation," *The American Political Science Review*, II, No. 4 (December 1957), 995–1008. Padgett observes that an increasingly literate public opinion and the growing complexity of governing an industrialized society have elicited new pressures upon the president, resulting in a drastic change in the use of his authority to remove incompetent politicos from office. He is now more responsive to public pressures and less likely to act in terms of personal whims.

[2] His arbitrary tax policy, his alleged control of vice in C. Juarez, and personal quarrels with certain businessmen about a variety of issues.

important segments of business and the professions in several cities of the state. A number of his opponents banded together against him when he selected the mayoral candidate for C. Juarez in the 1952 elections. They joined forces with the small *Partido Nacionalista Mexicano* (Mexican Nationalist Party), and entered a slate of candidates for the municipal elections. The PNM ticket was led by a distinguished physician and supported by some of the outstanding businessmen and professionals in the city. In fact, a majority of the candidates, including those who ran for aldermen, were subsequently identified as business influentials in 1955 and general influentials in 1958. The PNM slate was not politically sophisticated, and it was badly defeated at the polls.[3] The leaders of PNM did not protest strongly that PRI had won by fraud, a common face-saving device used by losing parties in Mexican politics. They decided soon after the elections to form a "Civic Association" to develop a more informed public opinion in C. Juarez. During the first four years of its existence, the Association fluctuated between thirty and eighty members. Eleven of these were key business influentials in the city, including Sr. Francisco Porvenir, one of the founders of the Association. These men were also on the executive board of the Chamber of Commerce, and many, including Rodrigo Leal and Ramón Torres, were members of Rotary. As far as could be ascertained, no member of PRI was in the Association until 1956, when Porvenir and his followers joined the party. By mid-1954 this group had clearly established itself in opposition to the local and state governments.

During 1954 and 1955 the Association led a state-wide movement to urge the president of Mexico, Ruiz Cortines, to remove the governor from office. Three events, among others, precipitated this action: the arbitrary levying of new state

[3] The leaders admitted that they had naively assumed the people would vote for them simply because they had a prestigeful slate of candidates. They also assumed that the public was alienated from PRI, thus completely misassessing the strength of the PRI organization.

taxes against business; the mysterious murder of a taxi cab driver in Chihuahua City, in which it was alleged that a member of the governor's family was implicated, and in which the governor became further involved by ordering hasty arrests of innocent persons; and an attempt to upset the business exposition held in C. Juarez during October 1954. Many people also asserted that the governor directly controlled prostitution in C. Juarez, and that the money collected from medical inspections and licensing of prostitutes was being siphoned into his private accounts rather than into the public treasury.

The event which brought the conflict into the open was an attempt by local politicians, allegedly spurred on by the governor, to disrupt the business exposition and thus discredit its leaders, particularly Sr. Porvenir, whose growing political influence was becoming a matter of concern to old-line PRI leaders.

It will be recalled that Sr. Porvenir and the other leaders of the Chamber of Commerce had decided that a business exposition which dramatized Mexican industrialization would be a boon to Juarez business and perhaps reduce the flow of money being spent in El Paso.[4] In making plans for the exposition, the directors hired a group of private detectives to guard the many expensive items on the exposition grounds, including paintings by some of Mexico's foremost artists. Permits to carry arms were obtained from the general in charge of the federal army garrison in C. Juarez. A few days after the fair opened and three weeks after the guards had begun working, the mayor ordered all the guards arrested for bearing arms illegally and threatened to arrest those in charge of the exposition. He asserted that the law empowered the municipal government and not the federal garrison to grant arms permits. The violators were charged with illegally arming men, con-

[4] For other details on the Exposition and the business implications surrounding it see Chapter 2, pp. 45ff.

stituting a threat to civil authority and a revolutionary movement against the government.

Sr. Porvenir argued that the guards had been on duty for twenty-one days before their arrest, and that if he had erred in judgment as to whose permission was necessary to obtain gun permits, that it had been an honest mistake. He noted that the mayor had sat next to him at the formal exercises opening the exposition. He complained that the means employed to rectify the error were neither legal nor proper, and were, in fact, efforts to disgrace him and to ruin the exposition. The newspapers, which were part of a national syndicate, had been generally favorable to PRI, but they strongly supported the businessmen on this issue. Most businessmen and professionals believed that the mayor was following orders of the governor, but this did little to alleviate the situation locally. The businessmen carried their case to Mexico City and the president,[5] who finally sent a representative to the city to settle the dispute quietly. The principals could not agree on terms, and the case was settled eventually when the courts decided to drop the charges.

The importance of this issue was that it gave the businessmen and the professionals who supported them a cause to symbolize their opposition to the state and local governments. By January 1955, the move to oust the governor had gathered momentum and rallies were being held in various cities of the state. When it appeared that the Civic Association might succeed, the tide suddenly turned against it. The local newspapers abruptly ceased their attacks on the governor and the mayor just before a major rally was to be held in C. Juarez on Sunday, February 20. One of the leaders of the Civic Association explained the situation as follows:

[5] The president was seen as above partisan disputes, and the businessmen expected him to act dispassionately in this case.

You know, up to a year ago, the papers were always against us and for whatever PRI did. Then a new editor was sent here, and he got interested in our attempts to improve the city, and saw that our program was good and began to back us. So we accepted their support and now we're in a real fix. You see, the governor is a close friend of an ex-president, and so is the owner of these papers. The governor went to the ex-president and asked him to speak to the owner to get him to stop the attacks against the state administration. So that is what has happened. . . . Also, you have probably seen the ads that have been appearing in the papers giving us the works. They are all being paid for by the government; we know that for a fact. They are really plastering us. We can't possibly compete with the public treasury. Whatever we put into the paper we pay for out of our own pockets. And these full page ads cost 2,000 pesos ($180.00) apiece. For every ad we can put in, they put in four or five. So we are laying low for awhile until they ease up, and then we'll bring up our artillery. But it is tough. For instance, there are two bar and restaurant unions here. We know the larger one was always against us. But the smaller one was definitely with us. But they both came out against us in an ad. Why? They had to. This is the time of the year when taxes are paid and licenses are renewed. The pressure was on them, we know it. They were given the choice of signing the statement supporting the governor or of not getting a license. I don't blame them, they have got to live.

Even the PNM party which the Civic Association leaders had joined and led in the previous election came out with an advertisement supporting the governor. A businessman confessed:

We hadn't kept up with the party since the election. But we know for a fact that the two local [party] leaders were paid 2,000 pesos each to sign that ad, plus the fact that the government actually paid for the paper cost.

Despite the obstacles, the rally was held on February 20. While estimates of the attendance varied according to the political feelings of the observers, a fair estimate would be that between four and six thousand persons appeared. Although the leaders insisted that the rally had achieved its purpose, opposition to the governor sharply declined shortly after.

The Civic Association sent a delegation to Mexico City to persuade the president to intercede against the governor. Although he allegedly wavered, he did not intervene. One explanation for the president's behavior came from a man who was caught in the center of the controversy:

> There is a great influence here (on the border) because of the United States. This Tabasco case [Tabasco is a state in southern Mexico] is a good one to illustrate. I know the governor there. He is a good, honest man, a poet and philosopher. What happened? They [the government] raised bus fares. The people protested, there were riots, and a couple of people were killed and windows were smashed. In eight days they had a new governor. Bloodshed and rioting aroused the president to quick action. Here there have been abuses by the government for the past year; they [the businessmen-professionals] have been protesting for more than three months, with rallies, campaigns, etc. And they have many charges, not just one. But the people in this state have the new concept of democracy, that everything must be done by peaceful means, that bloodshed must be avoided. As all the rallies have been held strictly according to the law, there have been no outbreaks. So the federal government is not moved to action because, as long as there is no real crisis, they will go along with the governor.

By mid-April it appeared that the Civic Association had lost its battle to have the governor ousted.[6] Its leaders turned to a new project, presenting weekly programs in the various *barrios* of the city. The programs which were given in the open air generally consisted of: a movie feature, usually dealing with a patriotic or civic theme; a talk by a lawyer or other learned person on parts of the Mexican Constitution and/or Mexican law; and a raffle of food and other items. The programs were so well-attended that PRI's Committee on Moral, Civic and Material Improvement began to sponsor competing

[6] One of its leaders admitted, "Our open political fight against the mayor and the governor is lost. Quite a few members of the Association have begun to waver, and attendance at meetings has fallen off." At the same time, he asserted that other members had become more determined than ever and had increased their activities.

programs. Dances were scheduled on the same nights and in the same *barrios* where the Civic Association was holding its programs.

In July 1955, a member of the Civic Association who had been nominated for federal deputy on the PAN ticket won a surprising victory over the heavily favored PRI candidate. Apparently the work of the Civic Association in support of the PAN candidate had resulted in its first tangible victory. This was confirmed when the Congressional Credentials Committee of PRI accepted the credentials of the PAN candidate, making him the first Panista from Northern Mexico to be elected to the federal congress.

Early in August the governor attempted to assess a special tax on business, and the conflict between him and the business-civic groups in the state flared anew. On August 7, the president of Mexico announced that the governor had requested a "leave of absence," which was granted. He then appointed a distinguished physician as interim governor. Most of the state-appointed officials in C. Juarez also took "leaves," or were transferred to posts in other cities.

Thus culminated a protest movement which was almost a year old. It demonstrated that people not holding governmental offices and not belonging to PRI could wield political influence. It further revealed that the president still had the power to intercede at all levels of Mexican government. Nevertheless, as Padgett has pointed out, the president was much more likely to intercede when public opinion strongly supported such a move.[7] The removal of the governor in this case was very remarkable in view of his strong personal ties to people in the highest circles of PRI. The success of his opposition clearly signifies that members of the Civic Association also had access to highest sources of influence and power in the national government and politics.

[7] See Padgett, *op. cit.*

Municipal Elections of 1956: Test Case for Local Democracy

In 1955 the state electoral code was revised to permit municipal and gubernatorial elections to coincide more often.[8] Toward the end of the Pérez administration, Luis Muñoz, mayor
pro tem under Pérez, was selected as interim mayor. The interim governor who replaced Montones, had selected Porvenir
to head the hospital building committee. At the same time,
Porvenir was given the impression that national leaders might
consider him as PRI's mayoral candidate for the 1956 elections. This led to a hotly contested battle for control of the
local party between Porvenir and a leading political influential
who was trying to obtain the nomination for himself and thus
keep the old guard in power.

This situation provoked a heated controversy within the
Civic Association on the advisability of one of its members
accepting political office in PRI. Everyone in the Association
agreed on the need for radical political and social reform in
C. Juarez, but they were almost evenly split on the possibility
of instituting these reforms within PRI. Porvenir finally decided to work with PRI while his closest friend and business
partner, Rodrigo Leal, continued to insist that no lasting bene-
fits to C. Juarez could come from such a move.

PAN held its nominating convention in late April 1956, a
week before PRI held its convention. The PAN leaders approached Leal and asked him to be their candidate for mayor.
Leal had not been a member of PAN but was sympathetic
with its principles and knew many of its local and national
leaders. He was also well known in PRI circles, and had relatives in the party. Furthermore, he knew that Porvenir, his
compadre, business partner, and friend of almost twenty years
would almost surely be the PRI candidate. Because he was

[8] The mayors and other local officials are elected for single three-year terms,
while the governor is elected for a single six-year term.

entirely convinced that reform was not possible within PRI, and because he believed so strongly in the cause of reform for which he had fought in the Civic Association, he decided to accept the PAN nomination. This influenced other Association members to accept PAN candidacies for other offices, the most notable being Jesús Blanco for mayor pro tem and Ramón Torres for state governor. These moves widened the breach in the Association.

Meanwhile, last minute efforts were being made within PRI to forestall Porvenir's nomination. His opponents claimed that Porvenir had always been a Panista at heart, and thus didn't deserve the nomination. Actually, more than a year before we had asked Porvenir for his assessment of PAN. His impression was that PAN could not become a strong, effective second party of Mexico with its "present conservative program," and for this reason he wouldn't join the party. He continued, "Sure, it has some of the ideals that I believe in, but it is behind the times in its thinking. The Republicans in the U. S. were getting too conservative also, but they're changing. They have to, if they want to remain alive. Unless PAN becomes more liberal, it will never get anywhere."

Mexico City decided in favor of Porvenir, and he was able to choose his mayor pro tem running mate, and three of the ten city aldermen. The other seven were selected from the various PRI organizations by the gubernatorial candidate, Domingo Castro, a former mayor of C. Juarez, who was just finishing his term as national senator. Castro was a popular old-line PRI politician, and it was clear that national leaders had no intention of putting the entire state in new hands.[9]

The decision by Leal and Torres to seek public office through PAN meant that former friends and associates were now struggling for control of the city and state. Despite attempts to

[9] Thus, control of state politics was still firmly held by the "old-line" PRI leaders.

keep the Civic Association alive as a nonpolitical organization, the breach became wider as the campaign progressed, and the Association finally split asunder. Long friendships were terminated, and in several cases family members became personal as well as political enemies.

The campaign for mayor was not friendly jousting. Both candidates were determined to win, and both strongly believed that they were acting in the best interests of the community. Both men had strong personalities, were imaginative, and had financial and other resources at their command. And both had to overcome handicaps. Porvenir had to find a way to end the internal dissension within PRI which his nomination had provoked, and Leal had to overcome the handicap of running for a party that had never been able to elect a mayor in any major city in the country. PAN was not well organized and it suffered from being labeled a party for clerics and bankers.

Leal's greatest resource was his widespread reputation among all classes of the city as a man of integrity, intelligence and ability. His *abrazo* (embrace) was taken as a sign of true friendship. In addition to holding the usual mass rallies, Leal and his supporters instituted the practice of meeting voters in their own homes in various sections of the city, but especially in the poorer sections. Here the candidates and party leaders would address small groups of twenty or so persons for about an hour in a very informal give-and-take atmosphere. Teams of party members would make three or four such visits in an evening.

Porvenir was not as well known as Leal, but this was not his most pressing problem; it was rather the task of convincing various sectors of PRI that he was a legitimate candidate. He had to convince them that, although he was a newcomer to the party, he was a firm believer in its principles and was completely committed to it. This was not easy, and he early became aware of the fact that his past association with the Civic

Association was a political liability. Nevertheless, his determination and ability gradually won him acceptance from the Labor, Agrarian and Popular sectors of PRI. Although he could not hope to heal all the wounds caused by his previous attacks on the old-line party organization, he hoped that party loyalty would insure him sufficient votes to win. A behind-the-scenes influence in his favor was the respect his brother-in-law had in PRI by virtue of his position as general manager of the government-run Mexican Petroleum Industry.

Early in May both candidates announced extensive reform programs for the city. As might be expected, given their close relationship during the preceding years, there were very few differences in their programs. Porvenir's program envisioned more extensive public works, and he intended to raise the budget from seven million to twenty million pesos, while Leal intended only to double the budget. One of the most interesting observations of the campaign was the fact that Leal and PAN received about as much coverage in the local newspapers as did Porvenir and PRI. In all previous elections, PAN had to purchase most of its space. The editor of the major newspaper, *El Fronterizo*, in particular, felt that this campaign was different. On May 24 he announced that he had interviewed both candidates and would present the results of the interviews on two successive days. He editorialized that no matter who won, C. Juarez itself would be the winner because two such distinguished persons were candidates. The two interviews were published on May 25 and 26, and both men had received equal space and photo coverage. One section of each article was devoted to family background and careers, and the other to their views on political matters. The articles emphasized the striking similarity between the two men in their administrative and leadership qualities and in their attitudes toward public issues. Probably the greatest difference between the two was that Leal appeared to be more informal and more concerned with interpersonal relations than Porvenir.

The campaign was not without controversy. PAN complained several times that the local government was giving preferences to PRI in use of the Plaza for major rallies. However, the most serious charge in the campaign involved the special printing of some 16,000 ballots in addition to those legally assigned to C. Juarez. One of the PAN leaders received word that an El Paso printing plant had received an order to print some 16,000 ballots for the coming election. The order had been brought over by two PRI leaders. PAN notified the United States Customs authorities that some materials might be smuggled into Mexico, and they were able to pinpoint the time of delivery of the ballots to the PRI leaders in El Paso. The Customs officials were notified that a certain car would be carrying these materials and should be stopped. When the car was stopped, the PRI leaders were unable to produce documents authorizing the transportation of these ballots from El Paso to C. Juarez, and they were subsequently taken into custody. When the Juarez officials were informed of this, they made proper arrangements for the transfer of the ballots to C. Juarez.

The official explanation of this situation was that the excitement engendered by the campaign between Porvenir and Leal had increased the number of registered voters beyond the estimates of the electoral commission so that the available ballots were insufficient. In this emergency, quality ballots had to be printed in a hurry. A plant in El Paso was found to have the best facilities for this emergency operation. In commenting on the way that the electoral commission and its president had handled the situation, *El Fronterizo* accepted the story but added that printing ballots without public notification was bound to cause bad feelings. The commission also acted unwisely when it asked members of PRI to have the ballots printed and to transport them back to C. Juarez. PAN leaders were never convinced of the veracity of the official account.

On July 2, the "closest and most bitterly fought campaign in the city's history" came to an end. A record of more than

40,000 persons went to the polls to elect a mayor, a board of aldermen, a governor and a state representative. The election was closely contested in almost every precinct. On July 3 the press announced that unofficial results showed that Porvenir was leading Leal by 737 votes, 21,830 to 21,093. This total did not include the votes from Precinct 19, which had not yet been counted, and which had, in fact, been tentatively declared null and void. PAN claimed that its own figures showed that PRI was ahead by only 189 votes in the race for mayor, with Precinct 19 unreported. On July 4 the president of the electoral commission issued a clarifying statement covering the situation in Precinct 19. He revealed that there had been many procedural errors in the voting operations; that voting continued beyond the legal time, almost to midnight; and that the recount procedure had not conformed to the law. He announced that the ballot boxes had been removed to the commission's headquarters with the consent of the two PAN representatives who were stationed at the Precinct. Because of all the legal infractions which allegedly occurred, the commission had not yet decided what to do about the ballots. However, it did insist that the votes had not yet been counted, and that PAN had no reason to claim that it had garnered a majority of the votes in the precinct and thus had won the election.

PAN immediately announced that it was going to organize a protest caravan to Mexico City to see the president of the nation. It claimed the following violations in its official protest: (1) PRI had issued voting credentials falsely to hundreds of persons; (2) PRI had the 16,000 ballots printed in El Paso under its control; (3) the officials of the voting precincts were not neutrals who gave both parties equal treatment but were all PRI members who did not permit PAN members to hold posts in the precinct committees; (4) some voting booths were closed early in areas where officials suspected that PAN had greater strength; (5) voters were intimidated because the PRI officials in charge of the voting booths would not permit them to vote in secret. A protest rally was held, but as expected, the election results were not altered. On Sunday, July 15, as prescribed by law, the electoral commission met to recount the votes and to announce officially the winner of the mayoralty campaign. Porvenir was declared winner by 555 votes, 21,998 to 21,443. Nothing was said about the votes of Precinct 19.

Whatever the truth of the situation, an important fact stands out—that a vigorous two-party electoral contest had been waged according to the democratic model. Undoubtedly the Civic Association had played a decisive role in causing a situation of creative conflict and in stimulating PRI to respond to grass-roots feelings to institute responsive government. In addition, the Association provided a training ground for active political participation. The new adherents to PRI and the PAN adherents both admitted that their membership in the Association had been a turning point in their lives. One of them said, "Working with the Civic Association opened my eyes on civic affairs. We had 84 men, but what a group! If only we could have kept united . . . the Association gave me my first experience in politics and my first clear realization about how bad Mexico's social problems are."

By the summer of 1958, there were three clearly defined political units in C. Juarez: the old-line PRI, the new PRI, and PAN, which had emerged as a formal, organized party with mass following. Opposition to the local government, which had been formerly concentrated in the Civic Association, was now predominately in PAN and to a lesser extent in the ousted PRI faction.[10]

Municipal Elections of 1959: A Return to Old Ways?

PAN was the first party to select candidates for the local and state offices in 1959. Its candidate for mayor was the former

[10] About half of the members of the Civic Association supported Sr. Porvenir, and some of these joined PRI in order to be able to accept key posts in his administration.

federal deputy who had won the 1955 campaign. All candidates who had been considered for mayor were business influentials. None in the remainder of the slate were influentials.

The selection of PRI's candidate for mayor was a tumultuous affair. After much bargaining, after many visits to Mexico City and Chihuahua, after considering almost a dozen names, and after several postponements of the party convention, PRI arrived at a "unanimous" choice. Although the candidate had not been considered an influential, he seemed to be a popular choice of the Labor, Popular, and Agrarian sectors of PRI. He was described by an old-line PRI influential as a "man who has worked within the Party in favor of the poor. He is a simple man and a hard worker." Porvenir had fought hard to secure a man from his own group to succeed him, but could not overcome the opposition of the PRI professionals. The best he could do was to name five of the ten city aldermanic candidates.

By 1959, PRI had been completely reorganized at the local level. Porvenir had spent 500,000 pesos to give the party a modern headquarters building, and the party had conducted an active campaign to register new party members. It could now count on almost 40,000 votes. PAN was now at a relatively greater disadvantage. Leal himself was not in position to run again, and the new candidate lacked his appeal.

In a record turnout of more than 60,000 voters, PRI won an overwhelming victory, swamping PAN by more than three to one. The newspaper attributed the victory as much to a vote of thanks to the outgoing administration as to the popularity of the PRI candidate. At the last minute, PAN tried to withdraw from the elections, charging irregularities by the electoral commission. Many PAN adherents were not informed of this step and voted. Confusion reigned.

Despite PRI's easy victory, the officials who supervised the elections were accused of employing devious tactics to keep PAN voters from registering. PAN protested the election on two counts: (1) that the census of citizens eligible to vote had been compiled by PRI workers who deliberately avoided the homes of many Panistas, and (2) that the PRI officials conducted registration in such a manner as to prevent many Panistas from registering, even if they had been included in the census. The local newspaper which supported the PRI slate acknowledged that the charges might have some validity, and chided PRI for using such tactics, especially in a situation where an easy victory was certain. The official PAN protest to the state government was disallowed.

The analysis of politics in C. Juarez from 1952-1959 presents a situation of multi-group conflict. The Mexican political system was not found to be a single, monolithic, hierarchically controlled bureaucracy. To be sure, policy making was generally centralized in higher levels of government and co-ordinated in localities through PRI. Nevertheless, changes in both governmental and party behavior could be induced by forces outside of the government and party.

All of the political influentials and half of the business influentials were involved in one or more of the electoral campaigns of 1952-1959. Just as in El Paso, where an ethnic minority was able to win an electoral victory by having good organization, despite the opposition of a powerful group of business influentials, so did businessmen come to power in C. Juarez in 1956-1959 by overcoming the power of an entrenched group within PRI. In doing so, however, the business group was split, with one faction gaining temporary control of PRI and the other joining PAN.

The cleavages alluded to in Chapters 3, 4, and 5 were clearly manifested in these elections. Whereas a share in political power by the ethnic minority in El Paso was followed by a gradual rapprochement between its leaders and those of the CCC, there was no such rapprochement in C. Juarez. Strong ideological commitments continued to separate PAN and PRI, and no reduction of hostility was in sight. In this situation, PRI, with its broader organizations of workers, farmers, and small businessmen, may be expected to dominate the local power scene in the immediate future. How long this domination will endure depends on the growth, reform-appeals of PAN, and the willingness of PRI to risk loss of major national, state, and local offices through open and honest elections.

The ability of organized groups to appeal to the Mexican president reveals some flexibility of PRI in handling inter-group tensions.[11] The fact that PRI was able to absorb opposing interest groups into its organization was a sign that it might become more responsive to a wider set of interests including those of local business and professional groups. Acceding to pressure to run candidates who have not come up through party ranks may both represent an increasing outward orientation of the party, and it may also signify an ability to co-opt a potentially annoying opponent.[12] Both interpretations represent the party's determination to remain in power.

It is difficult to arrive at firm conclusions about two-party politics in the city. The fact that the 1956 mayoral election was won by fewer than 600 votes, and that PAN elected a federal deputy in 1955, suggest that the traditional supporters of PRI do not always follow the "party line." Perhaps the independence they exhibited in 1956 was due to the unusual situation of having two outstanding local businessmen as political opponents. Whether this represented a first step toward significant socio-political change or a unique occurrence, could not be decisively established from the pattern of the 1959 elections.

[11] The president has the authority to remove state and local officials if the situation demands it. Persons outside of PRI may exert pressure upon him to do so. This device is not only legitimate in Mexican decision-making; it also reduces the monolithic character of PRI.

[12] It may also reveal the awareness by PRI that big business is fast becoming a powerful independent force, outside of the party.

Influentials and Special Fund Drives

Analysis of local elections in C. Juarez between 1952 and 1959 showed that not all who were called political and/or business influentials in 1955 or general influentials in 1958 were involved in the political campaigns. However, the candidates in these campaigns and all who played leading roles were influentials in both time periods. As we turn to examine special fund drives, some evidence is available to explain why certain individuals are identified as influentials even though their participation in local affairs is limited. There is also some evidence on the linkage between participation in the political and private sectors of community life.

C. Juarez was not without its philanthropists. Men like Jaime García, Miguel Aguirre, Alfredo González, and Luis Viejo were among generous contributors to the Red Cross and to special fund drives. Two influentials occupied roles similar to those of Mr. Cofield and Mr. Stillman in El Paso, and they both managed to transcend social cleavage in the city.

Sr. Miguel Aguirre, who was frequently chosen as a business influential, was reputed one of the city's wealthiest men. He was considered an influential not because he participated actively in community affairs, nor because he had informal power. Actually he was almost a recluse, and he refused to engage in local politics. He was respected because he was a philanthropist who could be counted upon to contribute regularly and handsomely to every worthy charity. He generously supported both governmental and nongovernmental welfare efforts. Respondents insisted that this was a kind of "influence" which had to be recognized.

Sr. Manuel López had served as mayor of C. Juarez in the early 1940's. He was remembered for his honest and progressive administration, and for his extraordinary success in business. Actually, he had not resided in the city in recent years, since he had become one of the most influential men in the federal government as manager of the state-owned Mexican Petroleum Industry. While it was generally conceded that he had not exerted direct influence in local affairs in recent years, he was nonetheless considered a local influential because of his national eminence and his past local accomplishments. Although he was closely identified with the local group headed by Porvenir and Navárez, he transcended local business and politics, and was respected in both camps. Most local influentials believed that his unique personality and not his role enabled him to transcend local cleavages.

While Aguirre was a generous supporter of worthy drives and López had led and supported such drives in the past, neither man initiated drives in the 1950's.[13] Issues were initiated at various times by the Civic Association under the leadership of Porvenir and by local government influentials. Let us consider several welfare issues and how they were handled in the city.

The Rio Grande flood

During the late spring of 1954, a flash flood raged along the Rio Grande causing severe damage to several United States and Mexican border towns east of C. Juarez.[14] Sr. Porvenir quickly called on the Chamber of Commerce and the Civic Association to raise more than 30,000 pesos, which they distributed in equal proportions to the Chambers of Commerce of the three Mexican cities most badly hit. They also collected a considerable

[13] Sr. López returned to an active role in Juarez affairs in 1961 when President Adolfo López Mateos appointed him Director General of the National Border Program, a special development program designed to improve the economic, social and recreational level of the nine major cities on the U.S.-Mexico border. Among the projects underway by 1962 were a new shopping center removed from the old center, a horse- and dog-race track, Frontón for Jai Alai, and a new cultural center including museums and theaters. Porvenir was also playing a leading role in this activity.

[14] See Roy Clifford, "Rio Grande Flood Disaster Study No. 7," *National Academy of Sciences*, National Research Council, 1956.

amount of clothing which was dispatched to the flooded area. The local government objected to these activities and accused the leaders of the Chamber of meddling in affairs that were properly within the area of local government. The fact that the Chamber had acted with such alacrity and completely independently of local government revealed that the two groups were not willing to work together, even in such a nonpolitical cause as a flood disaster.

School breakfast program

The rapid population growth of C. Juarez as a consequence of heavy immigration from southern Mexico and a high birth rate taxed the ability and resources of local government to the utmost. It was widely recognized that the children of the poorest families were badly undernourished, and that a school breakfast program would at least help the children enrolled in the schools. In the fall of 1954, Porvenir, through the Civic Association, proposed to the local and state governments that local businessmen would be willing to raise one third of the money needed for such a program if the governments would supply the other two thirds. Without waiting for government approval, the businessmen quickly raised 180,000 pesos which they deposited in a bank, and then called upon the municipal and state governments to match the funds. Government officials objected that this was not the proper way to approach the problem, and that they would not bow to the dictates of a group of businessmen.

The result was a stalemate, and the school children went without the much-needed breakfast program. A front-page editorial in *El Fronterizo* in November 1954 attacked the government for letting the breakfast program die and praised the business group which had "tried to get something done." This case demonstrates that the Civic Association would do little to ease tension with local government and that the latter would not be coerced into a status-testing contest no matter how worthy the cause.

Not until Porvenir became mayor in 1957 were funds provided for the breakfast program. This time the program was completely financed by municipal funds and the breakfasts were served by mothers' clubs, which were organized in the various *barrios*.

Schools and teachers

The rapid population growth in C. Juarez also led to a great shortage of teachers and schools. The responsibility for building classrooms and providing teachers belonged officially to the state and federal governments. On occasion either the Rotary or the Lions Club raised enough funds to build a small school in one of the "depressed" *barrios*, but no effective overall planning for educational expansion had ever been attempted. By 1954 more than 2,000 children of school age were not in school, and the local government felt compelled by public pressure to take some action.[15] Lacking resources, the government called upon businessmen like Jaime García who had maintained a neutral position in the dispute between the political and business influentials to raise additional funds for teachers.

[15] The state and federal governments had not been able, since the Revolution, to achieve the goal of national literacy. They were completely unprepared to handle a crisis such as that which arose in C. Juarez in 1954. Recently, the federal government has permitted the opening of Catholic parochial schools on the pragmatic grounds that without private aid it can not meet the nation's school needs. For his part, Mayor Pérez was caught in an intolerable situation. He was not powerful enough to persuade state or federal governments to engage in a crash program, partly because educational expansion was a national problem. Nevertheless, increasing pressure from a hostile press was forcing him to take some action in an area in which he was not legally responsible, and for which he lacked funds. With a large segment of the business-professional groups hostile to his government, he simply could not obtain the resources necessary to resolve the problem. That he did succeed in alleviating it to some degree is testimony to the existence of a substantial number of neutral and pro-PRI business leaders.

A small number of individuals contributed most of the funds. Several complained privately that raising school funds was the proper concern of the government, and that asking for donations demonstrated that government was not doing its proper job. Mayor Pérez was faced with other problems which the government could not meet, for lack of resources. The hostility of the Civic Association made their solution all the more difficult.

The main effort of the businessmen during the educational crisis resulted in the building of a private parochial school. They also supported a Boy's Town (*Ciudad del Niño*) under the auspices of the local Catholic monsignor. Under his direction they also established a reclamation school for wayward girls and women. Although Porvenir participated in these projects, the main effort was borne by other business and professional influentials, particularly Leal, Torres, and Blanco, who later became the leaders of PAN. As far as could be ascertained, no governmental official helped organize these projects, although some political influentials like Alberto Rico made financial contributions to Boy's Town. Generally the political influentials thought that Boy's Town was a good project, and that the monsignor was a good man, an exception among Mexican clergy. Most of the neutral businessmen, including García, Banco, González and O'Higgins also supported these private efforts.

An analysis of the above issues documents the absence of effective linkages between the government and the business-professional sector of the community. Very few people were able to transcend this cleavage, and those who did were not active in the struggle for power. The efforts of the Civic Association and the Chamber of Commerce to raise funds for community welfare programs represented a new trend in Mexico, where relief and welfare programs have traditionally been the responsibility of government. It is thus understandable that

government officials resented this "intrusion" into their legitimate sphere of action. Since the leaders of the Association and
Chamber had "taken a leaf" from the United States private
welfare pattern, clash with local politicos was almost inevitable.
Mutual mistrust led to the struggle for control of the decision-
making process. This struggle so completely blocked co-operative welfare projects that each group embarked on independent
programs. Although both factions claimed to be sincere in their
desires for community welfare, many neutral observers felt
that they were more concerned with embarrassing the opposition than with helping the needy. The conflicts precipitated in
1954–1955 became increasingly politicized and finally found
their institutional expression in the activities of PRI and PAN.

The bitter party conflicts benefited the public in an unexpected way. It began to see that important local programs
could be successfully organized by various sectors of the community. Even the PRI-oriented newspapers participated in
this informal educational campaign by calling for a rise in the
level of governmental performance and by encouraging organizational experimentation in various arenas. In such an
unstable situation where new political alternatives were being
offered, the conditions for the emergence of charismatic leadership were present. Sr. Porvenir, as the initiator of new ideas
and programs for the community, seemed to be such a leader.
One of the promises he made in his campaign for mayor was
that the general hospital that was long a-building would be
opened during his administration. How he behaved in this
thorny issue is shown below.

The Juarez General Hospital

The rapid growth of C. Juarez not only taxed its school system but its hospital facilities as well. Government monies supported an obsolete Civil-Liberty hospital built in the first
quarter of the century to serve a community of less than 50,000
persons. There was also a small, well-staffed and well-equipped

private sanitarium which had been jointly built by physicians and businessmen about ten years ago. Other Juarenses who could afford it patronized one of the private hospitals in El Paso and a few even managed to obtain services from the El Paso General Hospital.

One of the first projects which the researchers observed in 1954 was the shell of a building about a mile from the center of the city. This was to be the new General Hospital. No one was certain when it would open, but government officials indicated that construction was proceeding as rapidly as funds permitted. With no long-range public or private funding program in operation, the prospects for opening the hospital in the near future were dim. Since the hospital had not been completed in the summer of 1958, the researchers decided to study the entire project to gain further insight into how projects of community-wide significance were carried out.

The call to action: The mayor speaks

Local residents agreed that former mayor Alberto Rico had decided that the city needed a new hospital. His administration had run from 1946 to 1949, and had been marked by the greatest public-building campaign which C. Juarez had ever seen. The building of the general hospital was a part of that campaign. The following comments by a banker refer to initiation of the project:

> The mayor called a meeting to tell us what he wanted. We were not asked about planning or anything else. That is the way it is in Mexico. A mayor starts a project that he's interested in, and only asks private enterprise for monetary help. Then the next mayor comes along and doesn't feel that it's his project, so he drags his feet. Perhaps some day the project gets finished.

A merchant commented:

> The mayor chose a bad location. He paid no attention to architectural details. He really wanted to build a visible monument to himself. The

governor ordered the work stopped when the mayors changed. There was no committee capable of keeping the thing going.

The above picture was confirmed by a political influential:

> The mayor decided that C. Juarez needed a new hospital, but without plans. All he got done was the frame. The following administration did nothing. The next administration changed plans with state government aid. But still there was no overall plan. Then in 1955 the interim governor set up a new committee . . . This represents a 14 million peso investment: 4½ million in equipment; 5–6 million in construction; and about 2 million to go.

As far as could be ascertained, only ten of the influentials had been contacted on this hospital issue either originally or at some time during the ensuing ten years. Initiation of action generally came from politicos who contacted others for financial support. Advice or other type of involvement from businessmen or physicians were rarely solicited because it was felt that the project was mainly governmental, and not the concern of the private sector. The drives for funds appeared to be poorly planned and they relied too often on street collections near the international bridges. Poor overall planning and lack of co-ordination among the interested groups stalled the project at various points. The difficulties in surmounting these drawbacks were described by a physician who played an important role in trying to get the hospital functioning in 1958:

> It was begun under the administration of Rico who was concerned only with getting a hospital built, not with how it was to be constructed. It was poorly done. Other mayors contributed to the building of the hospital, but—like Rico—they were not concerned with architectural details.
>
> When Porvenir was president of the Patronato (Hospital Planning Committee), he convinced the mayor that some attention should be paid to the functioning of the structure. An architect was called in from outside Juarez and this man—an expert in hospital construction—made suggestions for changes. Since that time—and especially during

his administration—Porvenir has worked to make the building more functional.

Porvenir's original plan for operating the hospital was to get together funds from city, state and federal governments: 100,000 pesos per month from each. However, this plan failed when state and federal officials balked. Then Porvenir decided to interest the Seguro Social in renting about 50 beds. The rental money thus derived would provide operating funds for the hospital. Seguro Social has not officially replied to Porvenir's request and a meeting is to be held early in September in Mexico City.

A survey conducted by outside "experts" revealed that operating costs of the hospital will be about 360,000 pesos ($28,800) per month.

The physician did not refer to an obvious fact that the hospital would be serving the city's most indigent families, and thus could not expect to recover operating costs from its patients. Since the city budget was less than 2,000,000 pesos per month, the municipality obviously could not spend another 300,000 pesos. Porvenir evidently had to seek outside help. Under these conditions only the optimistic felt that the hospital would soon be completed and put into operation.

An industrialist who had been close to some of the political influentials and had tried unsuccessfully to help, admitted:

I suggested to the governor and to the mayor that they let the nuns run the hospital. They would do an honest job. But they (the politicians) are afraid to let the Church run it for fear they'll be called pro-religion or something. The Church is the only real solution without graft. But it's up to the government to do what they think is best . . . . How will it be solved? Either through help from the federal government or some kind of local fund-raising campaign—maybe the money will come out of the mayor's own pocket.

Issue resolution: The mayor keeps his promise

In the course of ten years, from 1949 to 1959, more than one million dollars had been spent to build the hospital. This was a formidable sum for a community whose total municipal budget during most of this period was less than one million dollars a year. As indicated above, the project had been conceived and pushed mainly by local government officials, and the business-professional segment of the community had not been deeply involved until Porvenir became chairman of the Hospital Committee late in 1955, in which capacity he served until he became mayor in 1956. Despite his position of business leadership and despite the fact that he had at least temporary control of the local political system, Porvenir could not entirely overcome the business-political cleavage which had persisted so long in the community. He became increasingly anxious because, as we have seen, he had made the completion of the General Hospital a primary obligation of his administration. By the summer of 1958 it was apparent that sufficient funds to open the hospital would not be available at either the local or state level. Mayor Porvenir approached the National Social Security Agency, which operates many hospitals throughout Mexico, to loan the city funds which would be repaid later from hospital fees. The Agency declined on the grounds that the hospital was badly located and too poorly constructed to meet modern hospital needs. Shortly thereafter, the Agency announced its intention to build another hospital in C. Juarez, since the city needed more beds than the new hospital would provide.

Though the mayor needed no reminders of his promise to open the hospital, the press regularly reminded him of it. He made several visits to Mexico City to consult with the president, and finally, in the spring of 1959, he announced that the president of Mexico had agreed to loan the city one million pesos so that a portion of the hospital could be put into operation by July 1959. The mayor's personal influence with the president and his driving determination to get the hospital into operation were decisive in obtaining this unusual loan. After some delay and after ten years of inadequate planning, insufficient resources, and many frustrations, the General Hospital of C. Juarez began to function in September 1959.

The hospital project was, from its inception, a concern of government officials. Although they alone had the authority to carry it out, they were without institutional resources to complete the task. It remained for a career businessman who had personal influence with the president to meet a need which the legitimate mechanisms of local government could not provide.

Ideal and Real Hospital Committees

Can a community characterized by institutional factions launch a successful private project, such as building a hospital? This question was posed in 1959 to twenty influentials and three physicians who were involved in hospital and public medical assistance programs in C. Juarez. They were given the perhaps unrealistic task of selecting the members of a committee that would put across a hospital project.[16] The pattern of their response was strikingly similar to that obtained in El Paso. If they had a choice, they would place the project in the hands of those who had successfully managed private fund drives in the past. They had no doubt about the ability of Juarez businessmen to carry out projects which were strictly within the private sector. However, an ideal hospital committee, they felt, had to include members from all major factions. If such a committee could find a *modus operandi*, it would have a better chance of succeeding than any committee thus far created.

Ten years of struggle and frustration had made them suspicious of governmental efforts to resolve such problems, but these experiences had not taught them how to co-operate with government projects benefiting the community. Similarly local governmental officials had not learned that when they needed the financial resources of the private sector, they had to involve it also in the planning and execution phases of the project. In short, voluntary projects involving the co-operation

[16] For further details on the significance of the response to this question, see Chapter 5, pp. 122ff.

of two or more institutions are community projects and new organizational devices must be invented to achieve community goals. The hospital issue, more than any other, revealed the basic weakness in the social fabric of the Mexican community. Lacking the structural requisites for common efforts, the attainment of community goals resulted from the almost accidental appearance of charismatic leaders like Porvenir. The question remained whether such leadership could produce long-lasting changes in the community.

In considering the role which the business and political influentials have played in community decision-making in C. Juarez during the 1950's, we attempted to answer two basic questions: (1) How solidary were the influentials, i.e., would the data on institutional cleavage be supported by analysis of actual situations? and (2) were influentials generally effective on all issues or was their influence functionally specific?

The answer to the first question was clear. Not once during the seven-year period covered by this study did the business influentials as a group work with the political influentials as a group to resolve a common problem. Whether the issues were electoral, concerned with a school breakfast program, or the building of a new hospital, conflict and cleavage was ubiquitous.[17] Even in 1955, when the local and state officials took "leaves of absence," a large proportion of the business influentials found it impossible to work with PRI for purely ideological reasons. Out of this split within business a fairly strong PAN organization emerged.

The reduction of conflict to the point which would make a stable, democratic process possible depends on the resolution of two problems. First, can the party which has controlled Mexican politics and changed much of Mexican life since the

[17] Although effective opposition is a necessary condition of political democracy, the kind of opposition observed in C. Juarez during this period was not conducive to political democracy. Here the groups opposed each other even in situations where cooperation would enhance their respective positions.

Revolution of 1910 be expected to give up some of its power to an opponent? In particular, will it relinquish some power to an opponent such as PAN which, although it has strong links to Christian-Democratic principles, has been identified rightly or wrongly as the party of clericalism and big business? Despite the fact that relations between the present president and the head of the Mexican religious hierarchy have become almost cordial of late, considerable suspicion and conflict persist at the local levels. If PAN continues to be identified as the spokesman of the Church and big business, and PRI insists on this identification, intelligent opposition tempered by the desire to work together for the common good may be impossible.[18]

The second question revolves around the apparent paradox of a simultaneous diffusion and a concentration of power in Mexico. Diffusion of power was manifested by: (a) the victory of the PAN deputy in the 1955 elections; (b) the ability of the Civic Association in conjunction with others to get the president to intervene in state and local politics; and (c) the victory and temporary control of PRI by a group of business influentials from 1956 to 1959. These instances demonstrate that segments of the public can, on occasion, marshall effective opposition against those who traditionally control PRI in the state and in the city. While the intervention of the president demonstrated that PRI was not an inflexible bureaucracy, it also revealed the absence of an independent community power structure capable of resolving local impasses.

A dilemma faces the Mexican community

The problems and issues confronting Mexican communities are so grave that they require the marshalling of all institutional

[18] PAN spokesmen continually asserted that the allegations that it represented clerical, nineteenth-century reactionary thinking were smoke screens motivated to block their attempts to become a legitimate political force. Two things seem clear: that the clergy and some wealthy conservatives have supported PAN in the past, and that PAN leaders recognize that the open support of these groups is inimical to their efforts to become a major political party.

facilities in joint efforts. Yet deep-seated cleavages prevent such co-operation. In such a situation the emergence of political figures like Porvenir may become a possible way out. Porvenir was a career businessman who entered politics because of a fierce determination to do something for his city and a firm conviction that business had an important role to play in community life. He met his first setback when some of his closest friends and supporters would not join him in a movement to reform PRI. This split within business almost cost him the election in 1956 and harassed him during his first year in office. However, he did succeed in more than doubling taxes in three years, in order to give the city a health, education and welfare program never before realized. Perhaps his most unusual and important innovation was his weekly tour through the city in the company of 30 to 40 business, professional and working-class people, to show them what was being done with their tax money. This increased interest in community affairs and perhaps created a new respect for local government.

During these seven turbulent years, the mayors and their supporters were influential in office, as were the two regular and one interim governors, and some of the members of the Civic Association. However, there can be no doubt that the one man who dominated Juarez politics and business during this period was Porvenir. Whether his influence will last is highly problematic, for PRI had shown itself to be a complex and stable structure resistant to internal reforms; and business has yet to find a balanced perspective on its role in community decision-making.

CHAPTER 8

Decision-Making in an International Context

INTRODUCTION

IN THE ANALYSIS OF the decision-making process in the two cities we found that some influentials played decisive roles in some issues while others were not involved at all. In both cities businessmen were active in politics, and they met with a number of successes as well as some failures. In El Paso the animosities generated during the contests for political power never led to serious institutional cleavages. In C. Juarez, the ideological cleavages which traditionally separated church-men from anticlerics and liberals from conservatives were ubiquitous in the struggle for power between the business and political influentials. In short, there was much greater co-operation among the El Paso influentials than among their Juarez counterparts.

Our final task is to try to ascertain whether this same pattern of relative harmony in one city and conflict in the other would persist in a project requiring the co-operation of all four groups of influentials. This project was the resolution of one of the most persistent problems which had plagued the two cities in the last ten years, namely, providing adequate border-crossing facilities. This international project presented a challenge to analyze the articulation of systems having different values, structures and internal integration. Since we were early aware of the long-standing concern with the bridge issue in both communities, we interviewed influentials about it in 1954, 1958, and subsequently. An attempt was made to learn what they knew about the issue and in what ways they were involved in its resolution.

Linking the Two Borders

The bridges over the Rio Grande symbolize the tie between the two countries and the two communities. Up to 1958 there were two operating bridges, which were about half a mile apart and served as one-way entrances to the respective cities. Only one bridge permitted two-way pedestrian traffic. With the ever-increasing volume of traffic the bridges became more and more congested. Several influentials on both sides of the border said that they did not visit the other city more frequently because they hated to get ensnarled in the traffic, which at certain times of the day might cause them to spend two hours in their cars (see Figures 3 and 4).

The auto-trolley bridge which permitted two-way pedestrian traffic connected directly with Juarez Avenue in the Mexican City. This street contained the main tourist attractions. On the El Paso side the bridge led into the Chamizal, a generally run-down area of warehouses and tenements which bordered the heart of the main business district. Stanton Street in El Paso led to the bridge which permitted only one-way traffic to C. Juarez. It was lined with grocery stores and other small businesses. The corresponding street in C. Juarez was Lerdo, which opened into a transitional area of mixed residential and busi-

FIGURE 3. Aerial view of international boundary showing public and railroad bridges. (El Paso on the left; C. Juarez on the right.) Courtesy of El Paso Department of Planning.

FIGURE 4. *Typical traffic congestion on the International Bridge in El Paso. Courtesy of El Paso Department of Planning.*

ness use. While these two bridges had been adequate when the cities had a combined population of under 100,000, in recent years they had become completely inadequate for the increasing traffic. The two bridges had to serve the 15,000 Juarez workers who daily made the round trip to El Paso on foot, in trollies, or in private cars, the innumerable Mexican shoppers who patronized El Paso stores, the many American tourists who went to C. Juarez and the interior, the businessmen and government officials on daily visits to the other city and the countless truck drivers who delivered goods in both communities.

A New Bridge: The Issue Arises

It is not clear how the issue of increasing the crossing facilities first arose. Most Juarenses asserted that the former mayor, Rico, who started the construction of the General Hospital in the late 1940's, was the first official who attempted to increase the border-crossing facilities. By seeking donations from all those who crossed the Juarez Avenue bridge into El Paso, he gradually raised enough money to build a two-lane bridge across the Rio Grande about two miles east of the present bridges, connecting the Mexican mainland with "Cordova Island." Cordova Island (Figure 5) was a piece of land owned by Mexico which jutted out onto the American side of the Rio Grande,[1] and was contiguous to the Chamizal area of El Paso.

[1] During the nineteenth century the Rio Grande (Rio Bravo to the Mexicans) shifted its bed several times. Apparently one such shift left a piece of land (Cordova Island) to the north of the river, and this has been recognized as Mexican territory. The "Island" is not now surrounded by water. Other shifts in the river have created the area now called the Chamizal.

As the figure shows, the Cordova entry would take traffic east of the downtown business districts of both cities. As a matter of coincidence it takes traffic near the two new General Hospitals. Sears-Roebuck of El Paso, which is almost two miles east of the center of El Paso, would certainly benefit by the new traffic flow. Since the eastern sectors of both cities have been expanding rapidly in recent years, the Cordova entry clearly promised to ease the flow of vehicular traffic. The El Paso City Lines would continue to transport the overwhelming majority of non-auto owning Juarez workers.

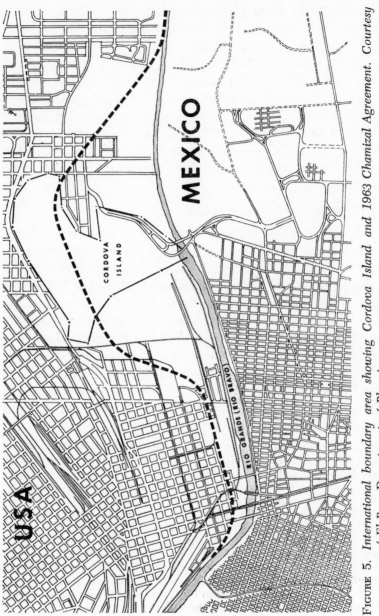

FIGURE 5. *International boundary area showing Cordova Island and 1963 Chamizal Agreement. Courtesy of El Paso Department of Planning.*

Two immediate problems became apparent as soon as the bridge was completed: The mayor had not obtained commitments from either federal government to staff the bridge with Customs and Immigration officials. Neither had he made provisions to establish access highways to the bridge on either side of the border. Almost a mile of highway was needed on the Mexican side alone. The federal governments ignored the bridge and it went unused.

The following comments illustrate the views of the Juarez influentials with respect to what had happened. An industrialist who looked with favor upon increased commerce between the two cities said:

> The mayor wanted to build a bridge; he formed a committee to get funds; the drive was successful and the bridge constructed. Certain El Pasoans objected and the bridge has not been opened to traffic. The bridge has been a project upon which Juarez and El Paso have not agreed (the marriage has not been consummated, so to speak.) Yet forward-thinking people of both towns know that such a project is necessary. There is also the fact that the U.S. government doesn't want the free bridge [Cordova] opened because it would encourage Mexico to develop the island.

A more cynical view was expressed by a PRI politician who had had nothing to do with the construction of the Cordova bridge:

> That bridge is too narrow for human beings—only fit for driving cattle and hogs over. And it is located at the wrong place. Planning for new projects is usually very deficient here. Each administration tries to do too much and to build monuments to itself. This is another obvious white-elephant monument.

The El Paso influentials were not clear about the origin of the bridge issue. While recognizing the long-standing need for new facilities, as late as in the summer of 1958 the influentials we interviewed did not mention that a bridge had been built connecting Cordova Island to the mainland of Mexico, and that the present issue traced its origin to a decision made by a Juarez mayor some ten years before. One fourth (12) of the El Paso respondents said that the issue had originated within the El Paso Chamber of Commerce, and one fifth insisted that the morning newspaper had "revived" the issue. Another fourth said that the government, either local or federal, had initiated the issue as a result of the constant traffic tieups that had been occurring.

Actually, there had been considerable discussion about the need for new bridge facilities since the late 1940's, and several groups had tackled the problem in one form or another. In 1955 next to water shortage, the problem of inter-city traffic was mentioned more often than any other by both El Paso influential groups. The influentials in C. Juarez also recognized this need for bridges as a crucial problem in 1955.

One El Pasoan explained in 1955:

> Ever since I've been here I've been aware of the need for two new ports of entry in the area, one at the other end of town, and one on the New Mexico side. But there are political and business forces of considerable magnitude which are opposed to this expansion. The El Paso merchants are happy to see the Mexicans coming right into their business district, and the Juarez merchants along the Avenue leading to the bridge feel the same way. They don't want the customers to move to other entries.

An El Paso political influential emphasized the importance of the weight of numbers when he said:

> For myself, I think I could manage to get the entry ports built on this side, but what good would that be if the Mexicans weren't willing to put them up on their side. And so far there's no sure sign that they will go along with this. But the expansion has to come, and the bridge will come. It's not just an idle dream; it will come about soon over all the political and economic objections and pressures, because the sheer weight of numbers crossing these two little bridges will make it necessary.

In 1955 the United States federal government was already completing plans to enlarge its customs and immigration facilities on the Juarez Avenue bridge. Officials hoped that this would remove about half of the pedestrian and auto traffic from the immediate egress point and permit a more rapid traffic flow. Although the expansion was completed in 1956, it did not sufficiently relieve traffic conditions, and by the summer of 1958 the problem of locating new facilities had again become critical. Our respondents reported that both ambassadors had visited the cities in 1958 and had personally experienced the traffic tieup at the bridges. They both seemed to be in favor of a new bridge, and the only problem seemed to be where the new facilities should be located.

Working for and against New Facilities

Only a small minority of the Juarez influentials were active in the issue between 1949 when the Cordova bridge was built and 1958. Two of them had been members of the original committee that had raised funds to build the Cordova Island bridge. PRI had made no plans to open a new bridge or to secure other crossing facilities. In C. Juarez in 1955 only the International Committee of the Chamber of Commerce under the leadership of Porvenir was displaying any activity on the bridge issue. Porvenir and his committee met frequently with the El Paso Committee to work out short-range solutions. Some successes were realized in 1956, but since these had been planned by the two federal governments, the committees had done little more than to encourage government action.

Here, then, was an international problem which the C. Juarez government attempted to resolve in the late 1940's. Since the issue had been ignored by two successive administrations, and since a grave cleavage existed between local government and business, it was not surprising that the C. Juarez Chamber of

Commerce did not receive active support from the government. However, since this issue involved relations with El Paso influentials, the Juarez government did not hamper the work of the Chamber. After 1956 the International Committee of the Chamber and the city government did co-operate because Porvenir headed both groups.

On the American side, twelve influentials said that they had been contacted on the bridge issue at one time or another. Half of these indicated they would actively support a drive for new facilities, while the others decided to remain neutral. However, as we shall see, while there was widespread support for new facilities, there was considerable variation of opinion on what the facilities should be.

In C. Juarez, the influentials generally agreed that almost everyone locally wanted new facilities which would be a boon to both cities. They were generally informed about the history of the Cordova Island bridge and the activities of the Chamber to seek a workable solution with El Paso officials. They also felt that the downtown businessmen of El Paso constituted the main opposition to radical improvements in crossing facilities. They further charged that the El Paso City Lines (which owned the operating bridges and the streetcars which used these bridges), and the United States federal government were opposed to opening the Cordova Island bridge to traffic.

Perhaps the statement below best summarizes the frustration which Juarez influentials felt:

U.S. doesn't want the free bridge opened because of Cordova. Private enterprise could build one in any one of a dozen spots. I would be happy to build one next to the railroad bridge; the El Paso City Lines makes a hellava profit on their bridges. I don't know what the government is going to do; they (U.S.) have been dragging their feet. Would they man a bridge if it were built? The Ambassadors of both countries were here and seemed to favor a new bridge, but that doesn't mean anything. The downtown businessmen of El Paso are also against it because they're afraid of losing some business if a new bridge is built elsewhere. Personally, I don't think they'll lose anything. We ought to have three new bridges.

On the El Paso side most of the influentials asserted that the Chamber of Commerce, through its special International Committee, was trying to work out a practical solution to this problem. They identified certain influential businessmen and the newspaper editors as actively working on the issue. Some businessmen were accused of having selfish interests in wanting improvements restricted to the present bridge sites, and others for wanting the Cordova Island bridge. The influentials agreed that the Mexican federal government and "its people" were generally in favor of the Cordova Island bridge opening. An El Paso businessman said:

> We are in favor of a Cordova Island entrance on the east of Cordova Island without a shopping center. I think that most people prefer Cordova Island, and it's very necessary that this bridge be opened. The Mexicans are being herded like cattle right now; it's a shame. Unfortunately, the Chamber of Commerce is getting nowhere because those businessmen near the present bridges want things to stay the same. Since the businessmen cannot agree, the city will probably take no action now.

One downtown businessman defended his position by charging vested interests on the part of those favoring Cordova. He said that "I'm going to fight against the Cordova Island entrance because the only reason anyone wants it there is for personal profit." As in the case with the Juarez influentials, almost all El Paso influentials felt that the United States federal government was opposed to the Cordova entry. An El Paso banker, while admitting that Cordova would be ideal, asserted that "the state department is against it. They [the backers of Cordova] will never get it through." Indeed, this sentiment was generally accepted on both sides of the border.

The downtown businessmen themselves were the most hesitant to speak on the issue. As expected, they completely avoided mentioning the fear of losing business should the new entries be opened. One even put the blame for inaction on the Juarez government:

> Nothing will be done with Cordova Island until the boundary issue is settled. For the U.S. State Department to build at Cordova Island would be to recognize Mexico's right to the land. This the State Department will not do for quite some time. Actually, the Transportation Company which owns the present bridges will build another adequate one anytime. They are making a mint down there. Or the bridge could be easily financed here in El Paso. However, this is not the problem. The difficulty is that Juarez city government will do nothing on their side. Thus, what good would it do to have a twelve-lane bridge opening on a two-lane street?

Doubt and Delay

The influentials in both cities were asked how they thought the issue would finally be resolved. While most of them were certain that more adequate facilities would have to be forthcoming soon, they did not know where these facilities would be located and how they would be obtained. A strong minority of the El Paso influentials flatly asserted that the Cordova Island entry would never be accepted because a federal problem was involved. Both sides agreed that the United States federal government would be most influential in making the final decision, but occasionally the Mexican government was also mentioned. The ex-mayor who had built the bridge at Cordova and the "people of Juarez" were commonly mentioned by the C. Juarez respondents as most influential in resolving the problem, but they were rarely mentioned by the El Paso informants. With one notable exception, the El Pasoans omitted reference to any Juarez influentials who might play a role in the issue. Finally, it may be noted that while the two bridges were used by more than 65,000 persons daily, and while all citizens were concerned about the problem, no one felt that a popular referendum would be a useful device to activate the issue. The complexity of the international situation presumably precluded such a possibility.

The results of our interviewing clearly revealed that in August 1958 influentials and knowledgeables both felt that the issue would not be resolved within the foreseeable future. However, a small group of the El Paso and Juarez businessmen, through the International Committee of the Chambers of Commerce, continued to work for the opening of the Cordova Island bridge, and another group was opposing them. Meanwhile, most people believed that nothing would be done until the federal government in Washington decided to act and even the most ardent advocates of the Cordova Island entry conceded that Washington was not about to act.

The Cordova Island Issue, One Year Later

The Cordova Island bridge, built in 1949, was opened to international traffic almost a decade later on August 27, 1959. In addition, it appeared that at least one and perhaps more new bridges would be built in the near future. How was this issue resolved so suddenly?

In late August 1958, the *El Paso Post* stated in an editorial that it preferred the Cordova Island gateway, and recommended a specific street in south El Paso as the "logical" approach to the Mexican line. Shortly after, the chairman of the International Committee of the Chamber of Commerce in El Paso (an influential) issued a supporting statement. At the same time, he urged the City Planning Commission to study possible entrances into El Paso for vehicular traffic which might make use of the Cordova Island bridge. He said: "We would like a presentation, complete with maps, and showing the best possible route, that we can carry to Washington."[2]

During the month of September *The Times* also urged action, but with somewhat greater caution. It asked why Cordova Is-

[2] From *The Times*, August 28, 1958.

land was not acceptable or why it was opposed, suggesting, among other possibilities, that the State Department opposition was the major obstacle in the stalemate. The State Department promptly denied that it opposed opening of the Cordova Island bridge because it hoped to acquire the territory by trade with Mexico.[3] In October, the governors of Texas and Chihuahua met at an international ceremony and Governor Daniels of Texas promised to study the bridge problem. He then asked the interested El Paso parties to furnish him all relevant documents, plans and maps. Meanwhile, Porvenir, the mayor of C. Juarez, also obtained local newspaper support for the Cordova Island opening, and the governor of Chihuahua was also reported to be studying the issue seriously. Two months passed with no action.

In January 1959, the board of directors of the El Paso Chamber of Commerce was asked by the International Committee to support the Cordova project. It complied, stating that this solution to the problem was the "best one in sight." The documents were then turned over to the city council with a request for endorsement. The mayor agreed to assume leadership on the project, but refused to commit himself to any preselected site. He wanted to reserve his decision until the City Planning Commission submitted its report in approximately 60 days. Meanwhile, the Juarez mayor urged that a delegation from both cities go to Mexico City and urge federal approval of the Cordova crossing.

Then on January 19, in a surprise move, the county commissioners' court in El Paso, led by County Judge Nall, proposed that the county build a bridge or bridges across the Rio Grande. A formal proposal was forwarded to congressional leaders for immediate action. No specific site was suggested by the judge because he wanted congressional approval before

[3] *The Times*, through this public questioning, cautious though it was, did lead the State Department to make a formal, public statement on the issue, something which had been avoided up to that time.

taking further action. The El Paso congressman in Washington immediately indicated his willingness to "work with any responsible political sub-division or group."

The newspapers hailed the decisive, bold approach of the county judge, and gave his proposal prominent headlines. The judge then announced that the county would be willing to build an access road to meet a Mexican road from Cordova Island. This solution would be in addition to other new bridges he was proposing to build.

As if in response to the clamor for the opening of new bridges, the National City Lines, the private utility company which owned the El Paso City Lines and the two operating bridges announced its plans to add two new lanes to its bridge into Mexico. This "commitment" was hailed by the mayor of El Paso. The newspapers agreed that while the new lanes would alleviate the problem somewhat, they were not a solution. The campaign for the Cordova project was given new impetus by the county judge who flew to meet with Lyndon Johnson, then senator from Texas, to obtain his support for federal action to build new bridges and to open the Cordova crossing.

The initiative of the county judge galvanized support from most groups in favor of the Cordova solution. Despite this, the mayor of El Paso remained unwilling to commit the city without a statement from the federal governments that they would support port of entry facilities at Cordova. The county judge insisted that the momentum for action should be maintained, and the mayor finally consented to donate city land for an approach road to be built by the county. Again, urging caution, the mayor wrote the El Paso congressman that, "It is our firm and business-like belief that before the location of a new bridge is selected we should wait for the information from the origin-destination survey [of the City Planning Commission] that will be available in four to six weeks."

Editorials from both El Paso newspapers praised the "positive leadership" of the county judge and questioned the "stalling" tactics of the mayor. The two officials, who were allegedly friends and who had the same sources of political support, soon found themselves in conflict. They made claims and counter-claims about the most effective means of getting action on border-crossing facilities. The conflict was finally resolved when the City Planning Commission's origin-destination survey confirmed the choice of the Cordova entry and the approximate approach route already selected by the county.

In early March the president of Mexico at the urging of the Juarez mayor gave his approval for a new port of entry at Cordova with the necessary approach roads and facilities. El Paso County began to construct its approach roads almost immediately, but the Washington officials expressed concern about the cost of maintaining the port. The approval of the Mexican authorities now made it appear that the State Department was the single remaining stumbling block. After a few days it announced tentative approval of the port, and sent an official to El Paso to make cost estimates. Meanwhile, the county judge and the mayor of Juarez made plans to open the new entry on July 4, 1959.

By May almost all preparations had been completed on the El Paso side, but unexpected difficulties appeared on the Juarez side. Although the Mexican president had approved, no work on approach roads had begun because Cordova Island was the property of the federal government. Although the president had appropriated eight million pesos ($640,000.00) for developing Cordova Island as a "Cultural Center," no funds had been approved for road construction. Two major problems were noted: (1) that about 30 families were living on Cordova Island, and the president wanted to relocate them before beginning construction; and (2) the Mexican government had not decided on the location of its approach road to the border from the bridge (see Figure 5). The mayor of Juarez offered to build a temporary approach road at city expense, but the federal government did not respond to his offer.

By July, the two federal governments were reported to be near agreement. The El Paso county approach was a reality, but nothing had been done on the Mexican side. July 4 passed quietly. Meanwhile, the United States House of Representatives had passed a bill authorizing El Paso County to build a toll bridge(s) across the Rio Grande, east of Cordova Island. This location had been designated earlier by the federal government, which had wanted to avoid complications over the Chamizal question, which could have occurred were bridges built west of Cordova Island (see Figure 5). By mid-July Juarez Mayor Porvenir was concerned that the Cordova bridge would not open prior to the end of his administration (October 1, 1959), but he promised to continue supporting the project as a private citizen and as chairman of the Juarez International Relations Committee. The El Paso newspapers and influentials maintained a courteous silence about the unexpected delays in Mexico. Late in July, after Porvenir had made another trip to Mexico City to plead for action, the Mexican federal government made restitution of land to the inhabitants of Cordova Island and appropriated money for a highway and other necessary facilities. Work was completed in mid-August, and the new gateway to the cities was formally opened on August 27 with a great deal of fanfare.

Problems in International Decision-Making

To understand the behavior of the various groups involved in this issue, one should know how the decision to open a new gateway would affect them and what consequences would follow the opening.

First, the opening of a new port of entry meant that more links were being established between the two nations, a situation much desired by the more than 65,000 people who daily used the bridges. This public never became organized to resolve the issue. Neither were there dramatic incidents or riots at the bridges, despite the daily frustrations aroused by congestion. The situation was nearing a climax. Either new facilities had to be provided or the American government had to consider retracting many border-crossing permits of Juaranses working in El Paso. Such a decision would have been repugnant to the business influentials of both cities. It could have easily resulted in strong anti-American attitudes in Mexico.

Secondly, opening the Cordova Island approach would partially recognize Mexico's claim to land on the northern side of the Rio Grande, an asset for Mexico in any settlement involving the Chamizal dispute. Traditionally, the United States government discouraged new bridge proposals because this might aggravate the Chamizal question. Local business and political influentials also were concerned that new federal action might disturb the harmonious relations which they had struggled so long and so hard to achieve.

Third, were the United States to accept the Cordova opening, it would be partially acceding to Mexico's land claim, and enlarge the spirit of "good neighborliness" prior to negotiating on the Chamizal question.

Fourth, the bridge at Cordova had been built and paid for by C. Juarez. It was their "free bridge," a matter of local pride not to be underestimated. It was understood that no tolls would be charged at this bridge. The bridges owned by the El Paso City Lines were toll bridges.

Fifth, the proposal by the Mexican federal government to make Cordova Island a major cultural and sports center could have important consequences for certain business and political influentials. At the time of the study, it was not clear who exactly in C. Juarez would benefit from these long-range plans. Certainly, at present, no large vested interests were being threatened by the new bridge. This situation contrasted sharply with El Paso, where specific interests would undoubtedly profit or lose by the new bridge opening. The Downtown Businessmen's Group and the El Paso City Lines believed that new bridges would adversely affect their business. Although political fortunes were not heavily involved, the mayor feared losing his newly-won respect from some business influentials. Yet other businessmen were interested in the Cordova Island entrance either because their businesses were located nearby or because they could open new enterprises nearby. Clearly the El Paso business community was not united on this issue, but neither were the political influentials. Under these conditions the support which both newspapers gave the Cordova site was formidable.

Influentials in International Decision-Making

What role did influentials play in the bridge issue? It will be recalled that the issue of the Cordova port of entry originated as a project of Mayor Rico. He remained one of the city's most influential citizens, and was considered by several fellow influentials as the most important person in the current controversy. Since Rico's work was not pursued by succeeding administrations, the initiative passed quietly from government to business in 1954 when the International Committee of the Juarez Chamber of Commerce became interested in better border-crossing facilities. Until about 1956 the businessmen on both sides concentrated on obtaining better facilities at the already established bridges. This was a period of maximum co-operation among all influentials on both sides because there were no conflicts of interests, and because the Juarez political leaders did not believe the businessmen could accomplish anything by themselves.

Only when a group of El Paso businessmen began to study the feasibility of a new opening at Cordova Island did the project emerge as a genuine issue in El Paso. Among those most interested in this opening were two businessmen who had been political influentials in 1955. They were well acquainted with the local political and business scenes on both sides of the border. Our respondents frequently named them as being involved in the bridge issue. Moreover, the organizations with which Broon and Jiménez were associated were named by about a fourth of the influentials as heavily involved in the bridge issue. Although the downtown businessmen were allegedly opposed to opening the Cordova bridge there was no evidence that they used the Downtown Businessmen's Association (DBA), or any organization to fight their case. However, three of "the downtown group" opposed to the new bridge were top influentials both in 1955 and 1958. The manager of the El Paso City Lines was not an influential. Only two of the 30 influentials interviewed felt that the DBA and the City Lines were among the most powerful organizations involved in this issue. Although other influentials often cited these organizations as heavily involved, they did not attribute to them decisive power.

The mayor of El Paso, who was a key influential, never took the initiative in the bridge issue, nor did anyone ascribe to him a decisive role in the case. While his consent was necessary to construct an approach to Cordova, he insisted on following traditional governmental procedures of acting on the recommendations of the City Planning Commission. The fact that at one point he was very enthusiastic about expanding existing bridge facilities points to his desire to avoid conflict with the downtown businessmen.

The El Paso newspapers played major roles in bringing the issue to the public. The editors, who were key influentials, had been early supporters of the Cordova site which had been proposed by the International Commerce Committee. Yet, only one influential listed the newspaper as being among the most important organizations in resolving this issue.

In C. Juarez, from 1954 on, the Cordova project was championed by the International Commerce Committee and particularly by its chairman, Porvenir. In 1956, he became mayor and championed the cause in both capacities—this was one of the few business connections he maintained while he was mayor. Porvenir recognized that the decision of the United States would be crucial in this issue, and that certain El Paso leaders would have to get that decision. It is important to point out that during his administration Porvenir did not have the support of any businessman associated with PAN, the opposing political party. As far as they were concerned it was the mayor's problem and that of a small clique of business influentials loyal to him. However united the local influentials, the final resolution of the bridge issue rested on favorable federal action. Porvenir had to convince the leaders in Mexico City of the value of his project. His success was supreme evidence of his influence. The federal government or its agencies were mentioned most frequently by influentials in both cities as being ultimately responsible for solving the bridge issue. However, these judgments refer to the instrumentality of decision, and not to the process of activating this instrumentality. Our proper focus remains therefore on the local community power arena. In this connection it is significant that no one mentioned the Consul General of either country or other federal officials as being generally influential in this issue.

No one in El Paso seemed to know just how the Washington officials should be approached to resolve the issue. That the county judge turned out to provide the effective link between the various interest groups on the border, the State Department, as well as the Congress, was a surprise to almost everyone—

except the judge himself.[4] Although the judge, who had been formerly the chairman of the Democratic Party in El Paso, was a political influential, he was in the bottom half of the list. His party position was not evidently perceived as critical by the other influentials because he had never before held public office and had not done anything to demonstrate his influence.

The judge made the ranks of the general influentials in 1958, just after he had been elected county judge. Even though no one had earlier mentioned him as being important with respect to this issue, in less than one month after taking office he assumed overall responsibility for the project. Within six months he obtained federal approval of the Cordova site and tentative approval for building new bridges. His particular position as county judge did not necessarily call for a leadership role in this issue. In fact, while the people waited for the mayor to act, the judge pushed the project through in surprisingly short time. The evidence suggests that the businessmen in El Paso were not directly responsible for resolving the issue. Similarly on the Juarez side, it was Porvenir's role as mayor rather than as businessman that was decisive.

The interview data reveal that over half of the influentials and half of the key influentials in both cities had no association whatever with this project at any stage. Clearly, the businessmen do not make all the decisions, even when some of them are centrally involved in them. This is especially the case if the decision involves nonlocal units of government. Such units seem to have their own dynamics, which are somewhat independent of other institutional pressures. The evidence in this case also shows that local officials may be influential

---

[4] When County Judge Nall was interviewed just before he took office in 1958, he asserted his belief that the issue of new gateways to Mexico could be resolved by resolute political action. There was no reason why he could not take the initiative in bringing about resolution if others failed to act.

in their own right in both Mexico and the United States.[5] The county judge was able to seize the initiative because the businessmen were in disagreement, the mayor was cautious, and the issue could fall within the bounds of county authority. In addition to his political access into the federal structure, the judge could count on the support of both newspapers and the general public. Moreover, he was personally willing to gamble for high stakes. He found in Porvenir an enthusiastic and able counterpart.

In comparing decision-making in an issue of international dimensions, striking similarities and differences are seen between the American and Mexican cases. In C. Juarez, issues of a local nature were often resolved in the interlocking systems of local, state and federal governments. The bridge issue was the first illustration of this phenomenon in El Paso. The manner of resolving the issue was rather similar in both countries, for local key political influentials were able to gain access into high governmental and political circles to get a local issue resolved.

An important observation in the Cordova issue deals with the private expression of negative attitudes which had long been directed at certain American groups. Had the Mexicans chosen to express these attitudes publicly, hope for a successful resolution of the issue would have died. Overeager

[5] This finding suggests that federal government involvement in community decision-making, at least in the United States, provides opportunity for local government officials to increase their power vis à vis businessmen and other community leaders. Thus, depending on the nature of the federal government involvement it would seem that democratic decision-making would be enhanced rather than restricted at the local community level. For further evidence on this see Robert Presthus, *Men at the Top* (New York: Oxford University Press, 1964), and M. Kent Jennings, *Community Influentials* (New York: The Free Press, 1964).

politicos might have easily accused the downtown businessmen of El Paso, the El Paso City Lines, and the United States government of blocking action. Juarez newspapers and leaders kept a discreet public silence during all of this time. The diplomatic silence on the part of the El Paso newspapers with respect to the delays on the Mexican side after El Paso County had completed its access road, is equally notable evidence of restraint. A situation which could have exploded in bitter recriminations on both sides was handled in a way to encourage closer and more friendly contacts in the future. It demonstrated that leaders of both countries could work together despite national differences and despite some divided local opposition. Perhaps a factor as important as any was that Porvenir and Nall had strong drives to succeed in the issue, and considerable respect for and confidence in each other as persons capable of decisive leadership. The confidence of the Americans in Porvenir was aptly expressed by one of its influentials who said: "If there were 100 men like him in C. Juarez, they would leave El Paso far behind." To Porvenir himself, the resolution of this issue represented another step in the effort of leaders of both cities "to keep alive the spirit of understanding and brotherhood among the peoples of these two neighboring and friendly communities."

CHAPTER 9

Influentials, Community Power and Democracy

UNRAVELING THE STRUCTURE OF power in two cities has been a difficult but intriguing task. We have tried to describe both the unique and common characteristics of the two cities, their independence and their interdependence. It has been a partial study because only the two basic institutions of business and politics and their influentials have been studied. The research first concentrated on how these influentials perceived the power structures of their own communities and their place in them. Later we examined their roles in decision making, both in their own communities and in the international area. As far as we are aware, such an analysis of two interdependent communities representing different cultures is nowhere else available.

International Relations Among Influentials

One of the difficulties constantly facing the researchers was to consider simultaneously the independent and interdependent character of the two cities. It became apparent that the long common history of the two cities may have produced an overriding border culture which contained certain structural ambiguities and anomalies not ordinarily found in cities clearly imbedded in a distinct culture. Such a situation may foreshadow the future as societies come into increasing contact with one another.

Daily contact between the peoples of Mexico and the United States is routine in El Paso and C. Juarez. It occurs on all socio-economic levels, and involves a wide complex of activities. Thousands of Juarenses leave their homes every morning to work in El Paso. Members of their families go to El Paso daily to shop and visit relatives. Movement in the other direction is also constant. Hundreds of "Yankees" cross daily into C. Juarez to spend a few hours, or to go south into Mexico. One may hear English spoken in Juarez as often as Spanish in El Paso. In short these two cities have developed a network of relationships which has resulted in a high degree of interdependence.

The control of these relationships, and indeed the very nature and extent of their existence, depend to a large degree on the business and political influentials who help guide the destinies of their communities. The business leaders of both cities, and the local, state and federal governmental officials, have all contributed to the development of this functionally interdependent community. Whatever its historical origins, and despite the many problems involved in interdependence, the influentials of both cities generally agreed that their interdependence was a good and necessary thing. Yet the El Paso influentials did not look to Mexico for new values, social contacts, new ideas or intellectual challenge. They recognized the importance of being good neighbors and were willing to help C. Juarez develop into a more vital community. In general they did not speak Spanish well; they had very few close friends in C. Juarez and they visited there rather infrequently. In short, they had worked out a *modus vivendi* with the city but had not internalized much of the Mexican culture.

To the Mexican influentials, especially the businessmen, the border represented more than economic opportunity. Although they profited from the tourist trade, they also looked to the United States as a source of values, ideas, and ideals. A majority had studied in American schools, learned English, observed how the American system worked, and made some strong friends in the States. In the process they had developed a cultural sophistication not found among many Americans. It was possible to interview many Mexicans as objective observers of both the American and Mexican social scene because they had become very knowledgeable of both cultures and their linkages.

Vigorous business relations between the two cities depended on government co-operation. Local politicos did everything possible to foster good relations. Their main concern was that state and federal officials might do something to upset the good local relationships which they had so carefully nourished. Their dominant mood was an overriding determination to get along. Both El Paso business and political influentials felt committed to the idea of being "good neighbors," and they patterned their behavior accordingly. This was something more than formally correct conduct or protocol. Despite the rejection of certain national norms and cultural values on both sides, influentials did develop certain international ties which were not instrumentally mediated. These continued to operate even when international friction occurred over such common problems as handling narcotics, traffic, escaping criminals, bridge crossings, and prostitution.

In fact this very situation of handling conflict may account for the emergence of situational understandings in a context of cultural diversity. This is most forcibly underscored in the emerging community of economic fate. In 1961 there were about 15,000 Juarenses legally working in El Paso. This situation was advantageous to both communities, and it is unlikely that even a protracted recession or depression could alter it without serious international consequences. Closing the border would completely disrupt the Juarez economy and visibly shake the El Paso economy. It would, moreover, alter trends in the acculturation processes occurring along the border and within the Spanish-name community of El Paso.

Influentials in Community Decision-Making

The comparative study of community influentials in El Paso and C. Juarez was designed to probe questions dealing with monolithic vs. pluralistic patterns of power, business vs. political control, integration or cleavage between differing institutional sectors, and the relationship between reputed and actual power. We shall try to summarize our findings on these questions, relate our findings to the growing body of theory on community power structures, and discuss the implications of our findings for the democratic urban life.

Bankers, industrialists, and merchants were predominant among the business influentials in both cities. In C. Juarez all the major governmental officials, both elected and appointed, were the key political influentials. Labor leaders and certain PRI officials at the state and national levels comprised most of the remaining. In El Paso a majority of the political influentials were lawyers and some were important businessmen. This composition of business and political influentials remained substantially unchanged over a four-year period.

The image of business power in El Paso reflects the fact that El Paso is a modern, urban, industrial, bureaucratized community. Most of the business influentials were presidents or chairmen of the board of their corporation. Many of them had withdrawn from government office-holding and direct participation in politics. Neither labor leaders, clergymen, nor educators were influentials, and this reflected the weak character of their institutions. On the other hand, lawyers were very active politically, and many held important posts in government. Their conservative political orientation enabled them to link the business and political systems effectively. The Spanish-name population had limited representation among the influentials.

Examination of a variety of community issues revealed that many businessmen were active and tried to influence local decisions. Often working closely with lawyers, they achieved notable success in welfare fund drives and at times in the political arena. But as a group, they were not always of one mind. Sometimes they belonged to shifting factions, and even when they were united, they did not always win. Moreover, they were not interested in all the issues facing the community, and in these cases, decisions were largely in the hands of government officials. Perhaps the decisions were not telling for business and they did not affect their economic welfare. Occasionally the citizens as voters demonstrated their power but this was usually in a decisional context previously set by the influentials.

Municipal elections, private and public welfare drives, and the building of general hospitals were the projects examined in both cities. In El Paso the businessmen were vitally interested in municipal elections, and they had organized a City-County Committee of 200 to select "the most qualified man for office." They were generally successful up to about 1955. But they did not always win the elections, for they lost in 1957 and 1958, and in 1959 they supported the mayor they had opposed in the previous elections. However, when they did not succeed in naming the mayor, they found no change in the city administration which affected them adversely. Their conflict seemed more concerned with status than with ideology and power.

Businessmen were also interested in community welfare programs. They took the lead in establishing the United Fund and in building a new private hospital for the city. They were able to achieve these aims without help from government. They also succeeded in building stadiums and sponsoring fund drives for various causes which did not seem to be the province of any particular institutional sector. No one felt that he had illegitimately assumed a community responsibility.

The development of a new public hospital was primarily the achievement of the county government, the Medical Society, and the newspapers. The majority of the business influentials were not involved, although they did express approval of the project and supported the campaign. But the voters made the final decision in an election.

The Cordova Island bridge issue revealed the degree to which the businessmen could be split over an issue which affected the economic interests of some of them. The issue was finally resolved by government officials at the county and federal levels. In the process of deciding, business as a whole was not split against government as a whole. Rather the sides were each composed of a coalition of business, political, and other interests, a rather common arrangement in the United States.

In conclusion, it seems that in a dynamic metropolitan American community, there is little probability that a single co-ordinated power elite consciously controls all the decisions in the community. The findings did not sustain a picture of El Paso as a monolithic power structure dominated by a small group of businessmen who kept surveillance over all decisions. The very complexity of the community social structure itself mitigated against overall control. Many issues arose, many decisions were made, and many groups got involved in various decisions. No single group kept track of all local issues and no single group was concerned about the outcome of all of the community issues. While a small number of men made decisions which affected the entire community, the same men were not involved in all issues, and no group always succeeded in imposing its will against the majority. However, it is important to stress that the political influentials rarely opposed businessmen ideologically and rarely threatened their local interests. Businessmen exerted such great influence in El Paso simply because no other organized group was willing to challenge them. When one did, it was at least possible to share in the personnel of power, as when the Spanish-surname groups elected a mayor. Even in this contest, however, there was no disagreement on community goals and no ideological cleavages. The problem for El Paso indeed was and perhaps will be one of fostering sufficient diversity of interests to create alternatives to the traditional decision-making process. There is a very real danger of overconsensus in the city. The existence of two opposing newspapers favors the probability that alternatives can be presented in issues requiring public support. The disappearance of an opposition newspaper could be disastrous for this type of community.

The profile of power which emerged in C. Juarez showed that business influentials and career politicians were vying with each other for control of community decision-making. The businessmen represented a variety of small and medium enterprises in the early stages of bureaucratization. As true believers in the free enterprise system, they were struggling to free themselves from governmental controls. The political influentials were mostly office holders, some local party officials, and a few small businessmen. Although ideological issues such as, for instance, government control vs. free enterprise, and the proper role of religion in politics, were played down, they were nonetheless present. Local business had partially freed itself from local political control, but no mechanisms had emerged through which the two institutions of business and government could co-operate in community endeavors. Unlike El Paso, lawyers were split in their ideological loyalties, and they did not provide an effective link between the two institutions. PRI itself was internally oriented and had developed a centralized

bureaucracy which responded to internal forces. Groups outside the party could only influence its operation locally by
successfully appealing to higher echelons in the party. Although
the latter had broader conceptions of government and party
responsibility to interests in the wider community, they were
not ready to undermine the local party to the point where outside forces could capture it. Nor would they foster a climate to
enable opposition parties to arise and prosper.

An examination of a variety of issues in C. Juarez supports
this profile of local power. Business influentials were organized politically both to oppose the local PRI and to influence it
by appealing to the president of the country to intervene locally
in their favor. By these methods they actually gained some
measure of influence over the local party for a period of three
years. However, this unstable pattern was incapable of sustain-
ing efforts to meet the welfare and other important community
needs, with the result that the traditional cleavages remained
stronger than the integrative forces. So basic was the cleavage
between business and political influentials that they were unable to co-operate even in situations where there was no ideological conflict. Conflict had become its own end, and the
public weal had become secondary.

The hypothesis that C. Juarez was controlled by a monolithic
power structure dominated by PRI was not found corresponding to current reality. Businessmen and professionals were able
to form voluntary associations which sometimes opposed local
government successfully. Moreover, they were able to act independently of government especially in private welfare matters.
On the whole, however, power was strongly centralized, and
local problems were often solved at the federal level by a trium-
virate consisting of the president of the nation, the national
president of PRI, and the minister of government. Close to a
true power elite, they have become increasingly responsive to a
wider set of influences.

The institutional conflict between the businessmen and the

politicos in C. Juarez had disastrous consequences for the community. Communities in early stages of industrial development which have burgeoning populations and many problems, can not afford institutional conflicts which immobilize community action by pitting the energies of its most talented citizens against each other in a bitter struggle for power. The development of a stable democracy for C. Juarez depends on the ability of its leaders to overcome this historical pattern of conflict. In part this can be accomplished by changes within PRI and the emergence of a strong opposition party. If PAN is to be that party, it must shed its reputation of being a mouthpiece of the clergy and big business. At the same time PRI must be ready to absorb within its leadership capable men who also happen to be practicing Catholics. At the national level, PRI leaders and the Catholic hierarchy have been showing increasing respect for each other in their "proper" areas of interest. PRI has also become more friendly toward big business, while PAN has made an effort to respond to the interests of the working classes. However, these are only slight trends, and the future remains uncertain and fraught with dangers. A two-party system may not be possible in view of the facts that PRI and the government tend to merge into one entity, and that PRI's para-structure includes a wide range of occupational groups in the community. While democratic tendencies can be fostered within a one-party system, a two-party system is more easily linked to a wide range of associations found in the entire institutional structure of the nation.

Comparative Analysis of Decision-Making

In comparing decision-making and power in El Paso and in C. Juarez, a number of observations come to the fore. First, power seems to be more concentrated and less representative of diverse groups in C. Juarez than in El Paso because formal governmental authority is more closely associated with community decisions in the Mexican city. Thus, the mayor in C.

Juarez is expected to make and execute all major decisions. The mayor, for example, decides what programs will be developed in the community during his administration, and he does not feel obligated to carry out the projects of previous administrations. His behavior is influenced by pressure brought upon him through the party. Thus a local businessman or a professional can influence the mayor because of his party contacts and not because he represents a legitimate occupational interest group. This does not apply to the president of the nation who is the ultimate source of political power and who can be influenced by non-PRI members. His willingness to listen to the opposition makes possible decisions which might otherwise be impossible. The use of such a mechanism to resolve community problems has limited effectiveness, for it does not institutionalize interest group politics locally.

Second, the two communities differed in the limits of institutional authority. In El Paso businessmen could initiate projects and influence political decisions without feeling that they were exceeding their legitimate rights. In fact, they were not certain just how far governmental authority should extend. Neither were local governmental officials certain just what should be the role and limits of governmental authority in the community. Yet both groups felt an obligation for what happened locally, and they accepted help from each other and from others. In such a situation other organized groups and individuals could and did exert influence on community projects and issues.

Third, limits of authority were less problematic in C. Juarez because all community-wide programs were the proper responsibility of government.[1] However, businessmen felt that govern-

[1] Although the United States community is in a different governmental context, Presthus found in his study of two New York State communities that the community which had a less cohesive group of decision-makers was more exposed to influences from the state and federal governments. See Robert Presthus, *Men at the Top* (New York: Oxford University Press, 1964), pp. 221–236.

ment did not anticipate community problems and could not resolve them with the resources at its disposal. As businessmen slowly redefined the limits of their authority and responsibility to include community problems, institutional cleavages became aggravated. After the Revolution, businessmen were on the defensive, for they were preoccupied with the struggle of the right of private capital to exist. Having achieved success here, they are now attempting to redefine and augment their role in community affairs. Their probings are forcing career politicians on the defensive.

Fourth, in both cities citizens could and did exercise their influence by voting. At times they responded to *status quo* forces and at other times they opposed them. Powerful groups met electoral defeat in both cities; businessmen lost in El Paso and PRI politicos in C. Juarez. The election results reflected the different patterns of institutional articulation in the two communities. In El Paso the defeat of the position taken by businessmen did not create an institutional split. On the contrary, businessmen displayed remarkable flexibility in adjusting to the new political realities. Similarly politicos were flexible in their posture toward business. Thus, the newly-elected Spanish-name mayor was determined to demonstrate that he could perform his official obligations as well as any Anglo businessman, and he succeeded. The pattern which emerged in El Paso by 1959 was not unlike that which has developed in many eastern and midwestern American communities where minority groups have succeeded in gaining political power. The pattern of influence remains unchanged but the personnel in authority positions experiences turnover. Thus it was in El Paso where influentials could still say in 1959 what they said in 1955, that business and government got along very well.

In C. Juarez, on the other hand, the picture of cleavage and conflict between business and government persisted before, during, and after a series of victories and defeats on both sides. Sr. Porvenir's victory in the 1956 elections did not terminate the institutional strife. Some businessmen so strongly opposed PRI ideologically that they could not support his administration. They preferred instead to solidify their opposition in the ranks of PAN. Until PAN or some other second party becomes recognized throughout Mexico as a legitimate and virile opposition with a membership which cuts across institutional and occupational lines, ideological conflict will continue to forestall co-operative problem-solving on both the local and national levels.

Neutral observers may conclude that there was too much consensus in El Paso and too little in C. Juarez. Political democracy may suffer as much from overconsensus as from underconsensus. Neither extreme can indefinitely persist in either city, for stabilities are being threatened by social and economic changes. Population growth, growing literacy, urbanization, industrialization, and the rise of voluntary organizations committed to the principles of equality of opportunity and rising standards of living for all will tend to diffuse community power. Moreover the general acceptance of the principle that opposing groups have the right to express themselves through the electoral process further serves to undermine monolithic control by a single group of influentials.

The researchers repeatedly observed that interest in politics was more widespread in C. Juarez than in El Paso. Although ideological cleavage in the former city made consensual problem-solving improbable, it seemed to guarantee a high level of interest. Conceivably the problem of ethnic stratification could have given El Paso a persistent issue with deep ideological undertones. That it did not appear at the time of research points to a dialectic situation; the basic identification of Spanish-speaking leaders to American values and a malintegration of large masses into the cultural and organizational life of the city.

Community Power Structure

A growing body of data about community power structure has made it possible to test the validity of some of the theoretical formulations in the field. Whatever their exact formulations, students seem to agree that community power structures in the United States range from monolithic or oligarchic to pluralistic or amorphous. Three recent formulations are compared below.[2]

Dahl, Miller and Rossi each recognize a number of patterns along the continuum ranging from extreme monolithic power

Miller	Dahl	Rossi
A. Pyramidal: one person at top; autocratic; one industry town as a type. No form of counterpower.	A. An executive-centered grand coalition of coalitions: ephemeral, unstable; may be reformist; dependent on charismatic leadership; different institutional sectors involved, but power centers in one man. A hierarchical arrangement.	A. Pyramidal: lines of power are found in one man or a small group. Group at the apex makes the decision. (Middletown, Regional City)
B. Pyramidal: small, tightly knit group at top. Other interests may be able to challenge those in power. One group doesn't own the whole town. (Middletown)	B. A coalition of chieftains. Heavy reliance on negotiations among chiefs; decisions made on basis of agreement among chiefs.	B. Caucus Rule: power in a relatively large, loosely knit coalition. Typical of small towns. (Springdale, Cibola)

[2] See D. C. Miller, "Democracy and Decision-Making in the Community Power Structure," in *Power and Democracy in America* (Notre Dame: University of Notre Dame Press, 1961), pp. 62ff.; Robert A. Dahl, *Who Governs?* (New Haven: Yale University Press, 1961), pp. 184–189; and Peter H. Rossi, "Theory and Method in the Study of Power in the Local Community" (mimeographed, unpublished paper, 1960), pp. 37–38.

Miller	*Dahl*	*Rossi*

C. Stratified pyramidal structure; policy makers drawn largely from business class. Social aristocracy built on business values. (Regional City)

C. Covert control by economic notables: a unified group of wealthy men with high status. They don't hold office; they control those in office.

C. Polylithic structures: separate power groups for different spheres of community life. Government in the hands of politicians backed by working classes. (Stackton, Lorain)

D. Ring or cone model: many modern communities; 1-heterogeneous business sector; 2-countervailing powers (labor, second party); 3-autonomy of institutional sectors. No single focus of decision-making. (English City)

D. Independent sovereignties with spheres of influence: different sets of leaders for different sectors of policy; conflict avoided if possible. Power is sphere-limited.

D. Amorphous: no discernible enduring pattern of power. Perhaps exists where local autonomy is lacking. (Tijuana)

E. Segmented power pyramids: political parties form clearly opposing blocs. Community power breaks cleanly along party lines. (French politics)

E. Rival sovereignties fighting it out. Conflict is costly, but in this case it is the goal. Opposing political parties the classic example.

(one-man or one-party rule) to extreme pluralism (a multiparty system of balanced and/or unstable forces). Monolithic patterns seem to predominate in small, stable communities (Middletown of a generation ago), in communities built on values of a landed aristocracy (New Haven of 150 years ago), or in communities experiencing industrial growth, but which have working classes and/or ethnic groups which are unorganized and in a subordinate position (Regional City, New Haven 100 years ago).

It is possible to discern an evolutionary development in the structure of decision-making as communities move away from a pattern of landed aristocracy to industrialization. If such democratic guarantees exist as the right to a secret ballot, and the right to organize political parties, pressure groups and other voluntary associations, industrialization may have the effect of restructuring community power toward more pluralistic patterns. In this connection, Rossi states that "a monolithic power structure tends to go along with a very subordinate position for public officials and labor unions, while a prominent position for the latter implies a polylithic (pluralistic) patterning."[3]

Thus pluralism emerges in the American community when the business-professional groups are successfully challenged by the working class and ethnic groups. Until that occurs, much of what may pass as pluralism may be nothing but a struggle for status among competing business-professional factions, such as Hunter apparently found in Regional City.

In the case of El Paso it seemed that the decision of the CCC to nominate José Jiménez for one of the city council posts was only a token step toward recognizing the potential power of the Spanish-name masses, but it also represented an attempt to co-opt ethnic leadership. He was elected to office primarily because the business-professional clique had selected him. It was not until Rivera won the mayoralty race in 1957 that the ethnics could be said to have acted independently of the dominant business-professional coalition. Thus, power diffused because the rules permitted lower classes to place their representatives in public office, and when the representatives were in fact leaders who had the backing of groups independent of the traditional business-professional coalition. Whether this diffusion of office-holding represents a shift in the objectives of power holding remains an open question. At least the possibility now exists.

El Paso lacked certain important structural elements which might have enhanced the possibility of the diffusion of power.

[3] Rossi, *op. cit.*, p. 36.

Only the Democratic Party was functioning during the time of this study, and it was at best a loosely organized entity. Labor unions were weak, nonpolitical, or politically conservative. The Spanish-speaking had not, like ethnic groups in the North, erected a network of voluntary associations which could be articulated for political action. The best organized politically-oriented voluntary association appeared to be the City-County Committee of the business-professional group. On the other hand, the presence of two independently owned and controlled competing newspapers helped to mitigate against a monopoly in the flow of political communication.

The situation in C. Juarez differs considerably. The Mexican Revolution of 1910 substituted for a monolithic structure built around agriculture and incipient industry a "monolithic" structure built upon a political party dedicated to building a modern and industrial nation. While in the United States, power diffused into pluralistic patterns when working-class leaders gained public office, this was not entirely the case in Mexico. To be sure the Revolution gave the agricultural and industrial working classes representation in public office. In fact, PRI was so structured that a wide range of occupational interest groups gained some representatives in the seats of power. However, this did not result in a form of syndicalism or in a pluralistic democracy. If the problem in the United States was for the working classes to achieve power independent of the business-professional coalition, the problem in Mexico became one of the various classes achieving power independent of PRI.

The development of the Civic Association in C. Juarez marked one effort in this direction. No unions or voluntary associations representing the working or middle classes were able to achieve political office independent of PRI. Since, for all practical purposes PRI and the government tended to be identical, pluralistic forces tended to remain constricted. In conclusion, although neither community approximated the pluralistic model, both were tending in that direction. A review of the issues studied may clarify the situation:

		El Paso		*C. Juarez*
Elections	1955	Business won	1952	PRI won
	1957	Ethnics won	1955	Asociación Cívica helped depose governor
	1959	Unanimity with ethnic mayor	1956	PRI won—with support of business faction of Asociación Cívica
Private Welfare	1952	Providence Memorial Hospital Business - professionals dominate	1952–55	Boy's Town, private school built by business group.
	1957	United Fund Business - professionals dominate		Business-PRI stalemate on school lunch
Public Welfare	1958	General Community Hospital—county judge, Medical Societies, newspapers, voters decide	1954–55	School aid—local government with some business help
			1959	General Community Hospital — mayors, federal government
	1959	Cordova Bridge—county judge, federal officials, Chamber of Commerce, and newspapers influential	1959	Cordova Bridge— mayors, state and federal officials influential

A review of the issues resolved in El Paso during a decade reveals no absolute pattern. In 1955 businessmen seemed to be in control. A loose coalition of business chieftains was able to build a private hospital, win a mayoral election, and establish a United Fund program. But this loose coalition lost the 1957

mayoralty election, and played no discernible role in the establishment of the General Community Hospital in 1958. The
Cordova Bridge issue was resolved by a coalition which overlapped only slightly with the others. Whatever else might be
true, power was never broadly diffused. A small group of business and professional men were interested in the major areas
of community decision-making, but their interest, wealth, and
prestige were not sufficient to guarantee a victory in every
case. Political influentials could and did on occasion act independently.

With regard to C. Juarez it might at first appear that major
community issues were resolved through PRI more or less
unilaterally. PRI won all the elections, and PRI mayors were
responsible for building the General Hospital and opening the
Cordova entry into El Paso. But opposition groups did exist and
they could make decisions (disaster relief, building Boy's Town
and a parochial school) in the private sector. Opposition was
able to organize a Civic Association independent of government
control and able to win major concessions from PRI.[4] While
power patterns in C. Juarez were more highly structured than
in El Paso during the 1950's, there was some evidence of
emerging instabilities and pluralism. This was reflected in the
increasing interventions in the local control apparatus of PRI
by higher officials in the party and government.

Conflict was more open and bitter in C. Juarez, partly because institutionalized means were lacking whereby groups
opposing PRI could bargain with it in the community decision-
making process. In this regard Rossi, Coleman and others hy-
pothesize that conflict is more likely to occur where monolithic
power structures exist. In these cases, conflict is more likely to
be destructive "because there is no regularized means for the
expression and hence containment of conflict."[5]

----

[4] Seen from the local level, there were many changes within PRI between
1955 and 1958; seen from the national level, PRI was still very much in control.

[5] Rossi, *op. cit.*, p. 42.

The situation in El Paso may be clarified somewhat by another hypothesis proposed by Rossi. When political and economic elites no longer form a single unity, "then the economic elite will tend to develop a set of community institutions which they can dominate independently of popular approval."[6] Thus Rossi sees the growth of voluntary associations, particularly those concerned with private welfare, as a reaction to the loss of political power. This may be occurring in El Paso, although the data gathered are insufficient to support the hypothesis without qualification. The business-professional coalition did build a private hospital in 1952 while one of their own was mayor. It established the United Fund while Rivera was mayor, and gave tacit approval to the building of the new General Hospital, over which it did not exert control.

Clearly the coalition stimulated the growth of a wide variety of voluntary associations in recent years which were concerned with major community activities. Whether this was a response to a recognition that its days of political power were numbered is not at all clear. Possibly the matter goes deeper. It may well be that the growth of these voluntary associations represents an effort to demonstrate to the community and to the political sector the vitality of the free enterprise philosophy and the ability of the private sector to handle important community activities more effectively than government.

In summary, the power structures of both communities seemed to be in a state of flux during the 1950's. Neither community was ruled by one man, nor by a small united clique operating in secret. Nevertheless, on any single issue excepting those involving the voters only a few persons were involved. Although there was considerable change in the personnel involved in different issues, they did not represent a broad range of economic and political interests. This, of course, decreases the social and political significance of variability of personnel involved in decision-making.

[6] *Ibid.*, p. 42.

Reputed and Actual Power: The Problems of Reliability and Validity

The above observations on the structure of power are valid and reliable to the degree that the techniques of study were adequate to the task. Two research techniques were used: (1) finding persons who were reputed to be the most influential in each community, and then studying their social backgrounds and activities, and (2) ascertaining what role these influentials and others played in a number of important community issues. We now have to ask if these techniques provide us with a reliable and valid picture of power and decision-making during the 1950's. Let us consider first the question of reliability.

Reliability

The charge has been made that the reputational technique is unreliable, that it yields results which are at best inconsistent and ambiguous.[7] Two charges seem to be central: (a) that the concept "influence" is not and presumably cannot be operationally defined, and (b) that the lists of names obtained from questions seeking a community's most influential citizens seem to suggest a pyramidal, monolithic power structure.

Influence, like many other concepts, is indeed broad and diffuse. Perhaps this is true because influence can take so many forms, and because it is so ubiquitous. An individual or group can achieve its will in a problematic situation for any of a number of important reasons such as: occupying a position of authority, possessing wealth, possessing knowledge, and possessing appealing personality characteristics. The bases of influence may be restricted to a single sphere or to an institutional sector or may be extended to the whole community. Thus, a bank president may have authority in his bank and also be influential in a community's economic affairs. Under

---

[7] For a complete bibliography on these charges and the way they have been answered, see the *American Sociological Review*, XXVII, No. 6 (December 1962), 838–854.

certain conditions he may influence political and religious leaders even though his legitimate economic authority does not appear to extend to them.

Those interviewed clearly indicated that the persons they selected as "most influential" were not all influential for the same reason. Some were influential because they held important positions of authority, some because they were wealthy and could guarantee the financial success of certain projects, and others because they were active, interested and talented organizers who would direct projects successfully. Greater influence was attributed to authoritative positions in the Juarez executive political system and in the judicial branch in El Paso. There was little difference in the kinds of occupations represented by the business influentials in either city. The method of identifying influentials showed both similarity and difference in the two cities, and it was sensitive to both inter- and intra-institutional differences which other methods of observation verified.

The second charge against the reputational technique is that a pyramidal power structure inevitably results from its use. The observation in the above paragraph partly refutes this charge. The technique may be sensitive to differences in influential arrangements to the degree that it seeks additional information about the "influentials." Additional probing reveals a social structure among influentials made up of cliques, factions and competing groups. The nomination process may, if used judiciously, reveal leaders, competing cliques, and horizontal as well as vertical power relations among influentials.

A second observation, which deals with the variety of reputational techniques used, is of greater importance. We used "reputational" questions in four ways at two different time periods. In 1955 the judges were asked to nominate separate lists of persons most influential in business and most influential in politics. If the reputational technique inevitably yields monolithic power structures one might expect the two lists to contain the same names. However, the data not only showed that business and politics were perceived as separate spheres, but that there was a small group in each community whose influence was perceived to overlap these spheres.

In a third test of the question, we asked judges in one city to name the most influential persons in the other city. In general they named the same influentials who were selected by judges within each city.

In an attempt to check the stability or reliability of nominations over time, two other "reputational" questions were used in 1958. These dealt with (1) the nomination of an ideal hospital committee, and (2) the selection of general community-wide influentials. Now, in three and one-half years one might expect changes in rapidly growing communities such as El Paso and C. Juarez. Men retire, others die, some lose influence, others lose interest in public affairs, and a few may be consolidating their influence. Nonetheless, a high degree of stability in the influence structure should also be expected if a structure is indeed present. A comparison of our findings between 1955 and 1958 confirmed this expectation of a stable influence system. In both cities a majority of the persons nominated to the ideal hospital committee had been identified as influentials in 1955.[8] In both communities a majority of those who had been nominated as business and/or political influentials in 1955 were selected as general influentials in 1958. In fact, only one person from among all identified as both business and political influentials in 1955 was not a general influential in 1958, and he had retired.

Validity

The question may now be posed whether a person's reputation for influence means that he has actual influence in the com-

[8] A similar finding is reported by Presthus, *op. cit.*, where he further suggests that businessmen display greater *continuity* as decision-makers and influentials because of the stability of their economic position in the community.

munity decision-making process. Does the structure of influence as outlined in Chapters 3, 4 and 5 have predictive validity for the data on the resolution of issues described in Chapters 6, 7 and 8? In short, does reputation for influence measure what it is supposed to measure, namely, a person's ability to influence community decision-making?

The first observation is that there was some agreement on the identification of influentials according to the reputational and decision-making techniques (see Tables XXI and XXII). A large majority of the key decision-makers in El Paso and *all* of the decision-makers in C. Juarez were reputed influentials.[9] However, in every issue studied in El Paso there were individuals who were not reputed influentials, e.g., the physicians who worked for the new General Hospital. In every case their influence was limited to a single issue, a pattern found also by Dahl, Presthus and Jennings. The remaining decision-makers were not only reputed influentials but key influentials who had maintained their reputation over time. The more votes an influential received the more likely was he to play key roles in several issues.[10] This was true for both cities. The most notable exception was Judge Nall who had just been elected county judge in El Paso after having served as Democratic Party chairman earlier. Neither in 1955 nor in 1958 was he ranked as a key influential.

The data also reveal that business influentials in El Paso were the least active in decision-making (Table XXI). Only 30 per cent participated in one or more issues. Similarly, a majority of the political influentials were not involved in any

[9] Presthus found that the identification of decision-makers by event analysis and by the reputational technique in two New York State communities overlapped from 43 to 64 per cent. *Op. cit.*, p. 174.

[10] This is essentially the same finding as reported by M. E. Burgess in *Negro Leadership in a Southern City* (Chapel Hill: The University of North Carolina Press, 1962). See especially Chapter 5, pp. 108ff.

TABLE XXI
NUMBER OF ISSUES IN WHICH INFLUENTIALS PLAYED KEY ROLES IN TWO BORDER CITIES.

	El Paso				*C. Juarez*			
	Influentials in 1955		Influentials in 1958		Influentials in 1955			Influentials in 1958
	Business	B & P	Politics		Business	B & P	Politics	
No. of Issues	N-40	N-11	N-19	N-49	N-38	N-7	N-28	N-51
None	28	3	12	30	22	3	17	30
One	6	1	3	4	9	0	4	14
Two	3	2	3	6	4	1	2	2
Three	2	0	1	3	1	1	2	2
Four or more	1	5	0	6	2	2	3	3

Abbreviations:
  B—Business
  P—Politics

TABLE XXII

PERCENTAGES OF REPUTED INFLUENTIALS WHO PLAYED KEY ROLES IN THE RESOLUTION OF SIX ISSUES IN EACH OF TWO BORDER CITIES.*

El Paso

Issues	Influentials in 1955		Influentials in 1958
	Business B & P	Politics	
	N-40	N-11	N-19	N-49
Memorial Hospital	12.5	45.5	0.0	20.4
United Fund	15.0	45.5	0.0	22.4
Elections, 1955	10.0	63.6	21.1	24.5
Elections, 1957	7.5	72.7	15.8	24.5
General Hospital	2.5	18.2	10.5	10.2
Cordova Bridge	7.5	27.3	15.8	18.4

C. Juarez

	Influentials in 1955		Influentials in 1958
	Business B & P	Politics	
Boy's Town and the Parochial School	26.3	28.6	0.0	19.6
Public School Crisis	13.2	42.9	10.7	17.6
Elections, 1952	7.9	42.9	39.3	13.7
Elections, 1956	18.4	42.9	32.1	29.4
General Hospital	7.9	28.6	14.3	13.7
Cordova Bridge	5.3	28.6	7.1	11.7

Abbreviations:
B—Business
P—Politics

* The influentials in El Paso represented the following proportions of the total key decision-makers in each of the issues: Memorial Hospital—83%; United Fund—85%; Elections of 1955—83%; Elections of 1957—93%; General Hospital—71%; Cordova Bridge—90%.

issue. Those who were, restricted themselves to political issues, such as elections. The most active were those identified as influential in both business and politics in 1955. The majority of the eleven were deeply involved in four out of the six issues and five were involved in four or more issues. Their pervasive scope of influence was attested by the fact that they were selected as key influentials in 1958. About 40 per cent of the reputed general influentials in 1958 were active in one or more issues during the period of study.

The same general patterns held for C. Juarez. Those identified strictly as business influentials limited their activities to fund raising. A minority (18 per cent) played key roles in more than one issue. The pattern held generally for the political influentials. Again, the greatest proportion of influentials involved in issues were those who had been reputed influentials in both business and politics in 1955. About 40 per cent of the general influentials in 1958 were involved in one or more issues, a pattern remarkably similar to that of El Paso.

In both cities influentials were more involved in elections than in any other issue, although in El Paso a much smaller percentage of the politicos were actively involved (Table XXII). This may be explained by the fact that many of them were in the judiciary branch of government and felt restrained from active participation. In C. Juarez the crucial roles in the elections were played by the mayoral candidates, governors and party leaders who constituted a minority of the influentials.

The reputational technique netted most of the main actors in the issues we examined, but it also identified persons who were not active in these issues. Had we probed issues more directly related to business affairs, such as industrial development, there would have been more convergence between the results provided by the reputational and the decision-participation techniques.

The pattern which emerged in both cities may be summarized now as follows:

1. Only a small number of persons participated actively in any given issue.
2. A majority of the influentials were not active in any of the issues studied.
3. Business influentials tended to be less active than other types and more limited in their scope of influence.
4. Political influentials were slightly more likely to be active in more than one issue.
5. Multi-issue influence was demonstrated by those who were reputed to have inter-institutional influence.

Before a more adequate theory of community power can be developed, a more systematic and encompassing view is needed of community issues and the requisites for influence. With respect to the former, a typology of community issues must be built which includes all inter-institutional relations and their interest groups. The requisites of influence must relate to the types of issues found in a particular set of institutional patterns. Furthermore, it is necessary to consider how the requisites for influence vary with the different stages of the decision-making process. Despite the lack of a good theory of community power, the crude techniques used to examine community power in these two cities proved surprisingly reliable and valid.

Democracy in the Perspective of Two Border Cities

We conclude with an attempt to appraise the power structure of the two border cities in the context of current democratic theory. We have taken the position that democracy can best develop and maintain itself in a setting where (a) the middle class is the largest class and the class which validates most status claims; (b) controlled conflict exists within a larger framework of consensus for rules which prescribe the extent of legal and other authority, how authority will be exercised, and how change in authority may occur; and (c) strong voluntary associations exist independently of governmental or elitist control, and can affect policy decisions. Citizens must develop interest in joining these voluntary associations and must be free to form and join them. Without these associations the citizen feels detached from the community and develops a feeling of powerlessness in a world which is too big and complex to understand. Since participation in small groups is personalized, membership in voluntary associations links the small local unit to larger political structures in a psychologically meaningful way. To serve democracy best, these associations must not be controlled by those who have primary loyalty to larger political organizations.

It is not possible, at the present state of knowledge, to know whether economic equality, consensus on norms of conflict, or the presence of strong voluntary associations is most important for democratic decision-making.[11] Possibly they are equally important. To consider the first, there is great disparity in wealth in both cities, although it seems to be greater in C. Juarez than in El Paso. Were it not for the fact that 15,000 Juarenses are employed in El Paso, the disparities in economic inequalities of the two cities would be even greater. One reason why pluralistic politics is not more highly developed in El Paso is the fact that it has such a large lower class. This condition reflects both the rapid growth of the city and its large first and second generation Spanish-surname population. Both cities need great increases in income and educational levels before they can develop a citizenry capable of exercising intelligent choice and restraints necessary for stable pluralistic politics.

In the second requisite of democracy, again El Paso seems closer than C. Juarez to achieving a system of controlled con-

[11] Presthus presents strong evidence that greater economic resources, higher education, higher income, and general economic well-being tend to support pluralistic politics and healthy competition between economic and political leaders. *Op. cit.*, pp. 175–202.

flict within a broad consensual framework of democratic values. This is mainly due to the fact that El Paso is part of the United States and shares its legal traditions which permit and encourage political pluralism. That this was insufficient to guarantee democratic consensus is evident from the fact that city politics was mainly the avocation of the middle and upper classes. Unfortunately, a large proportion of the citizenry simply did not participate in decision-making or conceive that they could legitimately have political obligations. This was not due simply to citizen apathy but the neglect to socialize that part of the Spanish-name population with limited education into the political culture of the nation and community.

In C. Juarez the problem of arriving at consensus through orderly conflict was even graver because there was still some confusion on the national level how consensus should be structured. Even though the struggle of the revolution to eliminate the landed aristocracy and a paternalistic church has been almost achieved in urban Mexico, the social ruptures caused by decades of struggle still survive. For C. Juarez this situation meant an absence of sufficient consensus to make democratically controlled conflict possible. Until PRI and PAN (or some other political party) become nearly equal in strength and recognize the rules of political democracy, destructive conflict may continue to hamper the resolution of major problems. On the other hand, can democratic norms be institutionalized and protected from arbitrary interpretation as long as a large segment of the politically alert citizenry believe—as they apparently do now—that PRI is not willing to share its power?

The third requisite of democracy deals with voluntary organizations. Although these flourish in abundance in both cities, the result has not been a broadening democratic base. The strongest voluntary associations in El Paso, the Chamber of Commerce, Rotary, and Kiwanis, were run by the business-professional coalition. The coalition had also developed a highly effective directorate, the City-County Committee. Together they constituted a major source of opinion-formation and leadership development in the community. What the city lacked was a number of voluntary associations which would adequately represent or help develop the interests of the Spanish-surname population and other blue-collar workers.[12] Only one political party was functioning in the community. During the 1950's it did not encourage the Spanish-surname and working-class elements to develop political opinions or train leaders. Not even the labor unions played an innovating political role in the community. Such AFL unions as the Railroad Engineers were conservative, and did not vigorously organize the large number of Spanish-surname workers. The leftist International Mine-Mill and Smelter Workers Union had lost most of its influence by the mid 1950's and was struggling to survive as an organization. Clearly, the labor unions could not act as countervailing forces to the business-professional coalition.

The Spanish-speaking of the Southwest have organized a voluntary association called the League of United Latin American Citizens (LULAC). Unlike the NAACP, the league tends to be a social club with some welfare work concerns. Its leaders in El Paso have been split for several years over the question whether LULAC should become more politically aggressive. Apparently, it provided some support for Rivera when he ran for mayor in 1957. In general, however, unlike ethnic groups in northern and eastern cities, the Spanish-surname population had not formed clubs which could serve their political interests. Thus, it was not surprising that ethnic representation in community decision-making was so limited.[13]

[12] Organizational density *per se* is no guarantee of pluralistic politics because of the limited activity of many organizations. See Presthus, *op. cit.*, pp. 281, 319.

[13] As noted elsewhere this situation has changed. Not only has a Republican Party been established in El Paso, but so, also have been a host of ethnic-oriented political clubs. Intense factionalism threatens to reduce their political influence. *PASO*, the Political Association of Spanish-Speaking Organizations, is the most prominent of these clubs.

In C. Juarez, the situation seemed at first glance to be somewhat reversed. Voluntary associations appeared in abundance among all segments of the population. However, it soon became apparent that almost all of the working-class voluntary associations were in one way or another controlled by PRI. The organizations with any semblance of autonomy were the Chamber of Commerce, the Junior Chamber, Rotary, Lions, and a few other international civic-service clubs. The Civic Association, formed by the business-professional men, was the most politically oriented non-PRI interest group in the city between 1952 and 1956. Since then PAN has been trying to become the focus of political opposition. It has been largely unsuccessful because most of the major labor, agricultural, white-collar, professional and small business groups are controlled by PRI, and there is little likelihood that this situation will change in the near future. If anything, PRI's control over these groups has become more effective in the past few years. Such opinion formation as occurs in these associations is primarily oriented toward carrying out the policies of the national or state organizations.

Although some working-class leadership has developed in this political context (see Chapter 3) it lacks autonomy and tends to be expedient and opportunistic in character. Compared to El Paso, the lower-income groups in C. Juarez have greater representation in local politics, but they do not necessarily have greater influence in community decisions. On the other hand, business and professional people, while seemingly restricted in their local politics have at times exerted a strong if mainly negative influence. They have been effective in decision-making to the degree that they have worked with PRI. Meanwhile, PRI, claiming a singular relationship with the Revolution of 1910, continues to hold the loyalty of the masses by offering them basic social services. Practically, if not theoretically, it is difficult for other political parties or for independent voluntary associations to gain influence among the workers by also offering them social services.

In conclusion, the problem for El Paso is to make the rules of political democracy, which are a normal part of middle- and upper-class life, meaningful to those broad segments of its citizens who are only primitively assimilated to United States political culture. Steady employment, higher wages, and more education may be important preconditions for the assimilation. The development of voluntary associations which articulate to the political order are also needed to spread democracy throughout the community.

The problem for C. Juarez is much more complicated. A vast majority of its citizens live in economic privation, and there is little likelihood that an adequate economic level can be achieved in the years immediately ahead. In fact, rising expectations not met by a rising level of living could topple the benevolent PRI structure in favor of less benevolent forces. Under this threat it is even more difficult for a two-party system to arise. Attempts of voluntary associations to become more effective politically may simply lead to increased conflict. The one way out is to broaden the arena of "representative conflict" within PRI, but this too has its problems. In many respects the problems of C. Juarez are a microcosm of the problems of Mexico in general. This fact is at the same time mitigated and further strained by the border location of this, Mexico's fifth largest city. One can only ponder the long-range consequences for C. Juarez of being on the border next to a United States city in which democracy, if still far short of achieving its promise for the great majority of the people, is nevertheless relatively well equipped to tackle its problems.

Appendix: Methodology

THE IDEA OF USING the political boundaries of a country for social research was first proposed in 1954 by Professor Charles P. Loomis, then head of the Department of Sociology and Anthropology at Michigan State University. He received a grant from the Carnegie Foundation to carry out research along the United States-Mexico border.[1] Two lines of inquiry were proposed: analysis of (a) the value orientations, attitudes, evaluations, and national images of influential groups in both countries, and (b) formal and informal social systems whereby national images, attitudes and evaluations related to technological and social changes are internalized and maintained.

THE EXPLORATORY PHASE OF RESEARCH

The El Paso and C. Juarez area was chosen as the first research site in a five-year study of United States-Mexico bor-

[1] For a detailed statement of the project proposal, see "Processes of Technological and Social Change in the Inter-Cultural Setting of the Border Areas of the United States" (mimeographed pamphlet), Michigan State University, Department of Sociology and Anthropology, 1954.

der relations. This area was chosen because the cities are the largest "twin cities" along the border, a high degree of inter-action exists between them[2] and both cities were experienc-ing rapid rates of social and technological change. Moreover, the communities were known to possess parallel structures sufficiently complex and different culturally to make cross-cultural analysis fruitful.

The researchers arrived on the scene in early September 1954, and carried out an exploratory investigation until mid-December of the same year. The main objective of this early study was to become acquainted with the economic, political and other social systems in both communities. They studied the ecology of the two cities, the extent of their economic interde-pendence, the main outlines of their institutional structures, the joint organizations they had created, the identification of polit-ical and economic influentials, the dominant attitudes which influentials of each city had of each other, and areas of conflict between persons and agencies within and between the two cities. These data were gathered by direct observation, content analysis of various media, and exploratory interviews with institutional representatives of both communities.

The researchers also observed such items as land use, treat-ment of people at the inspection points on the international bridges, and shopping habits of Juarenses in El Paso and tour-ists in C. Juarez. Public officials, businessmen and union offi-cials gave us guided tours of the cities. Long discussions were held with knowledgeable people on the economic development of the cities, their political problems, past and future projects, and related areas. We also attended luncheons, banquets and holiday ceremonials.

It proved profitable to examine carefully the half dozen pa-

---

[2] It was reported that this was one of the most important points of entry along the entire United States border, a statement borne out by the research.

pers published in the border area. Systematic clippings were made of all economic and political activities within and between the cities. Of particular interest was information on the political campaigns within each city, issues which developed between the cities (such as tensions over border traffic congestion or the illegal entry of "wetbacks" into the United States), and activities of the various international committees. These materials proved helpful later in formulating questions used in our interviews which dealt with national imageries and intercity contacts.

EXPLORATORY INTERVIEWS

Doubtless the most important source of background data was the exploratory interviewing. It was necessary to determine whether the general objectives of the research could be achieved locally. Although it was obvious that there was a great deal of contact between the cities, we did not know its extent, direction, and importance. The problem was to find out whether identifiable groups were noticeably involved in technological or social interchange. Moreover, we wanted to know whether national images were sufficiently crystallized among change agents to be an important variable in their economic, political and social contacts.

Interviews were held with officials of formal organizations in the two cities because we felt that they might have extensive contacts across the border or have knowledge about them. Among those interviewed were the mayors and other public officials in both cities; the presidents and selected members of both Chambers of Commerce; leaders in finance, commerce and industry; small businessmen; and labor, religious and educational leaders. All of them willingly co-operated in the lengthy interviews which often lasted more than two hours.[3] They also promised full co-operation in the study. The data presented in Chapter 2 shows that contacts among some leaders of these formal organizations were extensive, that they were on a status equal level, and that leaders were willing to be studied.[4]

At the beginning of the exploratory interviews the researchers simply explained that the project was concerned with studying international relations on our border.[5] We were interested in learning about the kinds of contacts that took place between Mexicans and Americans and the way people felt about them.

[3] The following comments provide some indication of the data received in these interviews:

"When serious problems arise, joint committees are set up to work on them. There is a warmer attitude toward Americans in Juarez than in other Mexican border towns. We have been working hard on it for fifteen years. Mr. X is largely responsible for the cordial relationships."

"Eleven years ago when the Juarez market was open, it did not cater to American standards. Now they enforce certain health standards. The two Chambers of Commerce spearheaded this movement. There is a community of interest here, and our department stores realize this. We have keenly felt the devaluation of the peso."

"Historically, FDR's good-neighbor policy was the beginning of the new era in El Paso-C. Juarez relations."

"It is the attitude of Americans that creates the problem; Americans use blunt language at times, which may belittle. A courteous, respectful American can create good feeling."

"No top brass in any of these factories are Mexicans; within the last year a superintendent slapped a girl in the face with a pair of pants. He once insulted them by saying, 'you people are the same as niggers in my book.'"

[4] This notion of status equality was well expressed by one Juarez banker who said: "The social position of bankers in both cities is about the same. They have high esteem for us as we do for them. We often entertain each other at cocktail parties. . . . We carry local peso accounts for the American banks and vice-versa. There are no special problems." This same sentiment was voiced by at least several El Paso bankers. These sentiments contrast sharply with those expressed by the factory superintendent in footnote 3.

[5] One of the researchers was fluent in Spanish, while the other could understand Spanish well. In interviews, both were able to converse directly in Spanish with leaders of C. Juarez. Form has long been interested in urban sociology, industrial relations, community power structures, and self-images. D'Antonio had written a Master's thesis on "The Political Philosophy of the Mexican Revolution," had studied and traveled in Mexico, and had been specifically concerned with the political and economic aspects of Mexican life. These factors seemed to be of some importance in establishing rapport with Mexican respondents. Almost all exploratory interviews were conducted by tandem interviewing.

We also indicated we were interested in the business and political structures of the two cities. It was suggested that their own experiences as leaders might provide some insights into how to improve international relations. Overall, less than 5 per cent of those approached refused to co-operate, and most of them were in El Paso.

The exploratory interviews were broadly designed to obtain from the institutional sector leaders the following: (a) a summary picture of the internal structure of their institution and the problems facing its agencies; (b) a summary of the contacts institutional leaders and agencies had in the past and present with persons and agencies in parallel institutions of the other city; (c) evaluation of the agencies and activities of the other city in terms of norms of efficiency, growth and democracy; and (d) attitudinal and imagery material on the style of life of institutional personnel and citizenry in the other city. Certain conclusions from these interviews affected the subsequent research design, the institutional sectors to be studied and the sampling procedure.

We found that practically no formal or informal contacts existed between "leaders" of labor, education, religion and welfare in both cities. The lack of religious contacts was surprising in view of the fact that a majority of the population of both cities were at least nominal Catholics. Special historical and political problems in Mexico during the past century help to explain the lack of contact among religious leaders. The value orientations of the institutions of education and labor in the two communities were so different as to almost preclude meaningful communication between their leaders. Since both education and labor were closely tied to Mexican government and politics, El Paso leaders hesitated to initiate contacts with their Mexican counterparts for fear of the political consequences.[6]

[6] The situation has changed considerably in recent years. For example, teacher-student exchange programs have been established between Texas Western College and the University of Chihuahua.

On the other hand, we found considerable formal and informal contacts between leaders in the political and business systems of the two communities. However, there was very little evidence of consciously directed technological interchange in the area. Mexican businessmen, for example, borrowed ideas from Mexico City as often as from El Paso.

Out of the exploratory study emerged a research design formally focused on the business and political influential groups of the two cities, their structures, degree of interrelatedness, the nature and extent of their cross-cultural contacts, and the conceptions which they held of the world of business and politics within their own and the neighboring country. The following factors indicated that a fruitful study was possible in this area:

(1) good contacts had been established with business and political leaders in both cities;

(2) a mayoralty campaign was approaching in El Paso, which offered an opportunity to study the participation of businessmen in the electoral process;

(3) an open and bitter struggle had erupted in C. Juarez between a group of businessmen and professionals on the one hand and the municipal and state government leaders on the other, over matters of business, civic and political affairs and how they should be run;

(4) there was considerable evidence of a high rate of interaction between business and political leaders of the two cities on both a professional and social basis;

(5) leaders who had been already contacted appeared to be a highly articulate group, with definite but varying attitudes which they were willing to discuss;

(6) the conceptions of business and politics, which under other circumstances might be latent and difficult to clarify, might be made manifest under the above conditions. If there were indeed identifiable power groups, the events of the day seemed certain to bring them out.

Unfortunately our early focus was not made to study decision-making systematically, although we were concerned with outlining the broad power structures in the two communities. The primary focus at this stage was to use certain events which were occurring in both cities as an opportunity to examine self and national images, and how these images related to occupation, nationality, and international contacts. It was not until these data were fully analyzed that we decided to carry out a systematic analysis of decision-making in both cities.

Developing an Interview Schedule

The first schedule comprised three parts: (a) questions on personal background (age, education, occupation, membership in various types of voluntary associations, the nature and extent of actual contacts with members of the other systems under study, and evaluation of these contacts); (b) questions dealing with business and economics, including comparative questions on the business systems as they functioned within and between the two cities; and (c) questions dealing mostly with comparison of the political systems of the two countries. The schedule was pretested in both cities, and the Spanish translation was checked for accuracy of meaning. Although we were worried about its length, which required from one and one-half to two hours to complete, only five people of the nearly 200 interviewed complained about the time.

Selection and Validation of the Respondents

In the exploratory interviewing the respondents were asked to name the persons who were most influential in local community affairs as well as those most influential in the neighboring city. Master lists were then built up. We decided to ask similar questions in the systematic interviews, but modified the approach somewhat. We decided to interview the most obvious business and political influentials of the two cities, because the exploratory interviews showed that people in other institutional sectors were not generally influential in the community. Moreover, the use of Hunter's technique would have left us with an underrepresentation of political influentials, at least in El Paso.[7] This would have been a serious problem since we were concerned with the relations between the business and political systems. Thus, while the technique was designed along the reputational model, it called for two distinct areas of influence and two separate lists of names. Since the assumption was not made that men who were most influential in business were also the most influential in politics, we hoped to avoid some of the ambiguity inherent in Hunter's technique. Again, departing from Hunter, respondents were not given lists of names from which to choose the most influential. They simply named the persons whom they thought were the most influential in the political and business areas. These two questions were separated in the interview by twenty other questions. Respondents in El Paso seemed to have more difficulty nominating than those in C. Juarez. They also had more difficulty distinguishing between persons influential in business from those influential in politics. They occasionally forgot the names of alleged influentials and referred to their occupations or the corporations for which they worked.

We attempted to ascertain the extent to which there was consensus among the influentials of the two cities about who the most influential persons were. We asked: "Can you give us the names of a few people who have the greatest influence and power in the neighboring city?" Seldom were more than four or five names given. The results of this question, summarized in Chapter 3, show that within a rather narrowly restricted range there was a fairly high degree of consensus.

By the time that the exploratory phase of the study was com-

---

[7] See Floyd Hunter, *Community Power Structure* (Chapel Hill: University of North Carolina Press, 1953), see especially "Appendix: Methods."

pleted, between 15 and 20 influentials in each city were clearly identified, and these persons were interviewed first. Lists of additional potential influentials were derived on the basis of their responses. Persons were classified as influential if they had been nominated by three or more judges. We interviewed all the influentials who would agree to be interviewed.[8] The researchers were always aware of the possibility that certain cliques might name only themselves. For this reason knowledgeables as well as influentials were used as sources of nominations.

Toward the end of the first phase of the study it became apparent that there were more or less two distinct groups within the business and political systems, the "influentials" and the "knowledgeables."[9] The knowledgeables were often closely associated with the influentials, but they were not perceived to have their influence. Yet they sometimes seemed to have an even clearer view of the power structure and the problems of international contacts than the influentials themselves.

In attempting to validate this list of influentials, lists of names of all those chosen at least once were submitted to several judges in both cities. The judges were people whom the researchers had come to recognize as having extensive knowledge about the local situation and an ability to be objective. They represented widely divergent shades of opinion, and included both top influentials and knowledgeables. Each judge was asked to select in order of their influence, the top twenty

[8] Some of the people who were interviewed in the exploratory phase were also in the final sample, and thus were interviewed twice. There was a lapse of at least five weeks in all such cases. The only questions omitted in the second interview were those dealing with personal background data which had already been obtained.

[9] They were labeled "knowledgeables" because we used them to provide us knowledge and not as secondary elites, which they were. Thus, we have no systematic sample of secondary influentials. The knowledgeables in both cities consisted of businessmen, professionals, government officials, politicians, as well as labor and welfare leaders.

influentials in each group, and if need be, add names to the lists. There was almost complete agreement between the choices of these judges and the overall vote of the influentials and knowledgeables. The two techniques yielded almost identical results. In essence, then, the individuals selected and interviewed were the influentials of their respective systems insofar as the technique used was a valid one. Whatever else the technique does, it tends to provide the image which influentials have of the influence structures within their respective cities.

Special Problems Encountered

A study in a cross-cultural situation is fraught with difficulties not ordinarily encountered in research within a society and culture. Some limitations of the study will be apparent from the poor strategy used in trying to handle some of these difficulties in the following areas: language fluency and historical perspective, importance of residence, gaining rapport and defining the study for the respondents, allocation of the time for the study of each city, and objectivity of the researchers. Two extra interviewers were hired to help with the interviewing in El Paso.

Language Fluency and the Historical Perspective

The researchers could not have carried out this study without having fluency in Spanish. Only a small number of Mexican influentials spoke English well enough to converse in it freely. The ability to speak their language well meant being able to probe, to get beyond the pat answer, and to meet respondents on terms of status equality. Coupled with language fluency was the necessity to have a historical perspective especially of the Mexican scene. This perspective made the clash between the political and business influentials in C. Juarez understandable. It enabled the researchers to converse knowledgeably with the respondents on topics of special interest to them. Mexican respondents were generally pleased that Americans knew something about Mexican history, and this may have encouraged them to provide more information than they might have otherwise given.

The Problem of Residence

When presented with the possibility of residing in an American or a Mexican city, it is all too easy for the researcher with family to choose the American city. But aside from personal comfort, residence has symbolic significance. In 1955 several influentials in both cities asked where the researchers were living. We defended our choice on the ground that since we had to spend an equal amount of time in both cities, we simply rented the first place that seemed adequate in El Paso because we had arrived there first.

It was later learned that there was resentment in both communities directed against certain members of the United States Consulate who were living in El Paso while their jobs were in C. Juarez. Resentment was expressed also toward some Mexican businessmen who were residing in El Paso, because of the allegedly superior living conditions there. During the 1950's several of them returned to C. Juarez in response to pressures from their colleagues.

The researchers later considered moving to C. Juarez. By this time, however, they had discovered the existence of the two opposing groups in C. Juarez, both of whom had large amounts of real estate, and had offered "excellent" housing facilities. Since it seemed impossible to make the move without offending one of the parties, the researchers stayed in El Paso. Conceivably a decision to reside in C. Juarez upon first arrival prior to acquiring knowledge about local cleavages might have impaired rapport.

Gaining Rapport and Defining the Study for the Respondents

As indicated, the ability to speak Spanish and historical knowledge of Mexico helped establish rapport with the Mexican

leaders. Fortunately, the top leaders of the opposition groups in
Juarez were favorably disposed towards the study. They were
impressed that an American university should be interested in
them. They offered letters of introduction or signed calling
cards to fellow influentials or to neutrals who took no part in the
controversy. Ninety-five per cent of the interviews in C. Juarez
were obtained by the use of a letter of recommendation or the
personal calling card of one of the leaders.

The problem of gaining rapport in El Paso was considerably
different. While most of the leaders were willing to participate,
they were not so impressed by the presence of professors from
a northern university. Only one influential was willing to provide the researchers with a calling card or letter of introduction. While the general manager of the Juarez Chamber of
Commerce had offered to write letters of recommendation to
any businessman in C. Juarez, the El Paso general manager insisted from the beginning that he could not do this, and that we
would have to present ourselves to whomever we wanted to
speak without his official support.

In retrospect, the differences in reception seemed to illustrate the differing value orientations of the two systems. On
the Mexican side, it was preferable to have a note of introduction from one of the top leaders. With such a note, one could
count on the complete co-operation of the respondent, without
having to validate one's role and the purposes of the study.
Such a particularistic technique was alien to the El Pasoans.
The researcher had to validate himself and the study to each
respondent. Thus, it was much easier to reach the top men in
C. Juarez than in El Paso. The same pattern held during the
interviewing which took place during the summer of 1958.

Allotment of Time

As so many things going on in C. Juarez seemed so unusual,
there was always the temptation to slight research in El Paso

in favor of C. Juarez. Bridge-crossing problems kept this tendency under control. Getting caught in the traffic at certain times of the day meant waiting an hour or more in line. To arrange appointments in both cities for the same afternoon meant careful timing. We sometimes feared cutting a respondent short in order to give ourselves time to get back to the other city.[10] This problem was avoided in 1958 by having two teams of interviewers, one working in each city.

The researcher in such a cross-cultural setting is also caught up in the very concept of "time" and the varying cultural patterns related to "business" hours. One could reasonably expect that an appointment would be kept on time in El Paso, and that the working day would be from 8:00 A.M. to 5:00 P.M. Neither of these patterns held for C. Juarez. In many cases, the hour of appointment seemed merely a formality to please the Americans. The researchers spent many hours waiting for respondents to appear. They had the impression that most, if not all, of the late or completely forgotten appointments occurred with Mexican political influentials who had not internalized the time perspectives of businessmen.

The writers also had to become accustomed, and later enjoy, the fact that all influentials in C. Juarez took a two- or three-hour break in the afternoon. At times they found themselves in C. Juarez with a morning interview just completed and three hours for lunch before the afternoon interview. Frequently on such occasion the respondent would fail to be on time, so that a 4:00 P.M. interview did not begin until 5:15 or 5:30. Only once did a political influential apologize for having forgotten an

[10] Actually, an event of this nature occurred only once. One of the researchers was invited to a barbecue luncheon by a group of Juarez businessmen. After three delightful hours of "participant" observation the barbecue was still in progress but the writer had to leave to keep an El Paso appointment. Perhaps the Mexicans were left wondering about this peculiar American who was so concerned about an appointment.

This was not a major problem because two special interviewers were hired to handle most of the interviewing in El Paso.

appointment. To redeem himself, he insisted on being interviewed right in the middle of a busy morning schedule. Late afternoon interviews were preferred, especially for politicos, since their offices were generally quiet and free of visitors only at that time. This was as true in 1962 as in 1955. Most interviews took place in the offices of the respondents, although occasionally the researchers were invited to their homes. While these interviews proceeded at a more leisurely pace, there were obvious advantages to seeing the respondent in his place of work.

Objectivity

The researcher was faced with the important problem of establishing an adequate role in the field. The El Paso influentials were quite concerned lest anything said would disturb the harmonious relations which they had labored so long to develop. Some of the questions, especially those asking to compare political systems of the two countries, were upsetting. As one man put it, "Sure, there is a lot of corruption there, but we have to do business with them and live near them, and I don't want to lose any customers or friends over this." Others were doubly disturbed, since they wanted to point with pride to the superiority of their own system, but hesitated condemning another system. One businessman, after giving what he considered to be a fairly objective and complete answer to a "sensitive" question, said: "I'll bet you can't get that kind of information from those fellows in Juarez. "Actually, we tended to get more adequate answers to "sensitive" questions from Juarez influentials.

On the Juarez side, for businessmen who were outspoken against an allegedly corrupt government, there were no "sensitive" questions. Quite often they answered such questions before we asked them. The problem they posed was one of seeking support for their position from the interviewers. Understandably the researchers were very cautious in approaching the political influentials with these "sensitive" questions. They tended to spread them out more, and to add questions which would give the respondent a chance to expound on his political philosophy and accomplishments. As a result, only two respondents became visibly upset by certain questions, and both were businessmen friendly to the men in office at the time.

The best-phrased and thought-out questions are worthless if respondents will not answer them. It seemed difficult to determine a priori what questions they would refuse to answer. Some federal officials in both cities answered every question, while others insisted that their position prohibited their answering these same questions. The crucial factor appeared to be not the respondent's occupation but rather how he appraised the research project and the researcher.

Naturally, all of these events affected the researchers' own perceptions. The American influentials began to emerge as stand-offish, willing but not eager to co-operate, and generally afraid to speak out on controversial issues. Although we felt that many said: "Now, this is off the record," or "Don't quote me on this," a check of their interviews revealed that less than one third of the American respondents were timid.

In C. Juarez, we had the distinct impression that business and politics were in complete discord. At the same time, the top men of both groups were extremely co-operative, and gave the impression that they believed in the value of the study. Generally they were more willing to speak out frankly than were the El Pasoans. This same frankness may have magnified the differences between the businessmen on the one hand and the politicos on the other.

The Border Revisited

The field work of the first study was terminated in the fall of 1955. Through newspaper subscriptions and personal correspondence we were able to maintain contact with events on the border. No sooner had we left than some startling political changes began to take place in both cities. After following these events at a distance for three years we returned to the border in the summer of 1958 with the objective of examining the role of "influentials" in community decision-making. With the aid of an additional grant from the United States Public Health Service we decided to study decision-making not only in the original research site but in several Southwestern and Mexican communities. The aims were to examine the role of the influentials in: (a) the myriad health systems of their communities, such as United Fund, Red Cross committees, Cancer Drives, etc.; (b) decision-making with respect to hospital construction; and (c) health as opposed to nonhealth issues. We selected municipal elections and the Cordova Bridge Issue as the nonhealth issues for El Paso and C. Juarez.

This plan enabled us to give systematic attention to an aspect of research which was neglected in 1955. It also enabled us to discover whether the earlier data gathered on influence systems, national images, and international contacts would prove useful in analyzing the process of decision-making in the two communities.

Providing new hospital facilities had been a long-standing issue in C. Juarez, and we had already gathered considerable background data on it in the earlier research. Less background data were available on the hospital issue in El Paso because only a few people had foreseen it as a major unsolved problem in 1955. In order to relate our knowledge about across-the-border contacts and national images to decision-making we decided to study the problems of establishing new border-crossing facilities between the two cities. By the time we arrived at the border in summer 1958, the hospital and bridge issues had become major concerns in both cities. We also decided to study systematically the municipal elections in order to fill the gaps in our data on the two previous elections in each city and to obtain a comprehensive background for the forthcoming elections. Finally, we decided to examine and compare the way private fund drives were conducted in both cities.

In studying decision-making we wanted to find out how issues arose, how support and opposition were marshalled, and how issues were finally resolved. A key question was to discover the extent to which those persons who had the reputation for power actually participated in these issues.

Since only three weeks of field work were possible,[11] we could not reinterview all the influentials and knowledgeables. However, this was not crucial to our major concern of getting an adequate picture of the way certain specific issues arose and were resolved. It was essential that we interview all the top influentials and all others who were centrally involved in the issues selected for study. To help overcome the handicap of time, four interviewers were used, two in each city.

In preparation for field work the names of the influentials of the 1955 study were incorporated into separate lists for each city. To these lists were added the names of others whom we suspected might have become influentials. Immediately upon arrival, we contacted seven of the most reliable knowledgeables whom we knew from the previous study. They represented the press, local government, finance, commerce, the clergy, and civic leaders. We asked them to check the names of the persons most influential in their community, that is, men capable of initiating, carrying out or blocking issues or programs of community-wide significance. They were asked to add or remove names from the prepared lists and to include persons from any institutional segment of the community, as long as they were influential in resolving community issues.

[11] Three weeks is not a great length of time, but four researchers working together were able to achieve all major objectives. More recent site visits in 1961 and 1962 confirmed our belief that we had secured an accurate picture of leadership and decision-making in these border cities.

We asked them for the names of the top fifty influentials. They removed from the lists a dozen names of people who either had died or gone into retirement. The judges thought that most of the men who had been selected as influentials in 1955 were still the most influential in 1958. We found that there was a greater turnover of influential personnel in C. Juarez than in El Paso, and this was due mainly to the changing political tides. This modification of the Hunter technique also tended to reduce slightly the number of persons specifically representing government and political office, although in both cities these men were still among the top vote receivers.

We managed to interview 51 persons in El Paso and 25 in C. Juarez. Each person was asked to select from the list of 50 names developed from the judges' lists, the twelve most influential persons in the community. Not all of the persons interviewed in either city were influentials, but all of the influentials who were available were interviewed. Thus, in El Paso 31 of the 50 influentials selected by the judges were interviewed, and in C. Juarez 21 out of 50 were interviewed. The influentials who were interviewed agreed that 35 El Pasoans and 30 Juarenses who were influentials in business and politics in 1955 were still influential in 1958. Of these we managed to interview 29 in El Paso and 20 in C. Juarez. The others interviewed were involved in the issues under study. The results of this aspect of our study are found in Chapter 5.

Interviews took just over an hour to complete, largely because we already had the necessary background data on most of the respondents. The great majority of the interviewees of the 1955 study seemed pleased to renew contacts and they received us in a friendly and cordial manner. They were presented with a brief summary of the results of the previous study, and were told that they would be notified of future publications.[12]

[12] This promise has been honored, and several leaders have written to request additional reprints of published articles.

Necessary data were also obtained from local records, newspaper accounts, and other documents. In order to have complete coverage of the resolution of the bridge and hospital issues, both of which were in their final stages when we left the border in 1958, we continued subscriptions to the major newspapers of both cities through the summer of 1959. We also maintained extensive correspondence with some of the key decision-makers. To fill in the remaining gaps on the hospital issues, a special trip was made to the border in 1961. Again, in the summer of 1962 D'Antonio lived for almost two months in C. Juarez, studying local elections. During that time all the material for Chapters 6, 7 and 8 was reviewed with the major participants. Minor points were added to help enrich the presentation.

In this study we have tried to present the results of seven years of research which included four visits to the research site, as a single, more or less continuous analysis of some of the important events in which the influentials in business and politics in El Paso and C. Juarez participated during the hectic years of the 1950's.

Index

A

Agger, Robert, 84n
Anderson, Charles W., 10n
Authority, defined, 11
  and power, 11, 130

B

Barber, Bernard, 72n
Bernard, Jesse, 155n
Bermúdez, Antonio J., 33n
Bolio, Lic. Clemente, 43n
Burgess, M. E., 7n, 59n, 239n

C

Camacho, Avila, 44
Cárdenas, Lázaro, 8
Cárdenas, Leonard Jr., 9n, 37n
Chamizal, described, 20

maps of, 45
nature of problem, 43n, 44n
resolution of problem, 44n
C. Juarez, associational patterns
  of, 41–43
ecology and economy of, 31–36
elections in, 161–178
history of, 31ff
institutional patterns of, 25–29
issues in, 161ff
unions, 36
Cleavage, between business and
  politics, 86–87, 90–92, 98–101
within business and politics, 14,
    55, 227
ethnic, 128
ideological, 96–228
influentials and, 101–102
between PRI and PAN, 39–40
voluntary associations and, 88ff,
    101

Clifford, Roy, 180n
Cline, Howard F., 17n
Coleman, James S., 4n
Conflict, in the community, 2
  in community decisions, 14
  in politics, 3
  between PRI and business
    leaders, 14
Consensus, between business and
    government, 5
  and democracy, 243–245
  functions of, 3
  on local problems, 15
  perils of, 4
Cutright, P., 2n

D

Dahl, Robert A., 5n, 7n, 86n, 89n,
    229n–230
D'Antonio, William V., 2n, 23n,
    88n, 128n, 252n, 267
Decision-making, business domi-
    nance of, 102–103
  in C. Juarez, 160ff
  in the community, 2, 12–15,
    85–86
  comparative, 225–228
  democratic, 243–248
  in El Paso, 130ff
  and influentials, 10, 211–215,
    221–225
  power in, 1, 4, 10
  problems in international,
    209–211
De Leon, Juan María Ponce, 19
Democracy, future of, 243–248
  history of, 8
  ideals in, 96–98
  requisite for, 2–5, 243–246
Dentler, R., 7n
Díaz, Porfirio, 8, 18, 44

E

Education, in C. Juarez, 39
  in El Paso, 25–28
  school issue, 182n, 182–184
Ehrlich, H. J., 2n, 88n
El Paso, associational patterns of,
    29–31
  ecology of, 20–21
  elections in, 161–178
  history of, 18–20
  institutional patterns of, 25–29
  issues in, 161
  labor unions, 24–25
Elections and power structure, in
    C. Juarez, 177–178
  in El Paso, 145–146
  role of C.C.C. in, 131–141
Erickson, E. C., 88n, 128n

F

Form, William H., 89n, 157n, 252n

G

Glade, William P., 10n

H

Hunter, Floyd, 6n, 88n, 157n,
    256n, 266n
Hypotheses of the study, 14–17
  see also Methodology

I

Ideal hospital committee, 112–115,
    122–125, 156–159, 189–191
Influence, assumptions in delineat-
    ing, 13, 58–59
  as charisma, 11
  defined, 11

patterns of, 65–66
stability of;
see Influentials, longevity
Influentials, assumptions made in
delineating, 58–59
business, 63–73
business and political images of,
93–100
and changes in cities, 125–129
of C. Juarez and El Paso compared, 125–129
community leadership and, 2,
58–59
community problems perceived
by, 100–102
defined, 53–55
economic affiliation of, 68
and elections, 242
"general" defined, 107
identification of, 60–65
and institutional overlap, 102–
105
and international decisions, 211–
215
and international relations, 217–
220
"key" defined, 108
and labor unions, 25
and longevity in: C. Juarez,
115–122; El Paso, 107–115
nonelectoral strength of,
146–150
organizational affiliation of, 71
political, 73–83
social characteristics, 70, 90–93
sociometric leaders, 62, 110
Integration, 88*ff;* of business and
politics, 128
measures of, 90
of values, 90
Inter-city, economic contacts,
45–51
interdependence, 16, 45, 220

leadership contacts, 254
political contacts, 51–53
relations, 15
Issues, in C. Juarez: bridge, 193*ff*
education, 182–184
elections, 164–178
hospital, 184–189
sequence of, 233–234
welfare, 179–182
Issues, in El Paso: bridge, 193*ff*
elections, 131–146
hospital, 150–155
sequence of, 233–234
welfare, 17

J

Janowitz, Morris, 2*n*
Jennings, M. Kent, 86*n*, 159*n*,
215*n*
Juárez, Benito, 8, 18, 31

K

Knowledgeables, defined, 59*ff*, 60*n*
and influentials, 111*n*, 257*n*

L

Lewis, Oscar, 9*n*
Lipset, Seymour M., 2*n*, 5*n*, 159*n*
Loomis, Charles P., 249
Lynd, Helen and Robert, 6*n*, 88*n*

M

Maccoby, Herbert, 4*n*
Madero, Francisco, 8, 18
Maximillian, 18, 31
Methodology, exploratory research,
249–255
field experience, 13, 14, 258

gaining rapport, 259–260, 263
interviewing, 53n, 255
problems of, 258–263
see also Hunter, Floyd, and reputational technique
Miller, D. C., 6n, 7n, 15, 85n, 89n, 229n, 230
Mills, C. Wright, 6n, 85n, 157n
Mobility, patterns of, 5, 81–82
Mordida, defined, 74, 79, 83, 97

N

Nationalism and conflict in Mexico, 56
economic, 47
Newspapers, role in decision-making: in C. Juarez, 41–42, 172–173
in El Paso, 30–31, 152–153, 205–206

P

Padgett, L. V., 9n, 38n, 162n, 168n
Parties, C.C.C., 133–141
Democratic, 132, 232
PAN, 37ff, 162ff, 174, 225
PNM, 163, 166
PRI, 8, 14, 37, 162ff, 223–224
Peixotto, Ernest, 18n, 33n–34n
Power, and authority, 11
community, 13, 16, 59, 67
and decision-making, 1, 4, 10
defined, 10
distribution of, 11
and voluntary associations, 5
see also Influence
Power structure in C. Juarez, 224–225
community, 6–7
conflicts in, 2, 12
in El Paso, 222–223

hypotheses, 16, 90
models compared, 229–231
monolithic, 7, 14, 66, 88–90, 105, 178n, 230–232
pluralistic, 6, 7, 89–90, 105, 230–232
Press, Charles, 6n
Presthus, Robert, 7n, 15n, 86n, 88n, 215n, 226n, 238n, 239n, 244

R

Religion, composition in C. Juarez, 40–41
in El Paso, 28–30
international contacts, 253
Reputational Technique, defined, 11, 107
reliability of, 236–238
validity of, 238–243, 255–258
Revolution, 97, 245
Mexican, 8, 9, 95, 190–191
Rose, Arnold, 4n
Roosevelt, F. D., 44, 252n
Rossi, Peter, 7n, 85n, 89n, 145n, 229n, 230n, 231n, 234n, 235n

S

Samora, Julian, 23n
Schools, see education
Schulze, Robert O., 26n
Scott, Robert E., 9n, 38n, 84n
Spanish surname associations
education and, 27
employment of, 23, 26
LULAC, 29, 30n, 246
PASO, 246n
political activity of, 134ff
political strength of, 144
population in El Paso, 24

T

Taft, W. Howard, 18, 44
Tangent, Pierre, 6n
Tannenbaum, Frank, 85n
Trow, Martin A., 4n
Tucker, William P., 38n, 84n

U

Useem, John and Ruth, 6n

V

Villa, Pancho, 43–44
Voluntary associations, and the
    bridge issue, 201–216

and business, 49–51
and democracy, 2–3
in C. Juarez, 36, 41
in El Paso, 29–30, 36
and PAN, 37–39
political activity and Civic As-
    sociation, 165–168
political power and, 5
and PRI, 8, 37–39
social characteristics of, 90–92

W

Warner, W. Lloyd, 6n
West, James, 6n
Wise, George, 85n